MW01593549

THE SOUTHEAST FLORIDA GOLF GUIDE

Written by Daniel Wexler

Published by MT III Golf Media
El Segundo, CA   USA
Midd23@aol.com

Also by Daniel Wexler:

The Missing Links: America's Greatest Lost Golf Courses and Holes

Lost Links: Forgotten Treasures From Golf's Golden Age

The Golfer's Library: A Reader's Guide to Three Centuries of Golf Literature

The Book of Golfers: A Biographical History of the Royal & Ancient Game

The World Atlas of Golf (with Michael Clayton, Ran Morrissett, et al)

The Black Book

The American Private Golf Club Guide

The American Golf Resort Guide

The New York Metro Area Golf Guide

The Southern California Golf Guide

The Southeast Florida Golf Guide

The Phoenix Area Golf Guide

The Tropical Golf Guide

MT III Golf Media

In addition to producing our comprehensive golf course guidebooks ("The Black Book"), MT III Golf Media also offers customized public relations and promotional materials for public courses, resorts and private clubs. Please visit us at www.danielwexler.com.

TABLE OF CONTENTS

INTRODUCTION

By no means is this the first guidebook ever penned covering the golf courses of a particular region of the United States; such volumes are, in fact, fairly common, both in major metropolitan areas and destination locales readily identifiable as golfing hotbeds.

The Black Book, however, is different.

To begin with, this volume includes every facility within the five southernmost counties on Florida's east coast for which verifiable information was available at the time of its writing. From the ritziest private club to the tiniest nine-hole par 3, if it's open for business in Monroe, Miami-Dade, Broward, Palm Beach and Martin Counties (more than 270 courses in total), it is included here.

Second, these volumes are about the golf courses – their layouts, histories, architectural evolutions, great (and not-so-great) holes, and whatever other salient points come to mind on a course-by-course basis. What they are *not* about is all manner of ancillary items that often clog mainstream guidebooks. There will, for example, be no discussions of food, tennis facilities, nearby hotels or the quality of beverage cart service. These books are for avid, serious golfers; the course is what matters here.

But perhaps most importantly, these guidebooks are intended to live up to a pithy little phrase of my own creation:

"Candid, but not opinionated."

And this to me is the heart of the undertaking because what the golf world does not need is another book calling every layout a "gem," or passing off regurgitated public relations copy as insightful descriptive material. The goal of The Black Book, then, is to provide an accurate picture of each course's overall attributes based upon a mix of objective factors (e.g., style of design, USGA ratings and slope, invasiveness of hazards, etc.), and a consensus of less formalized ones (various published rankings and commentaries), while at the same time minimizing any personal preferences relative to designer, style, region or period. This goal is furthered by the book's use of our exclusive Collectability Rating (see page 3), a unique evaluation method that essentially measures how desirable a "get" each facility is for the discerning golfer's personal list of courses played.

As for The Black Book's accuracy, while periodic renovations of courses are inevitable, numerous sources have been utilized in order to present the most accurate information possible at the time of writing. One notable point, however, concerns individual hole yardages and course ratings. Where possible, the information herein comes directly from the courses themselves, generally via website. Failing this, it has been culled from either regional golf associations or the USGA's national database – sources which often show minor differences based on a variety of factors. Hole yardages can vary similarly, often due only to a recent re-measuring, or the addition of new tees. Therefore while the numbers presented are deemed substantially accurate, the occasional minor variance is unavoidable. And also unavoidable, particularly in golf's present economic climate, is the occasional variance in course classification, often in the form of traditionally private clubs allowing limited outside play. Thus, how a course is classified, while usually reliably accurate, is always subject to potential change.

Regarding "ratings" in the larger sense, at the end of each applicable entry are a course's current rankings in the three American publications that perform this service, *Golf* Magazine (biennial domestic and worldwide top 100s), *Golf Digest* (biennial domestic top 200, state-by-state rankings and top 100 public) and *Golfweek* (annual top 200s for both modern and classic layouts, plus resort courses). They are abbreviated as G, GD and GW respectively.

Now, a final, note regarding bias and perspective.

As mentioned above, the great majority of the material presented herein is *objective* – the scale and style of a course's bunkering, or the statement that a layout measures 7,700 yards, or has been hugely altered since the Golden Age, are all impartial facts and not matters of opinion. But to the extent that one's personal tastes must inevitably poke around at the edges, it seems only fair to lay out my own, as follows:

1) I place an enormous emphasis on strategic design. Being able to hit a golf ball solidly is one important skill that the game requires; being able to think one's way around a well-conceived layout is an entirely different one. For me, the game is infinitely more engaging when both are fully in play.

2) I place a similar level of emphasis on variety, because even the greatest hole would get dull if played repeatedly. Courses with varied lengths and strategic challenges are, to me, much more appealing.

3) I prefer my golf relatively gimmick-free. Granted, this is a somewhat more subjective area, but generally speaking, 700-yard par 5s and artificial waterfalls in the middle of deserts tend not to inspire.

4) Ambience and setting count – not, perhaps, in assessing the strategic merits of a layout, but certainly in weighing the overall experience.

Obviously, readers may disagree with any or all of these perspectives – indeed, that's part of what makes a book like this fun – but either way, at least you'll know which comments might best be taken with a grain of salt when our tastes differ.

Safe travels!

DW

COLLECTABILITY RATING

Among the many qualities that make golf unique, none stands out further than the endless variety of its playing fields. Indeed, for most avid golfers, the chance to experience the game's vast array of courses – layouts built by all sorts of designers, in all manner of styles and settings – represents the lynchpin of golf's visceral, lifelong appeal.

In this light, we are all, in effect, collectors of golf courses, hoping to add as many significant facilities to our personal portfolios as time and circumstance will allow. It is with such an acquisitive sense in mind that The Black Book employs its original Collectability Rating, a one-to-five diamond scale which assesses each profiled facility's relative importance to the golfer's personal collection, based upon the following criteria:

1) The general perception of a course's overall quality as determined by various published rankings and commentaries, both national and regional.

2) A course's historical significance, measured primarily in terms of major competitions held, as well as period or social prominence/prestige, famous professionals or members, etc.

3) A course's architectural significance, judged by its design pedigree, its place within a particular designer's portfolio and, for older facilities, how much of their original layout remains in play.

4) An especially high (or low) degree of scenery or golfing ambience.

Each club's rating appears in the initial line of its entry, and can be defined as follows:

One of the game's absolute elite. A must-see.

An internationally prominent facility. Well worth a special visit.

A nationally prominent facility. First-class design and/or major history.

A regionally prominent facility, often worth traveling for.

A significant facility worth finding, should one be in the neighborhood.

A stronger facility offering flashes of notable design or history.

A mid-range facility, perhaps standing out in a narrow market.

A basic facility, but one rated somewhat above the mundane.

It beats a driving range.

PROMINENT ARCHITECTS OF
SOUTHEAST FLORIDA

The following are the course designers who have left the largest footprints upon the golfing landscape of Southeast Florida, having built at least five courses in the region. Courses are referred to by their current names and are listed chronologically, with only those which remain in existence being included. Lists include only new courses or renovations large enough in scope to make the architect the new designer of record.

Pete Dye – Arguably the most influential golf course designer of the second half of the 20th century, Urbana, Ohio-born Paul B. "Pete" Dye (b.1925) played golf at Rollins College and competed in one British and five U.S. Amateurs. After marrying Alice O'Neal and excelling in, then leaving, the insurance business, Dye began a career in golf design by building several low-budget Midwestern layouts of limited repute. A 1963 visit to Scotland changed his entire philosophy, however, and his subsequent use of such Old World staples as pot bunkers, railroad ties and native grasses soon made his the most copied design style in the business.

Though Crooked Stick (IN) and The Golf Club (OH) were the first courses to reflect this new approach, it was 1969's Harbour Town Golf Links (built in partnership with Jack Nicklaus) that introduced it to the world stage – and began pushing architecture away from the bland, oversized courses of the postwar period. In 1981, Dye would again change architecture's face with his TPC at Sawgrass, a tough track built to serve as permanent host of the PGA Tour's Players Championship. With its much-imitated 132-yard 17th elevating the concept of the island green to an entirely new level, the TPC's creative use of waste areas and greens contoured to repel inferior approaches once again captured the design world's attention. Several years later, as equipment advances presaged changes in the game's fundamental balance, Dye stepped things up even further, first with the Stadium course at PGA West (1986), then, in 1990, with the windswept Ocean course at Kiawah Island.

Considering that he has maintained a home there for decades, Dye's work in Southeast Florida has been only moderate in volume. It has, however, included two highly significant entries in his portfolio, the environmentally groundbreaking Old Marsh and the Medalist Golf Club.

Pete Dye In Southeast Florida:	
Delray Dunes G&CC – Boynton Beach	1969
St. Andrews C – Delray Beach (Par 3, w/A. Dye)	1973
Old Marsh GC – Palm Beach Gardens	1987
Palm Beach Polo C (Cypress) – W. Palm Beach (w/P.B. Dye)	1989
The Medalist GC – Hobe Sound (w/G. Norman)	1995
Dye Preserve GC – Jupiter (Redesign)	2002
Boca West CC (No.4) – Boca Raton (Redesign)	2007

Tom Fazio – Standing among the biggest names in modern golf course design, Tom Fazio (b.1945) has been in the business since 1962 when he began working for his ex-PGA Tour Player uncle George. The firm enjoyed a good deal of success as Tom gradually replaced the aging George as its centerpiece, with much of "their" later output more resembling solo designs. Despite stylistically awkward alterations of Golden Age classics Inverness (1979) and Oak Hill (1980), it would be Fazio's polished aesthetics that would ultimately lead him to stardom, and by the early 1980s he was turning out attractive courses from coast to coast.

Frequently appearing more difficult than they actually played, such layouts became a favorite of real estate and resort developers – though numerous private clubs dot the Fazio résumé as well. A strong believer in moving tons of earth, Fazio has long prided himself on being able to build "quality" golf holes on virtually any terrain – an expensive philosophy but one which yielded Las Vegas' famed Shadow Creek, whose construction upon once-barren desert rates among the great accomplishments in the history of course design.

Though Fazio's layouts have frequently drawn lavish praise upon opening, a perceived emphasis on aesthetics over tactical excellence has made their staying power atop many rankings fleeting, and among Major championships, only the 1987 PGA (played over a since-redesigned Champion course at PGA National) has ever visited an original Fazio-designed course.

Tom Fazio in Southeast Florida:	
Palm Aire CC (Oaks) – Pompano Beach (w/G. Fazio)	1971
Riverbend GC – Tequesta (w/G. Fazio)	1971
Palm Aire CC (Cypress) – Pompano Beach (w/G. Fazio)	1972
Jupiter Hills C (Village) – Tequesta (w/G. Fazio)	1976
Jonathan's Landing GC (Village) – Jupiter (w/G. Fazio)	1978
PGA National GC (Haig) - Palm Beach Gardens	1980
Eastpointe CC (West) - Palm Beach Gardens	1981
Mariner Sands CC (Gold) – Stuart	1981
PGA National GC (Squire) - Palm Beach Gardens	1981
PGA National GC (Champion) - Palm Beach Gardens	1981
Jonathan's Landing GC (Fazio) – Jupiter	1987
Emerald Dunes GC – West Palm Beach	1989
Champions C at Summerfield – Stuart	1994
McArthur GC – Hobe Sound (w/N. Price)	2002
CC at Mirasol (Sunrise) – Palm Beach Gardens	2003

Robert Trent Jones – Arguably the most recognizable name in the history of golf design, Robert Trent Jones (1906-2000) was born in Lancashire, England but emigrated with his family to Rochester, New York in 1909. Though a talented young golfer, Jones did not to pursue a playing career after developing a stomach ulcer, instead turning his attention to the field of course design by studying agronomy, engineering and landscape architecture at Cornell. After spending most of the 1930s partnering with the flamboyant Canadian designer Stanley Thompson, Jones struck out on his own, eventually coming to dominate the postwar design world.

Quantifying his career is no easy task, for it encompassed more than 450 projects in 42 American states and 23 countries, including far-flung places like Japan, the Philippines and Morocco, as well as most of Europe and the Caribbean. Jones also performed renovations to at least nine U.S. Open sites (as well as to Augusta National), but his greatest impact on the game likely came from the style of his designs: big, brawny, palpably difficult and with an aesthetic all their own. Though his oft-cited philosophy of "a hard par or an easy bogey" certainly served him well, Jones's stylings have fallen somewhat out of favor over the last 30 years, leaving his better designs as landmarks of the postwar period – but seldom still rated among the world's elite. Notably, few of his Southeast Florida projects have been rated among his very best, though his work at Inverrary came to considerable fame as a PGA Tour stop from 1972-1983.

Robert Trent Jones in Southeast Florida:	
Coral Ridge CC – Ft. Lauderdale	1956
Royal Palm Yacht & CC – Boca Raton (BO)	1959
CC of Miami (East) – Hialeah	1962
CC of Miami (West) – Hialeah	1962
Inverrary Resort (East) – Lauderhill	1970
Inverrary Resort (West) – Lauderhill	1971
Turnberry Isle Resort (Miller) – Aventura	1971
Turnberry Isle Resort (Soffer) – Aventura	1971
Kings Point G (Executive) – Delray Beach (Executive)	1972
Kings Point G (Par 3) – Delray Beach (Par 3)	1973

Joe Lee – One of golf design's more popular men, Oviedo, Florida-born Joseph L. Lee (1922-2003) was brought into the design business by his friend Dick Wilson while working as a golf professional in Ohio. Returning to Florida, Lee handled construction for numerous Wilson designs, including a now-defunct 1957 project in Havana. The two became full partners by the late'50s with Lee having a hand in many of Wilson's trademark 1960s designs such as La Costa, Cog Hill (No.4), Bay Hill and the Blue Monster at Doral.

Following Wilson's death in 1965, Lee went into solo practice, ultimately becoming even more prolific than his celebrated mentor. Though his home state of Florida, where he worked on more than 80 projects, would forever be his primary stomping ground, Lee completed post-Wilson designs or alterations in 15 states and seven countries, with the Bahamas, Venezuela and Portugal all providing regular work. Lee had been a highly skilled player himself once upon a time, but his focus was on building courses that were manageable for the average golfer, featuring bunkers that looked tougher than they played, limited green contours and an overall minimum of flashy features.

All told, Joe Lee was involved with over 250 design projects, including the Trophy Club in Ft. Worth, Texas, where he enjoyed the honor of collaborating with Ben Hogan during Hogan's sole venture into the architectural field.

Joe Lee in Southeast Florida:

International Links – Miami (w/D. Wilson) (BO)	1962
The Little Club – Delray Beach (Par 3)	1969
Bonaventure CC (East) – Weston	1970
Turtle Creek GC – Tequesta	1970
Banyan GC – West Palm Beach	1973
Quail Ridge CC (South) – West Palm Beach	1973
Seagate CC – Delray Beach (fka The Hamlet CC)	1973
Poinciana CC – Lake Worth (Executive)	1974
Quail Ridge CC (North) – West Palm Beach	1975
Broken Sound C (Old) – Boca Raton	1976
Palm Beach National G&CC – Lake Worth (Redesign)	1978
Delaire CC – Delray Beach (27)	1979
Boca Greens CC – Boca Raton	1980
Boca Woods CC (Woods) – Boca Raton	1981
Boca West CC (No.4) – Boca Raton (BO)	1982
High Ridge CC – Lantana	1982
Piper's Landing CC – Palm City	1982
Bocaire CC – Boca Raton	1984
Atlantic National GC – Lake Worth	1985
Broken Sound C (Club) – Boca Raton	1985
Boca Raton Resort & C (Country Club) – Boca Raton (BO)	1986
Woodfield CC – Boca Raton	1987
Falls C – Lake Worth	1988
Hobe Sound GC – Hobe Sound	1988
C at Winston Trails – Lake Worth	1993
Abacoa GC – Jupiter	1999
Diplomat G Resort & Spa – Hallandale (Redesign)	2000

Karl Litten – A former civil engineer, Karl Litten (b.1933) changed careers in 1968 when he joined the golf course design firm of Robert von Hagge. Litten eventually went solo in 1979, though it would take eight years – and the signing-on of Gary Player as a consulting partner – before a substantial volume of new design work was obtained. Litten's list of American projects outside of Florida is limited but he gained international attention by building 1987's Emirates GC, a genuine desert oasis that hosts the PGA European Tour's annual Dubai Desert Classic. In 1992, Litten built a second 18 (the Dubai Creek GC) for the affluent Middle Eastern nation.

Karl Litten in Southeast Florida:

Boca Grove G&TC – Boca Raton	1982
Boca Delray G&CC – Delray Beach (Executive)	1983
Boca Woods CC (Lakes) – Boca Raton	1984
Gleneagles CC (Legends) – Delray Beach	1984
Gleneagles CC (Victory) – Delray Beach	1984
PGA National Resort (Estates) – Palm Beach Gardens	1984
Stonebridge G&CC – Boca Raton	1985
Polo C of Boca Raton (Equestrian) – Boca Raton	1986
Polo C of Boca Raton (Club) – Boca Raton	1986
Sugar Cane GC – Belle Glade (Add 9, w/G. Player)	1987
Westchester G&CC – Boynton Beach (27)	1988
Wycliffe G&CC (East) – Lake Worth (w/B. Devlin)	1989
Wycliffe G&CC (West) – Lake Worth	1989
Polo Trace G&CC – Delray Beach (w/J. Sindelar)	1990

Mark Mahannah – A native of Delta, Iowa, Charles Mark Mahannah (1906-1991) grew up in South Florida and got involved with golf by working on William Flynn's construction crew at the Boca Raton Resort & Club. Later becoming a greenkeeper, he shifted into course design in the early 1950s, eventually completing more than 30 projects, all but three of which were within the State of Florida. His son Charles would eventually follow in his footsteps, maintaining the family's practice right into the new millennium.

Mark Mahannah in Southeast Florida:

Normandy Shores GC – Miami Beach (Redesign)	1956
Florida Keys CC – Marathon (fka Sombrero CC)	1960
Greynolds Park GC – Miami (9)	1964
Lost Tree C – North Palm Beach	1964
Jacaranda GC (East) – Plantation	1970
Miccosukee G&CC – Miami (27)	1971
Miles Grant CC – Stuart	1972
Jacaranda GC (West) – Plantation	1975
Village GC – Royal Palm Beach	1975

Jack Nicklaus – By record the greatest golfer of all time, Jack William Nicklaus (b.1940) built a résumé which requires no amplification, his total of 18 professional Major championships (plus two U.S. Amateurs) remaining golf's gold standard, both now and for the foreseeable future. The son of a Columbus, Ohio pharmacist, Nicklaus was an excellent all-around athlete as a youth, giving up several other sports (most notably basketball) only when they began to conflict with golf. But as a golfer he was uniquely special, learning the game under Jack Grout at the Donald Ross-designed Scioto Country Club and establishing his competitive dominance early and often. Thus some 73 PGA Tour wins later, he turned his focus to a hugely successful course design business which has surely covered more ground worldwide than that of any other architect in the history of the profession.

Indeed, Nicklaus Design (which includes all manner of sons, in-laws and assorted family members) has completed over 400 courses in 41 countries on all six inhabited continents, with domestic projects marking the soil in 39 states. Though chided in its early years for building courses that either (A) favored long, high faders (like Jack himself) or (B) were somewhat formulaic, the company's work has seldom failed to be tactically engaging. Indeed, one would be hard pressed to find a Nicklaus layout that doesn't regularly engender a real degree of playing interest - even if, once upon a time, they often seemed to rely upon a checklist of reliable staples (e.g., split fairways, island and double greens, etc.) in order to do so.

Nicklaus's biggest early success came in his hometown at the Muirfield Village Golf Club, a highly thought of layout (built in partnership with Desmond Muirhead) which has hosted the PGA Tour's Memorial Tournament since 1976. In the years to follow, courses like Alabama's Shoal Creek (1977), Colorado's Castle Pines (1981) and Kentucky's Valhalla (1986) established themselves as big-event worthy, though recent entries like California's Mayacama (2001) and Long Island's Sebonack (2006, with Tom Doak), tend to grab more critical acclaim.

Jack Nicklaus in Southeast Florida:

Mayacoo Lakes CC – West Palm Beach (w/D. Muirhead)	1972
Cheeca Lodge GC – Islamorada (9 hole par 3) (Redesign)	1976
Sailfish Point GC – Stuart	1981
Bear Lakes CC (Lakes) – West Palm Beach	1984
Loxahatchee C – Jupiter	1985
Bear Lakes CC (Links) – West Palm Beach	1987
PGA Nat. Resort (Champion) – Palm Bch Gardens (Redesign)	1990
C at Ibis (Legend) - West Palm Beach	1991
C at Ibis (Heritage) - West Palm Beach	1991
La Gorce CC – Miami Beach (Redesign)	1995
Hammock Creek GC – Palm City	1996
The Bear's Club – Jupiter	1999
C at Ibis (Tradition) West Palm Beach	2001
Lost Tree C – North Palm Beach (Redesign)	2002
PGA Nat. Resort (Champion) – Palm Bch Gardens (Redesign)	2002
Trump National GC – Jupiter	2002
Royal Palm Yacht & CC – Boca Raton (Redesign)	2003
North Palm Beach CC – North Palm Beach (Redesign)	2006

Arnold Palmer – The son of a Latrobe, Pennsylvania course superintendent and professional, Arnold Daniel Palmer (b.1929) may not have been the post-World War II era's best golfer but he was very likely its most important, his aggressive, fan-friendly style going a long way towards rekindling the game's American popularity following the doldrums of Depression and war. After attending Wake Forest and spending three years in the Coast Guard, Palmer jumped onto the national stage by winning the 1954 U.S. Amateur , a triumph which led to a professional career which would come to include 62 PGA Tour wins, seven Major championships and a 22-8-2 record in six Ryder Cups.

Palmer was perhaps the single biggest reason for television's initial embrace of golf and his economic successes continued well after his game faltered. Among these, he established himself as a big-name golf course designer, partnering with Ed Seay to complete well over 200 projects worldwide. Though few of these layouts garner great favor among course raters, their modern, heavily bunkered stylings have appealed to developers enough to find a regular place upon the Southeast Florida landscape.

Arnold Palmer in Southeast Florida:

Mariner Sands GC (Green) – Stuart (w/F. Duane)	1973
PGA National Resort (Palmer) – Palm Beach Gardens	1984
Adios GC – Coconut Creek	1985
Monarch CC – Palm City	1987
Deering Bay Yacht & CC – Coral Gables	1991
Boca West CC (No.1) – Boca Raton (Redesign)	1997
Boca West CC (No.3) – Boca Raton (Redesign)	1999
Mizner CC – Delray Beach	1999
Frenchman's Reserve – Palm Beach Gardens	2002
St Andrews CC (Palmer) – Boca Raton (Redesign)	2003

Donald Ross – Among the most famous of prewar golf course designers, Donald James Ross (1872-1948) was born and raised in Dornoch, Scotland, but spent several years living at St Andrews where, like C.B. Macdonald before him and A.W. Tillinghast after, he fell under the influence of Old Tom Morris. Becoming well-versed in Old Tom's principles of sound course architecture, Ross returned home and served a stint as Royal Dornoch's professional and greenkeeper. Then, upon being invited to Boston by a vacationing Harvard professor, Ross emigrated to America in 1899.

It has been wrongly estimated that Ross designed as many as 600 courses in his career, though the actual number of just over 400 is certainly impressive enough. Ross's detractors have long accused him of laying out many courses from afar, using topographical maps to create drawings from which a third party – perhaps skilled, perhaps not – completed actual construction. And as there exists an obvious discrepancy between such high-profile classics as Seminole and Pinehurst No. 2 and many of Ross's lesser-known works, this argument likely holds some merit.

The most consistent stylistic aspect of Ross's actual, hands-on work was an attention to green positioning and contouring nearly unique in American history, resulting in green complexes that favor thoughtful approaches and, above all, an imaginative short game. Consequently, Ross's designs are seldom flashy, instead offering the sort of subtle, ground-level challenges often invisible on a course map and frequently requiring multiple playings (with different pin placements) to be fully appreciated.

Donald Ross in Southeast Florida:	
Palm Beach CC – Palm Beach	1917
Gulf Stream GC – Gulf Stream	1923
Biltmore GC – Coral Gables	1925
Delray Beach GC – Delray Beach (9)	1926
Seminole GC – Juno Beach	1929
Riviera CC – Coral Gables	1946

Robert von Hagge & Bruce Devlin – One of the game's more colorful modern characters, Robert von Hagge (1927-2010) was a fine player who, after failing on the PGA Tour, worked both as a club pro and an actor before gaining a degree of celebrity by marrying the LPGA's first glamour girl, Marlene Bauer – controversially divorcing her older sister Alice to do so.

Von Hagge entered the design business upon being hired by Dick Wilson in 1955, then formed his own Delray Beach, Florida-based company in 1962. Though hardly unsuccessful as a solo designer, his fortunes really soared after taking on popular Australian golfer Bruce Devlin as a partner in 1968. The son of a New South Wales plumber, the amiable Devlin (b.1937) was a nine-time winner on the PGA Tour and a 19-time champion Down Under, as well as a popular broadcaster prior to joining von Hagge.

Together von Hagge and Devlin designed more than 75 courses worldwide, with their largest stomping grounds – by far – being within the state of Florida. Following Devlin's 1987 departure for the Champions Tour, von Hagge formed a new firm with several younger designers, which helped him remain active until his 2010 death.

Robert von Hagge & Bruce Devlin in Southeast Florida:	
Doral G Resort & Spa (Gold) – Miami	1968
C at Emerald Hills – Hollywood	1969
Miami Beach GC – Miami Beach (Redesign)	1969
Ocean Reef C (Dolphin) – Hammock	1969
Ocean Reef C (Hammock) – Hammock	1969
Woodlands GC (East) – Tamarac	1969
Woodlands GC (West) – Tamarac	1969
Boca Dunes G&CC – Boca Raton	1970
Colony West CC (Championship) – Tamarac	1971

Robert von Hagge & Bruce Devlin Cont'd.	
Robert von Hagge & Bruce Devlin	
Crandon G Key Biscayne – Key Biscayne	1972
Fountains CC (South) – Lake Worth	1972
Via Mizner GC – Boca Raton	1972
Boca West CC (No.3) – Boca Raton	1974
Colony West CC (Glades) – Tamarac (Executive)	1974
Boca Lago CC – Boca Raton (27)	1975
Briar Bay GC – Miami (9, Executive)	1975
The Carolina C – Margate	1975
Indian Spring CC (East) – Boynton Beach	1975
Card Sound GC – Key Largo	1976
Woodmont CC – Tamarac	1976
Hunters Run (South) – Boynton Beach	1979
Hunters Run (North) – Boynton Beach	1979
Hunters Run (East) – Boynton Beach	1979
Indian Spring CC (West) – Boynton Beach	1980
Fountains CC (West) – Lake Worth	1981
Doral G Resort & Spa (Silver) – Miami (BO)	1984
Links at Boynton Beach – Boynton Beach	1984
Links at Boynton Beach (Family) – Boynton Beach (Par 3)	1984
Robert von Hagge	
Cypress Creek CC – Boynton Beach	1964
Boca Rio CC – Boca Raton	1967
Pompano Beach GC (Pines) – Pompano Beach	1967
Pompano Beach GC (Palms) – Pompano Beach (Redesign)	1967
C at Admiral's Cove (East) – Jupiter	1987
C at Admiral's Cove – Jupiter (Add 27)	1988

Dick Wilson – Though thoroughly associated with the modern, postwar era of golf course design, Philadelphia-born Louis Sibbett "Dick" Wilson (1904-1965) possessed a pedigree rooted in the ultra-classical. Following a football career at the University of Vermont, he took a job on the crew that handled construction of William Flynn's 1925 redesign of Merion, eventually turning it into full-time position with the firm of Toomey & Flynn, for whom he would oversee construction of a seminal 1931 rebuild of Shinnecock Hills.

Thus schooled by a Golden Age master, Wilson formed his own Florida-based design company shortly after World War II, hiring associates like Joe Lee and Robert von Hagge, and soon establishing himself as the prime challenger to Robert Trent Jones at the top of the American architectural market. His style, if not as aesthetically pleasing as his Golden Age predecessors, was certainly functional, with elevated green complexes, extensive bunkering and enough yardage – at least from the tips – to make any of his courses a challenge.

Wilson's base of operation and timing were perfect, for with golf's postwar explosion in Florida, he was able to fill out his résumé with all manner of Sunshine State designs including marquee facilities like Pine Tree, Doral's Blue Monster (as well as two more of the original Doral courses) and BallenIsles, site of the 1971 PGA Championship. But Wilson also built famous courses in the West (San Diego's La Costa CC), the Midwest (36 holes each at Cog Hill and NCR), the Northeast (Laurel Valley, Deepdale and Meadowbrook) and Canada (45 holes at Royal Montreal), as well as in South America, the Bahamas and even Cuba.

Dick Wilson in Southeast Florida:	
West Palm Beach GC – West Palm Beach	1947
Lake Worth Municipal GC – Lake Worth (Add 9)	1948

Dick Wilson Cont'd.

Tequesta CC – Tequesta	1957
Palmetto GC – Perrine	1960
Palm Beach Par 3 GC – Palm Beach (Par 3)	1961
Doral G Resort & Spa (Blue) – Miami	1962
Doral G Resort & Spa (Red) – Miami	1962
International Links – Miami (w/J. Lee) (BO)	1962
Pine Tree GC – Boynton Beach	1962
BallenIsles CC (East) – Palm Beach Gardens	1964
BallenIsles CC (North) – Palm Beach Gardens	1964

MONROE COUNTY

Card Sound Golf Club - Key Largo   ♦♦♦

Robert von Hagge & Bruce Devlin   www.cardsoundgolfclub.com
100 Country Club Rd, Key Largo, FL   33037   (305) 367-2555
               6,578 yds   Par 71   Rating: 71.9 / 143   (1976)

Situated near the northern tip of Key Largo, adjacent to the neighboring Ocean Reef resort's airstrip, the Card Sound Golf Club began its golfing life in 1976 with an open, heavily bunkered layout built by the popular team of Robert von Hagge and Bruce Devlin. Though essentially retaining their original routing today, the course has been renovated multiple times over the years, with its present version owing mostly to a 1999 Brian Silva makeover, the result of which is a tree-lined, classic-feeling test whose compact routing offers moments of both charm and challenge. It is also layout of two differently proportioned nines, with the far smaller front featuring several shorter par 4s wedged into the property's northern tip, plus a pair of pond-guarded closers, the 146-yard 8th (which bears some resemblance to a reverse Redan) and the 543-yard 9th. The back then stretches to a more imposing 3,542 yards and, after opening with the twisting 510-yard 10th, features two tricky, tree-narrowed dogleg rights, the 426-yard 11th and the 433-yard 14th. The 168-yard 15th plays to a shallow, lake-fronted target, kicking off a closing run which also boasts the 429-yard 16th (where the airstrip crowds the left side and the green is lake-fronted) and the 565-yard snake-like 18th. Though the course remains short by modern standards, Silva's work has made this a much more engaging test, and the most appealing of the relatively short list of golfing options available in the Florida Keys.

Ocean Reef Club (Dolphin) - Key Largo   ♦♦½

Robert von Hagge & Bruce Devlin   www.oceanreef.com
35 Ocean Reef Dr, Key Largo, FL 33037   (305) 367-2611
              6,433 yds   Par 71   Rating: 72.8 / 131   (1969)

Occupying a northern Key Largo location which is pleasantly remote yet also within real proximity of Miami, the Ocean Reef Club has been playing golf since 1955, but dates its present pair of von Hagge and Devlin-designed courses to 1969. As one might guess, squeezing so much golf onto the island's mangrove-laden *terra* not-so-*firma* posed a real challenge, resulting in a pair of short courses, the longer of which, the Dolphin, was renovated by Chip Powell in 2001. Teeing off adjacent to the private Card Sound Golf Club, and routed among houses, lakes and numerous man-made waste bunkers, this is a layout more pleasant than challenging, with some stylistic re-bunkering and tree growth giving von Hagge and Devlin's routing a more polished feel. Indeed, after opening with strong par 4s at the 429-yard dogleg left 1st and the 423-yard dogleg right 2nd, the scale of play ratchets down over the duration of the front nine, picking up a bit more brawn at the 405-yard pond-flanked 10th and the 420-yard 12th where water again flanks the left side. The finishing stretch, though still undersized by modern standards, does include the 497-yard par-5 14th (whose green angles closely along front-left water), the 416-yard out-of-bounds-lined 15th and the 218-yard 18th, a strong pond-guarded closer.

Ocean Reef Club (Hammock) - Key Largo   ♦♦

Robert von Hagge & Bruce Devlin   www.oceanreef.com
35 Ocean Reef Dr, Key Largo, FL 33037   (305) 367-2611
              6,116 yds   Par 71   Rating: 69.8 / 134   (1969)

The Ocean Reef Club's shorter Hammock (née Harbor) course sits across Gatehouse Road to the south and bears the oddity of having a substantially lower rating but a higher slope – this due mostly to a number of holes being flanked by thick, golf ball-eating mangroves. So thick is this native jungle, in fact, that a pair of tiny par 4s (the 249-yard 4th and the 297-yard 14th) actually play from astroturf tees suspended upon wooden platforms above the flora – utterly goofy but perhaps a necessity from an environmental perspective. The layout's routing is both expansive and highly disjointed, but with most holes being fairly short and basic, some of the extended cart rides may rate above the Hammock's most memorable features. Golf-wise, outbound favorites include the watery 333-yard opener and the 551-yard 8th, a long double dogleg which crosses a small patch of native sand. Coming home, the action peaks late, with both the 406-yard 16th and the 512-yard dogleg right 18th having water down the entirety of their right sides.

Florida Keys Country Club - Marathon   ◆◆½

Mark Mahannah   www.floridakeyscc.com
4000 Sombrero Blvd, Marathon, FL 33050   (305) 743-2551
              6,087 yds   Par 72   Rating: 71.9 / 127   (1960)

Originally known as the Sombrero Country Club, today's Florida Keys Country Club sits upon limited, housing-flanked acreage on Marathon Key, roughly two-thirds of the way along the remarkable over-sea drive from Miami to Key West. Palpably short and blessed with zero land upon which to expand, its Mark Mahannah-designed layout begins with a 3,014-yard front nine led by a pair of fairly engaging tests, the 480-yard par-5 3rd (where a small pond lies 30 yards shy of the green) and the 337-yard 9th, a gentle dogleg left around a wide inlet, daring longer hitters to perhaps try an all-carry blast off the tee. The back then occupies a large, man-made island to the west of the clubhouse where the golf continues to be mostly basic, save for the more heavily bunkered 448-yard 15th (which would make a strong two-shotter were it not a tiny par 5) and the 357-yard 18th, where the second must carry a narrow inlet to reach a green sitting back on the mainland.

Key West Golf Club - Key West   ◆◆◆½

Rees Jones   www.keywestgolf.com
6450 E. College Rd, Key West, FL 33040   (305) 294-5232
              6,512 yds   Par 70   Rating: 70.9 / 135   (1983)

A bit of history drives the Key West Golf Club's story, for today's course sits on the site of a lost William Langford-designed layout which dated to 1925 – a track which featured a spectacular, potentially driveable par-4 10th hole whose green occupied an small island among the mangroves. Remnants of that layout carried on for decades prior to Rees Jones' complete 1983 redesign, the result of which is shortish but often interesting track routed around several small residential developments that were not there in Langford's day. The front nine fills the eastern half of the property and includes notable longer entries like the 455-yard 2nd, the 486-yard par-5 3rd (whose green is closely guarded by left-side water) and the 434-yard 6th, an exceptionally demanding driving hole whose very narrow fairway is flanked on both sides by jungle. Most memorable, however, is the 185-yard 8th, an unforgiving, all-carry test played across marsh. The back nine then fills the site's western expanse, where favorites include the 455-yard dogleg right 11th, the 406-yard 15th (a pond-guarded dogleg left) and the 564-yard 18th, where water flanks the left side on all three shots. For the historically minded, Langford's late, lamented 10th sat mostly amidst the wide expanse of mangroves to the right of the 9th fairway.

Cheeca Lodge & Spa Golf Course - Islamorada   ♦♦

Unknown   www.cheeca.com
81801 Overseas Hwy, Islamorada, FL 33036   (305) 712-7166
          838 yds   Par 27   Rating: - / -   (1962)

An overlooked recreational centerpiece of this small seaside resort on Upper Matecumbe Key, the Cheeca Lodge Golf Course dates to the early 1960s, though multiple reports - and the resort website - credit Jack Nicklaus with redesigning it in 1976 (a project not listed on the Nicklaus Design website). But whatever its roots, this is highly engaging pitch-and-putt golf, with holes averaging 93 yards, and each being affected by either large swaths of open sand (six holes) or a pair of ponds which front the double green that houses the 97-yard 4th and the 111-yard 8th, as well as that of the 85-yard 7th. Hardly a must-see for skilled players, but this is back yard golf of the highest order.

Key Colony Beach Golf Course - Key Colony Beach   ♦

Phil Sadowski   www.keycolonybeach.net
460 8th St, Key Largo, FL 33037   (305) 289-9859
          962 yds   Par 27   Rating: - / -   (1962)

Originally an 18-hole par-3 layout which was reduced to nine during the late 1960s, the Key Colony Beach Golf Course is a municipally owned and operated facility occupying a rectangular, housing-ringed site less than 200 yards from the Atlantic Ocean. Essentially rudimentary in its design, the layout includes holes ranging in length from 66-132 yards, all routed over flat terrain, and around four largely decorative bunkers. Basic stuff.

MIAMI-DADE COUNTY

Deering Bay Yacht & Country Club - Coral Gables   ♦♦½

Arnold Palmer   www.dbycc.com
13610 Deering Bay Dr, Coral Gables, FL 33158   (305) 254-2111
            6,503 yds   Par 71   Rating: 72.0 / 144   (1991)

Situated in a surprisingly isolated waterfront location in the Miami area's southeastern reaches, the Deering Bay Yacht & Country Club is something of an architectural feat, for its 18 holes are shoehorned into a small, oddly shaped site, much of which is occupied by a residential community and a large yacht basin. The result is a somewhat disjointed layout whose outward half occupies a mangrove-protected peninsula while the back fills a prohibitively small tract on the mainland. The more engaging golf lies mostly on the peninsula, with the 418-yard 4th (the number one stroke hole), the 183-yard 5th (which juts out into the bay) and the 492-yard, watery 9th providing particularly interesting tests. The 400-yard dogleg left 3rd is also a challenge – though approaches played from the fairway's far left must fly dangerously close to adjacent houses. Following a massive cart ride through much of the development, the back nine is a bit more back-and-forth in nature, with the 334-yard 11th (with sand and water pinching the driving zone), the 199-yard 12th (whose bunkerless green sits between water hazards) and the 160-yard pond-crossing 16th rating among its best. A somewhat basic layout strategically, but the peninsula setting of the outward half is both memorable and fairly unique.

La Gorce Country Club - Miami Beach   ♦♦♦

H.C. Tippett   www.lagorcecc.com
5685 Alton Rd, Miami Beach, FL 33140   (305) 866-4021
            6,802 yds   Par 71   Rating: 73.9 / 131   (1927)

Originally built as part of automobile parts magnate Carl Fisher's ambitious Miami Beach development, the La Gorce Country Club was one of Florida's most prominent Golden Age tournament venues, witnessing victories by Gene Sarazen, Johnny Farrell, Horton Smith and Wild Bill Mehlhorn during the late 1920s and '30s. Neatly located amidst a pleasant residential neighborhood on one of Miami Beach's northernmost islands, the course underwent a substantial 1995 renovation by Jack Nicklaus, retaining much of its original routing (the front nine was slightly reconfigured) but being injected with more length and modernistic stylings. Among the most notable holes of a compact outward half are the 224-yard 4th (played to a very narrow green angled among bunkers), the 402-yard dogleg right 6th and the slightly goofy 363-yard split-fairway 7th. The back initially offers the 591-yard 11th (played to another very narrow putting surface) before closing with the 493-yard 15th (a reachable par 5 with green angled along left-side water), the 454-yard dogleg right 17th and the 452-yard pond-guarded 18th. Though historic, Captain H.C. Tippett's original design was fairly basic by Golden Age standards. Thus while Nicklaus's modern aesthetic might throw anyone expecting to find a classic facility, it can be argued that today's track is the more interesting, particularly given the flat, limited nature of the site. And the ever-present sea breeze only adds to the challenge.

Indian Creek Country Club - Indian Creek Village   ◆◆◆◆

William Flynn   www.indiancreekcountryclub.org
55 Indian Creek Island Rd, Indian Creek Village, FL 33154   (305) 866-1263
           6,851 yds   Par 72   Rating: 73.0 / 133   (1930)

The Indian Creek Country Club has long ranked among the most reclusive of American golfing institutions, its William Flynn-designed course (along with the nearly 40 private residences that encircle it) occupying its own 300-acre private island on the Miami Beach side of Biscayne Bay. Of course, this "island" actually began life as a mangrove swamp, only coming into its present form of inhabitable *terra firma* as a by-product of the U.S. Army Corps of Engineers dredging of the Intracoastal waterway, the excess sand and mud from which was shaped into a flat landmass four feet above the waterline. Flynn then added considerable contouring of his own in the form of mounding and elevated green complexes; indeed, not since Charles Blair Macdonald and Seth Raynor's legendary Lido Golf Club had a course had its every dip and roll so shaped by the hand of man. Also created was the 30-foot rise upon which the clubhouse was sited – a then-novel concept in generally flat South Florida, and one made especially noteworthy by this fabricated hilltop immediately becoming the highest point in Miami-Dade County. Flynn's layout is a fairly spacious affair with particularly wide fairways, most of which are flanked by his standard brand of angled bunkering; as with most Flynn designs, the golfer must be especially careful in selecting their line off the tee. Also notable is a complete lack of rough around the green complexes, with each being surrounded by generous areas of tightly mowed turf that both affords interesting chipping opportunities and allows errant shots to roll considerably further from their target than might otherwise be the case. Moderately altered over the years, the course retains virtually all of Flynn's routing and a grand dose of Golden Age ambience – though many original bunkers and sandy waste areas had, by the end of the 20th century, been reshaped or removed altogether. Modern restorative work by Ron Forse has reversed this trend, however, leaving a layout which, beyond the singular nature of its location, boasts some very fine golf holes. After an opening drive-and-pitch played to a typically elevated green, the front nine soon offers the 577-yard 3rd, a strong, seldom reachable par 5 which originally was buffered by a bit more open sand than remains today. Subsequent outgoing favorites include the 465-yard 6th (a classic Flynn two-shotter where a drive across a left-side bunker cluster opens the ideal line of approach), the 356-yard dogleg right 7th (which can be shortened via a tee shot flirting with plentiful right-side sand), and the tightly bunkered 218-yard 8th. Following the 548-yard 9th (which was actually a stiff 450-yard par 4 in Flynn's day), the back nine moves to the island's northern shoreline via the 427-yard 10th and the 536-yard 11th, setting up a pair of engaging waterside holes, the tightly bunkered 190-yard 12th (angled across an inlet to an attractively bunkered green) and the tempting 326-yard 13th, which dares a long carry across Indian Creek Lake to a small bulkheaded target guarded by five more bunkers. The homeward run is then led by the 448-yard 14th (a smartly bunkered dogleg right), the 165-yard bunker-ringed 15th and the 505-yard 18th, a reachable par 5 (or, potentially, a killer par 4) where highly invasive left-side sand threatens the lay-up zone. With its classic Flynn design, unique island location and timeless Florida atmosphere, Indian Creek – despite long existing beneath the national radar – rates among the region's most desirable visits. For the connoisseur, it will easily be Miami-Dade County's most coveted stop.   **(GD**: #25 State **GW**: #99 Classic)

1	2	3	4	5	6	7	8	9	Out
353	418	577	358	186	465	356	218	548	3479
4	4	5	4	3	4	4	3	5	36
10	11	12	13	14	15	16	17	18	In
427	536	190	326	448	165	379	396	505	3176
4	5	3	4	4	3	4	4	5	36

Riviera Country Club - Coral Gables   ♦♦½

Donald Ross   www.rivieracc.org
1155 Blue Rd, Coral Gables, FL 33146   (305) 661-5331
           6,603 yds   Par 72   Rating: 71.5 / 130   (1946)

Though often cited as having been built by Donald Ross in the mid-1920s (Ross did draw it up as a second 18 for the adjacent Biltmore Hotel in 1925), the Riviera Country Club actually came to life immediately after World War II, on a residence-lined tract just across SW 40th Street from the Biltmore's then-well-established 18. Altered many times since, today's facility still retains most of Ross's original corridors of play, with 14 housing-divided holes abutting the Biltmore property and four more situated across Blue Road to the south.   The layout itself, however, is quite different, with a pair of contemporary Brian Silva renovations having resulted in a well-bunkered, classic-feeling (if essentially modern) facility.   Silva's one big change was the addition of the property's lone water hazard, a narrow lake which greatly enlivens both the 541-yard 12th and the 355-yard 13th, the latter bending gently leftward between the water and a line of seven small bunkers.   The remaining 16 holes represent functional, attractive Florida golf, with notable entries including strong par 4s like the 438-yard 4th, the 416-yard 11th and the 421-yard dogleg right 18th, as well as the nicely bunkered 509-yard 7th.   Solid stuff throughout - but definitely not genuine Golden Age Donald Ross.

Biltmore Golf Course - Coral Gables   ♦♦♦

Donald Ross   www.biltmorehotel.com
1210 Anastasia Ave, Coral Gables, FL 33134   (305) 460-5364
                6,742 yds   Par 71   Rating: 72.1 / 126   (1925)

Though actually owned by the City of Coral Gables, the Biltmore Golf Course sits in the shadows of one of Florida's grandest surviving Golden Age hotels, a towering hybrid of Spanish and Italian architecture now known as the Biltmore Miami-Coral Gables. The golf course, though never among Donald Ross's elite, was a regular professional tournament venue from the 1920s through the early 1960s, counting Hagen, Sarazen, Snead, Hogan, Demaret, Guldahl, Middlecoff and Horton Smith among a dazzling roster of Hall-of-Fame winners. The layout's original Ross design was heavily altered by William Langford before World War II and multiple architects after, but was eventually returned to a classic style in 2007 via a Brian Silva renovation. The result is a pleasant track retaining virtually all of Ross's routing and many of his (restored) bunkers, all frequently enlivened by the waters of the Coral Gables Canal. The front nine initially runs out to the northwest before returning to the rear of the hotel, where the 400-yard 7th doglegs left across the canal, and the 229-yard 8th is a tough, tightly bunkered par 3. The back makes more aggressive use of the canal, first at the 211-yard 12th (where it angles left of the green), then especially at the 558-yard 15th and the 450-yard 17th, whose railroad-tied putting surface is perched dangerously above it. As the railroad ties suggest, this is hardly pure Ross, yet it remains an engaging – and highly historic – regional stop nonetheless.

Links at Fisher Island - Fisher Island   ♦♦

P.B. Dye   www.fisherislandclub.com
1 Fisher Island Dr, Fisher Island, FL 33109   (305) 535-6000
                3,069 yds   Par 35   Rating: 34.7 / 136   (1988)

Occupying an island that once served as a private winter home for the Vanderbilt family, the Links at Fisher Island lies just south of both Miami Beach and the Port of Miami, and features a creatively route P.B. Dye-designed nine wedged tightly within the property's residence-encircled center. What muscle there is lies in solid par 4s like the 435-yard 2nd and the 450-yard 4th, but more interesting are shorter entries like the 130-yard 3rd (played diagonally across a pond) and the 271-yard lake-flanked 8th. Most memorable, however, are a pair of holes isolated in the island's northwest corner, the 173-yard 6th (whose green juts leftward into a pond) and the 382-yard 7th, which lies directly along a shipping channel and doglegs left around the same water hazard, daring an aggressive line off the tee. By any measure, lots of golf for so confined (and limited) a site.

Miccosukee Golf & Country Club - Miami   ♦♦½

Mark Mahannah   www.miccosukee.com
6401 Kendale Lakes Dr, Miami, FL 33183   (305) 382-3930
        Marlin/Dolphin: 7,147 yds   Par 72   Rating: 74.9 / 138   (1971)
        Barracuda: 3,360 yds   Par 36   Rating: 35.9 / 131   (1971)

Owned since 2001 by the Miccosukee Indian Tribe, and serving as an amenity to their nearby hotel and casino, this Mark Mahannah-designed facility (known formerly as both Miami National and Kendale Lakes) hosted the LPGA five times during the 1970s as well as the Web.com Tour from 2003-2012. Its three nines fill a U-shaped tract whose arms flank a large residential neighborhood, with its highest-rated combination pairing the Marlin and Dolphin loops. The Marlin lies entirely south of the clubhouse and provides muscle with big par 4s like the 480-yard 2nd, the 470-yard 6th and the 450-yard 9th, though its strongest holes may well be the 210-yard 4th (whose narrow green is pinched between sand and water) and the 210-yard 8th. The Dolphin fills the property's western flank where it opens with a 532-yard water-crossed par 5, then later finds its strength in par 4s like the 440-yard 3rd and the 477-yard 6th, as well as the 615-yard par-5 7th, whose fairway slithers between a pair of large lakes. The 205-yard tightly bunkered 8th is another solid entry, but the 375-yard 9th (with interceding water suggesting a lay-up off the tee) is a relatively quiet closer. The Barracuda, meanwhile, is the club's shortest nine but starts with a bang, its 443-yard 1st doglegging sharply right, around a large lake. Thereafter, it builds around two very long par 5s (the 606-yard pond-crossed 4th and 585-yard 7th), with the remaining six holes being considerably shorter in nature.

Shula's Golf Club - Miami Lakes   ♦♦

William Watts   www.shulasgolfclub.com
7601 Miami Lakes Dr, Miami Lakes, FL 33014   (305) 821-1150
        6,757 yds   Par 72   Rating: 72.1 / 127   (1962)

Though named after the Miami Dolphin's legendary coach (and area resident) Don Shula, Shula's Golf Club has long been the property of Florida's powerful Graham family, who developed it (along with an adjacent resort hotel) in the early 1960s. Designed by local architect William Watts, the golf course is situated along the eastern flank of the Palmetto Expressway 14 miles northwest of downtown where, notwithstanding a 1990 renovation by Kipp Schulties, it retains nearly all of its original routing. The front nine is comfortably the less engaging half , offering largely basic golf prior to spreading its wings a bit at the 507-yard island-green 7th and the 550-yard dogleg right 9th. The back nine, though largely back-and-forth in nature, provides more playing interest largely due the network of lakes that separates its parallel fairways. Favorites here include the 535-yard 12th and a trio of long par 4s: the 439-yard water-fronted 11th, the 430-yard 14th (requiring a long water carry on approach) and the 454-yard 18th, a sweeping dogleg left around a pond. An adjoining nine-hole executive loop has been abandoned, but this remains pleasant resort golf – if not quite among the South Florida elite.

Trump National Doral (Red Tiger) - Miami   ◆◆◆

Dick Wilson   www.trumpgolfdoral.com
4400 NW 87th Ave, Miami, FL 33178   (305) 592-2000
        6,395 yds   Par 72   Rating: 71.8 / 136   (1962)

Joining the famed Blue Monster as half of Doral's original 36-hole complex back in 1962, this, the original Red course, was always intended to be a kinder and gentler Dick Wilson design – though it was strong enough in those early days to host the LPGA's Elizabeth Arden Classic in 1972-73. Altered a bit over the decades to accommodate the resort's expanding facilities, it underwent a significant Gil Hanse renovation in 2014, resulting in a still-short layout but one with greatly enhanced playing interest. Of course, "short" tends not to be the adjective of choice upon facing the 606-yard 1st (a lake-flanked test that would fit nicely on the Blue Monster) and the 231-yard 2nd, but the action scales down thereafter, with outbound favorites including the 296-yard watery 4th and the 487-yard par-5 5th, which doglegs sharply left around a lake before culminating in a narrow, elevated island green. The back opens with the slightly awkward 535-yard 10th (where right-side water reduces the lay-up zone to a sliver of fairway) but quickly picks up at the 185-yard over-water 11th, the 485-yard 12th (a tricky par 5 bothered by left-side water and a prominent tree) and the 173-yard 14th, which has a C.B. Macdonald-like depression with its bunker-ringed green. Also notable are the 301-yard 17th (driveable over short-right water) and the 526-yard 18th, a quirky closer whose triangular green is wedged between front-left sand and back-right water. There is enough room for the less-skilled player here, but better golfers will still find plenty to be entertained.   **(GW: #200 Resort)**

Trump National Doral (Golden Palm) - Miami   ◆◆◆

Robert von Hagge and Bruce Devlin   www.trumpgolfdoral.com
4400 NW 87th Ave, Miami, FL 33178   (305) 592-2000
        7,012 yds   Par 71   Rating: 74.2 / 139   (1968)

Originally built as Doral's third course by Robert von Hagge and Bruce Devlin in the late 1960s, today's Golden Palm layout was renovated several times (most prominently by Raymond Floyd in 1995) before joining both the Blue Monster and the Red in being overhauled by Gil Hanse in 2014. Hemmed in by property boundaries and copious water hazards, Hanse retained the existing routing but significantly altered the layout's green complexes and bunkering, creating a more stylish track that remains significantly long and challenging. One's attention is grabbed quickly at the 496-yard par-4 opener but the action takes on a tad more flavor at both the 430-yard 3rd (a tricky dogleg right whose long, narrow green sits flush against left-side water) and the 539-yard 4th, a water-lined double dogleg. The routing later crosses Northwest 97th Avenue for four outlying holes built around a central lake, the most engaging of which include the 425-yard 8th (where a small centerline bunker menaces the drive) and the 330-yard 10th, a dogleg left which dares one to drive the green via a long carry across water. Two more shorter back nine entries of note come at the 150-yard all-or-nothing 12th (played to a near-island green) and the 343-yard 13th, where left-side water greatly narrows the driving zone. But the most noteworthy test, easily, is the 469-yard 18th, a dangerous par 4 whose island green is so unforgiving that the hole's white tees lie at only 397-yards.   **(GW: #70 Resort)**

Trump National Doral (Blue Monster) - Miami   ◆◆◆◆

Dick Wilson   www.trumpgolfdoral.com
4400 NW 87th Ave, Miami, FL 33178   (305) 592-2000
            7,590 yds   Par 72   Rating: 77.4 / 146   (1962)

Largely the face of Southeast Florida golf since its opening in 1962, Doral's famed Blue Monster drew immediate attention to what was, in its infancy, a resort so mom-and-pop in nature that its moniker was actually just a blending of the names of its developers, Doris and Alfred Kaskel ("Dor" and "Al"). But naming issues aside, the Kaskels might well be considered visionaries as they brought to life a high-profile, highly successful resort on what was initially 2,400 acres of uninhabited semi-swamp two miles northwest of Miami International Airport. Though their first hotel actually lay on Miami Beach (with golfers being shuttled to the club), this inland property would eventually grow out to 90 holes of golf, over 700 hotel rooms and enough residential development that the adjacent City of Doral was incorporated in 2003. Golf-wise, the resort's calling card has forever been Dick Wilson's famed Blue Monster, a highly difficult layout at the time of its creation, and a course which came to fame upon hosting the PGA Tour beginning immediately after its opening in 1962. Though lengthened and rebunkered sporadically over the years, the lower scoring brought on by modern equipment made this a track in need of updating – a task performed impressively by Gil Hanse in 2013. Hanse's version retained Wilson's original routing but took on a more stylistic and strategic feel, all of which put a very nice face on a layout which also became considerably tougher. The 578-yard 1st may offer an opening birdie opportunity (though rather less than before) but thereafter the challenge ratchets upward quickly, with the 440-yard 3rd, the 227-yard 4th and the 472-yard 7th all playing to greens which are closely flanked by water, while the 430-yard 6th delivers one of the more tightly bunkered driving areas one is likely to encounter. One place where Hanse made a major change was at holes 8 and 9, with the 550-yard 8th having its green moved leftward, flush against a lake, which in turn allowed the dangerous 9th to grow from 169 to 216 yards – a major increase when we consider that its green now sits far more tightly against still more *agua*. Theoretically, the back nine opens with a handful of scoring opportunities, but the 608-yard dogleg left 10th features a scary drive across water, while the previously awkward 428-yard 11th has become far better balanced with Hanse's revised bunkering. The 245-yard 13th didn't require much alteration, but it is followed by a trio which underwent significant change: the par-4 14th (lengthened to 475 yards and played to a new, more tightly bunkered green), the 183-yard 15th (transformed from a basic, dry one-shotter to a dangerously watery one), and especially the 370-yard dogleg left 16th, where revised bunkering and the expansion of a lake have created an exciting, potentially drivable test. And then, of course, there is the famous 473-yard 18th, a lakeside finisher whose strength has long been such that it required little in the way of major alteration; indeed, now, as ever, there are few more demanding closers to be found in American golf. Sadly, the pros only got three cracks at the revised Blue Monster before politics pushed the PGA Tour to move on to less controversial pastures. Still, this remains something of a must-see in the world of Florida golf, for beyond Hanse's revitalized design, the roster of legendary golfers who have played and won here is among the most impressive to be found anywhere. Thus while we await the seemingly inevitable return of the Tour down the road, the Blue Monster remains a cornerstone of Southeast Florida golf. (**GD**: #24 State, #61 USA Public **GW**: #118 Modern, #28 Resort)

1	2	3	4	5	6	7	8	9	Out
578	446	440	227	419	430	472	550	216	3778
5	4	4	3	4	4	4	5	3	36
10	11	12	13	14	15	16	17	18	In
608	428	600	245	475	183	370	430	473	3812
5	4	5	3	4	3	4	4	4	36

Trump National Doral (Silver Fox) - Miami   ◆◆½

Robert von Hagge & Bruce Devlin   www.trumpgolfdoral.com
4400 NW 87th Ave, Miami, FL 33178   (305) 592-2000
         7,006 yds   Par 71   Rating: 74.9 / 148   (1984)

With Doral's former White course having been sold off for development, the resort's Silver Fox layout now bears the distinction of being its only track not to begin and end immediately adjacent to the hotel. Situated across Northwest 97th Avenue to the west, it began life as the unaffiliated von Hagge and Devlin-designed Doral Park Country Club, then was renovated by Jerry Pate after its purchase by the resort in 1997. More recently reworked by prominent instructor Jim McLean (and later resequenced to begin closer to the hotel), the Silver Fox is today marketed for its toughness, and with water having a major impact on no less than 12 holes, that assessment is a fair one. Housing-flanked in most directions, it begins with a front nine built around a three-hole stretch (marketed as the "Bermuda Triangle") which includes the 474-yard water-pinched 6th, the frightening 183-yard 7th (played to a scarily unforgiving island target) and the 429-yard 8th, which culminates in a narrow, false-fronted putting surface. The back then begins with two notably long par 4s (the 463-yard 10th and the 489-yard dogleg right 12th) before closing with a pair of short-but-very-watery tests, the 179-yard 17th and the narrow 389-yard 18th. The challenge is certainly present, but the more discerning golfer may find the polish of the resort's 54 Gil Hanse-redesigned holes a bit more to their liking.

Turnberry Isle (Soffer) - Aventura   ◆◆◆

Robert Trent Jones   www.turnberryislemiami.com
19999 West Country Club Dr, Aventura, FL 33180   (305) 932-6200
         7,047 yds   Par 71   Rating: 75.8 / 149   (1971)

An upscale residential community which also boasts a sizeable resort hotel, Turnberry Isle is located half a mile inland from the Atlantic and just north of Miami Beach, where it offers a pair of Robert Trent Jones-designed 18s which were renovated in 2006 by Hall-of-Famer Raymond Floyd. The Soffer (née South) course is the facility's tournament venue, having hosted the LPGA on eight occasions (with winners including Carner, Lopez, Sheehan and Alcott) as well as three playings of the Senior PGA Championship (1979-81) won by Don January, Arnold Palmer and Miller Barber. A heavily shaped, surprisingly compact layout with water meaningfully affecting play on 15 holes, it begins with a 3,617-yard front nine which features plenty of muscle, notably at the 558-yard 2nd, the 483-yard 4th (where ideal drives hug left-side water), the 452-yard dogleg right 5th and the 574-yard 6th, whose lake-fronted green returns to the clubhouse. The shorter inward half is initially led by the twisting 537-yard pond-guarded 11th before peaking over a compact, creatively routed finish that includes a trio of par 3s in the final six holes, the strongest being the 235-yard 15th (water left) and the 184-yard 17th, whose putting surface juts rightward into the same hazard. Most memorable, however, is the 571-yard 18th which, lacking a proper lay-up area, requires a long third to an island green framed, well to its left, by a large Disneyland-like waterfall. (**GW**: #89 Resort)

Turnberry Isle (Miller) - Aventura   ♦♦½

Robert Trent Jones   www.turnberryislemiami.com
19999 West Country Club Dr, Aventura, FL 33180   (305) 932-6200
                6,417 yds   Par 70   Rating: 72.0 / 143   (1971)

Turnberry Isle's much shorter Miller (née North) course occupies the property's upper half and is rated nearly three strokes easier – though as a 143 slope suggests, its Raymond Floyd-renovated layout is hardly a pushover. Its nines having been reversed since the renovation, the Miller today opens with its stronger half first, particularly over a stretch that surrounds Lake Julius, a huge water hazard named for Hall of Famer (and ex-club pro) Julius Boros. These include the 413-yard 4th (whose drive angles diagonally across water), the 577-yard 5th (which curves rightward to a peninsula green, and is easily the layout's most daunting entry), the 226-yard 6th (water lapping at the green's right edge) and the 388-yard 7th (ditto). The 3,130-yard inward half is considerably shorter and easier, with three of its first four being sub-400-yard two-shotters of only middling design. The strongest entries include the 246-yard 11th (on size alone), the 178-yard over-water 15th and the 515-yard 16th, a dogleg right featuring sand along the corner and a very narrow green extending rightward, into a pond. A very solid "second" course, but far kinder and gentler than the more tournament-ready Soffer.   (**GW**: #130 Resort)

Costa Del Sol Golf Club - Doral

Bob Cupp
100 Costa del Sol Blvd, Doral, FL 33178
6,011 yds   Par 72   Rating: 70.0 / 118   (1974)

www.cdsgolfclub.com
(305) 592-3300

Built two-and-a-half miles west of Miami International Airport, across the street from the sprawling Doral complex, the real estate-oriented Costa Del Sol Golf Club was one of the earliest entries in Bob Cupp's long-running design portfolio – so early, in fact, that it predated his career-making association with Jack Nicklaus. As such, it is more basic than much of his later work, though the confined nature of the housing-lined property surely had much to do with this. While the bunkering is largely decorative, water hazards are often more invasive, as are a number of trees which have filled out over the years. These latter two factors are apparent within a trio of solid par 5s: the 530-yard 1st (the number one stroke hole, with water affecting all three shots), the 497-yard straightaway 3rd (squeezed between trees and out-of-bounds, with a pond-fronted green), and the 482-yard 13th, where another pond consumes much of what should be the lay-up zone. Also notable are three somewhat similar over-water par 3s as well as each nine's closers, the 317-yard dogleg left 9th (theoretically driveable over water – and neighboring houses) and the 353-yard 18th, which makes an early right turn around one final lake.

Crandon Golf Key Biscayne - Key Biscayne

Robert von Hagge & Bruce Devlin
6700 Crandon Blvd, Key Biscayne, FL 33149
7,354 yds   Par 72   Rating: 76.5 / 151   (1972)

www.crandongolfclub.com
(305) 361-9129

One of America's more appealing (and splendidly situated) municipal facilities, Crandon Golf Key Biscayne sits in mangrove- and jungle-flanked seclusion on the eponymous key, three miles across the Rickenbacker Causeway from downtown Miami. But beyond its quiet-but-accessible location, this is also a big time golf course, boasting more than enough von Hagge & Devlin-designed challenge to have hosted the Champions Tour 18 times from 1987-2004. Touched up by von Hagge in 1993, it quickly grabs one's attention with a memorable opening trio: the 548-yard 1st (a heavily bunkered double dogleg along a lake), the 464-yard 2nd (a sweeping dogleg left around three bunkers) and the 193-yard 3rd, an all-carry test across a mangrove-framed inlet of the bay. Another inlet is crossed at the 453-yard 7th, which sets up the course's shortest hole, the 140-yard 8th, an isolated tests set within the mangroves at the property's western tip. The imposing 3,903-yard back nine lies to the north of the facility's entrance road and opens with a powerhouse trio of its own: the 556-yard 10th (which bends right, between two lakes), the 450-yard 11th (the number one stroke hole, with more water right) and the 187-yard 12th, an all-carry test played across a lagoon. The closers are equally testing, culminating in the tightly bunkered 255-yard 17th and the narrow 555-yard 18th, which runs along the mangrove-lined bayshore. Counting Major champions like Trevino, Player, David Graham and Larry Nelson among its winners, this is top-shelf municipal stuff.

Granada Golf Course - Coral Gables   ♦½

William Langford   www.coralgables.com
2001 Granada Blvd, Coral Gables, FL 33134   (305) 460-5367
2,986 yds   Par 36   Rating: 34.1 / 109   (1925)

Built by the prolific Chicago-based designer William Langford at the height of Florida's Golden Age real estate boom, the Granada Golf Course is today run by the City of Coral Gables as a municipal facility, marketed as the state's oldest nine-hole layout. A short and unassuming loop, it has changed comparatively little from Langford's day, with its first four holes running out and back to the east of Granada Boulevard and its last five following a similar pattern to the west. Some interior tree growth is apparent, and only 14 bunkers remain in play (few posing any real tactical questions) – but Langford's famed steep-and-deep bunkering and sharply elevated putting surfaces were little in evidence here from the beginning. Anyone hoping to find a hidden Golden Age classic may be disappointed, but the park-like setting still makes for an enjoyable, classical-feeling game.

Greynolds Park Golf Course - North Miami Beach   ♦½

Mark Mahannah   www.miamidade.gov
17530 West Dixie Hwy, North Miami Beach, FL 33160   (305) 949-1741
3,090 yds   Par 36   Rating: 34.4 / 118   (1964)

Part of a county park whose irregularly shaped boundaries lie just west of Biscayne Boulevard, the Greynolds Park Golf Course is a short nine-holer laid out by regional design stalwart Mark Mahannah in 1964. Its smallish site lends itself to a simple, back-and-forth routing, while leaving little room for longer holes; indeed, the 409-yard 9th is the only par 4 longer than 350 yards. Favorites include the well-bunkered 147-yard 3rd and a trio of stronger finishers: the 521-yard dogleg right 7th, the 308-yard 8th (a tempting two-shotter with a prominent left-side bunker impeding the direct route home) and the aforementioned 9th. Solid stuff relative to many a neighborhood municipal nine.

International Links Golf Club - Miami   ◆◆½

Dick Wilson & Joe Lee   www.internationallinksgolfclub.com
1802 North 37ᵗʰ Ave, Miami, FL 33125   (305) 633-4583
                7,173 yds   Par 71   Rating: 73.7 / 128   (1997)

Despite being flanked by several major roads and a tributary of the Miami River, and lying nearly adjacent to Miami International Airport, the International Links (née the Melreese Country Club) is one of the stronger municipal offerings in Southeast Florida. Originally built by Dick Wilson and Joe Lee in 1962 (and touched up by Trent Jones in 1966), it was substantially remodeled by Charles Mahannah in 1997, resulting in a challenging layout that is remarkably long given the compactness of its property. Thus bearing little resemblance to the layout upon which Betsy Rawls won the LPGA's 1963 Sunshine Open, it is a track whose size can be somewhat deceiving; indeed, fully one-third of this length is consumed by a quartet of par 5s *averaging* 592-yards, the best of which are the 608-yard dual-fairway 4ᵗʰ and the 602-yard 17ᵗʰ, an endless dogleg left along/around a narrow lake. The par 4s are thus left to include only two in excess of 440 yards, the 451-yard 3ʳᵈ (with sand – and the river – right, and water left) and the 460-yard 18ᵗʰ, which plays into the prevailing wind, to a narrow green angled behind front-right sand. A tad formulaic in spots, but with so much size, as well as 80+ bunkers in play, this is big municipal stuff.

Killian Greens Golf Club - Miami   ◆½

Unknown   www.killiangreens.com
9980 SW 104ᵗʰ St, Miami, FL 33176   (305) 271-0917
                6,449 yds   Par 72   Rating: 70.1 / 124   (1969)

Occupying an oddly shaped, power line-crossed tract immediately adjacent to the Don Shula Expressway, the Killian Greens Golf Club is a real estate-perforated layout which would appear to have been planned with housing considerations taking top priority. This is initially apparent at the 542-yard 2ⁿᵈ (a late-turning dogleg right where corner homes might creep into play) but is plainly visible at two later entries, the 375-yard 15ᵗʰ and 490-yard 16ᵗʰ, where flanking housing must surely field frequent incoming fire. Otherwise this is a functional facility whose most interesting holes include a trio of tree-bothered tests: the 395-yard 4ᵗʰ (where a line of right-side specimens severely narrows the line of play), the 380-yard 9ᵗʰ (where two more divide the fairway) and the 325-yard 10ᵗʰ, where both trees and sand pinch the approach. Functional neighborhood stuff.

Country Club of Miami (West) - Miami   ◆◆½

Robert Trent Jones   www.golfccmiami.com
6801 NW 186th St, Hialeah, FL 33015   (305) 829-8456
        6,970 yds   Par 72   Rating: 73.8 / 132   (1962)

Built upon a housing-lined, W-shaped tract three miles northwest of Opa Locka Airport, the Country Club of Miami sat literally at the edge of Miami-area civilization at the time of its 1962 opening. Yet despite such relative remoteness, it quickly established itself as a hot period golfing destination, simultaneously hosting the PGA Tour's National Airlines Open and the LPGA's Elizabeth Arden Classic from 1969-1971. Thus able to boast of winners like Trevino, Player, Carner and Mann (as well as having had Arnold Palmer as the club's first touring pro), it is today a somewhat less-heralded facility led by the layout upon which the pros competed, the 6,970-yard West course. Still playing over Jones' original routing, the West has evolved a bit over the decades, as it is today missing more than 20 Jones bunkers and has seen several greens reduced significantly in size. Thus it today weighs in as a mid-range Jones layout, with plenty of sand and water present – but much of it is less invasively placed. Some muscle appears at entries like the 462-yard 6th (the number one stroke hole), the 212-yard 8th and especially the 453-yard 17th, but most interesting is a trio of water-affected par 5s: the 560-yard pond-guarded 7th, the slightly awkward 540-yard 13th and the 523-yard creek-flanked 16th.

Country Club of Miami (East) - Miami   ◆◆

Robert Trent Jones   www.golfccmiami.com
6801 NW 186th St, Hialeah, FL 33015   (305) 829-8456
        6,409 yds   Par 70   Rating: 70.8 / 127   (1962)

Actually being, by several months, the older half of the Country Club of Miami's 36-hole facility, the Robert Trent Jones-designed East course today represents a second-tier entry next to the much longer West - but such was not always the case. Indeed, the East is missing more than 40 original bunkers and has actually been downsized, its 7th, 8th and 9th holes being heavily reconfigured circa 1990 to accommodate a new practice facility. It has also seen what remains of its bunkering morph considerably in appearance, joining the West in having its once-distinctive cape-and-bay shaping evolve into a blander, far less Jones-like look. But while only one par 4 (the 436-yard 3rd) measures in excess of 400 yards, there are several shorter holes that are comparably engaging to most anything on the West. Most notable among these are a pair of diminutive par 4s, the 285-yard 8th (a driveable water-crossing test that began life as a one-shotter) and the 364-yard 18th, which bends gently leftward along a lake. On the brawnier side, the 418-yard 10th, the watery 192-yard 13th and the 564-yard 16th are among the top entries.

Miami Beach Golf Club - Miami Beach   ◆◆◆

Robert von Hagge & Bruce Devlin   www.miamibeachgolfclub.com
2301 Alton Rd, Miami Beach, FL 33140   (305) 532-3350
          6,813 yds   Par 72   Rating: 73.1 / 131   (1969)

Today's municipally owned Miami Beach Golf Club occupies the site of the former Bayshore Golf Course, a 1923 creation (possibly by the legendary Willie Park Jr.) which hosted numerous PGA and LPGA Tour events from 1928-1961. Despite a multi-generational list of champions which included Sarazen, Snead, Player and Zaharias, Bayshore was completely rebuilt in 1969 by Robert von Hagge and Bruce Devlin, then subsequently renovated once more by Arthur Hills in 2002. The present layout is a compact test, but one which frequently offers somewhat more interesting golf than the average big city muni. The par-35 front side measures only 3,137 yards and, save for the 594-yard 1st (a typically long, water-flanked von Hagge opener), is led by straightforward holes like the watery 153-yard 3rd, the 370-yard pond-guarded 8th (where drives carrying a large, right-side bunker yield the ideal second) and the 233-yard 9th. However, the par-37 back nine is another story, measuring nearly 3,700 yards and featuring a trio of strong par 5s: the 523-yard 10th (where water can affect all three shots), the 567-yard 12th and the well-bunkered 553-yard 15th. But the most memorable entries, easily, are a pair of closers routed around the same lake, the 347-yard dogleg right 16th (a tactically rich par 4 which dares a 275-yard water carry to drive the green) and the 183-yard 17th, which plays across the water to a putting surface elevated above a massive fronting bunker.

Miami Shores Country Club - Miami Shores   ◆◆

Red Lawrence   www.miamishoresgolf.com
10000 Biscayne Blvd, Miami Shores, FL 33138   (305) 795-2360
          6,705 yds   Par 71   Rating: 71.2 / 131   (1939)

A 1939 Red Lawrence design which appropriated the name of a 1920s Donald Ross layout that previously existed nearby, the Miami Shores Country Club is an obviously venerable facility whose course is crossed by both railroad tracks and the waters of Biscayne Creek. Today's layout, however, is not quite consistent with Lawrence's original, with the most obvious changes being the 1990s construction of new 9th, 10th and 12th holes to make room for a new driving range, the addition of an incongruous waste bunker at the 530-yard 1st, and the construction of a creek to encircle the green complex (though not too closely) at the 432-yard 5th. Further, a 2012 renovation by John Sanford greatly reduced the scale of Lawrence's bunkering, presumably a concession to public course playability, but one which traditionalists will struggle to embrace. The river-like Biscayne Creek only really affects the 155-yard 2nd (which angles over it) as well as the par-5 7th and the reconfigured 12th, whose fairways it cuts across. A run of solid golf can be found over the home stretch, which includes the 419-yard dogleg right 15th, the 416-yard 16th, the imposing (if basic) 233-yard 17th and the 414-yard dogleg left 18th.

Miami Springs Golf & Country Club - Miami Springs ♦♦½

William Langford   www.miamispringsgolfcourse.com
650 Curtiss Pkwy, Miami Springs, FL 33166   (305) 805-5180
                6,755 yds   Par 71   Rating: 71.0 / 119   (1924)

Apparently pre-dated by an early nine holes designed by the site's original developers, today's Miami Springs Golf & Country Club was laid out by William Langford near the peak of the South Florida land boom, and soon went on to establish itself as a popular event venue. Indeed, it would host the PGA Tour's Miami Open from 1933-1955 (counting seven Hall-of-Famers among its winners), the Miami Four-Ball from 1945-1949 (Hogan and Demaret winning twice) and even the LPGA on three occasions (1959-1962). The outward half of Langford's design remains intact routing-wise, but much of his original bunkering is absent. Thus the back nine, though reconfigured to accommodate a practice range, is easily the better loop, finding early strength in the 395-yard 10th (a sharp dogleg left), the 449-yard 11th and the 248-yard 12th, a bunkerless one-shotter of obviously huge proportion. The 337-yard 14th is potentially driveable if one dares to carry a crossing creek, while the 439-yard 17th (affected by the same hazard) and the 429-yard 18th (a sweeping dogleg right) provide a big finish. Somewhat faded grandeur, to be sure, and in strictly golfing terms, there are several stronger public layouts to be found around Miami. But the list of legends who have competed here is an imposing one...

Normandy Shores Golf Club - Miami Beach ♦♦♦

William Flynn   www.normandyshoresgolfclub.com
2401 Biarritz Dr, Miami Beach, FL 33141   (305) 868-6502
                6,805 yds   Par 71   Rating: 72.5 / 129   (1941)

Joining the Miami Beach Golf Club as a second notably strong municipal facility operated by this famous resort city, Normandy Shores mirrors the nearby (and very private) Indian Creek in that it occupies its own island within Biscayne Bay, where its residence-lined course was similarly designed by Golden Age giant William Flynn in 1941. After hosting postwar PGA and LPGA tournaments that saw winners like Sam Snead, Jim Ferrier and Babe Zaharias, Flynn's creation was heavily renovated by Mark Mahannah in 1956, then again by Arthur Hills in 2008, resulting in a layout whose routing remains intact, but whose hazarding has been altered significantly. Despite playing to a par of 35, the front nine is actually the longer half, this owing to substantial par 4s like the 465-yard 4th (with water down its left side), the 452-yard 7th (ditto) and the 450-yard 9th, which plays to a smallish green angled behind sand. The back makes more invasive use of the property's many lakes, particularly at the 421-yard 11th (whose green slants leftward beyond a hazard) and the 325-yard waterside 12th, where centerline sand complicates aggressive drives. Easily the club's longest par 3, the 240-yard 17th is a well-bunkered test, while the 529-yard 18th slips between left-side water and right-side sand en route to the final green. Not Miami's top public-access facility, but few munis enjoy this sort of location and history – even if Flynn's original design would, for many, be preferable.

Palmetto Golf Course - Perrine   ♦♦♦½

Dick Wilson   www.golfpalmetto.com
9300 SW 152nd St, Perrine, FL 33157   (305) 238-2922
6,648 yds   Par 70   Rating: 72.2 / 128   (1960)

A municipally operated facility since 1967, the Palmetto Golf Course is located 14 miles southwest of downtown Miami along the west side of Dixie Highway, on an open, triangular tract crossed by the Cutler Canal. Owing to surrounding housing, the Dick Wilson-designed layout has remained close to its original size, but Wilson's standard heavy dose of sand (essentially flanking both sides of every green, often with multiple hazards) has helped to maintain a reasonable degree of challenge into the modern era. What keeps things user-friendly is Wilson's relatively benign use of the canal, particularly on a trio of par 4s whose greens are positioned a safe distance beyond the hazard: the 435-yard 3rd, the 419-yard 10th and the 374-yard 14th. Additional (dryer) two-shotters of note include the 430-yard 2nd (played to a green which angles leftward, beyond sand), the 451-yard heavily bunkered 12th, the 434-yard 18th, while more tactical golf can be found at the 319-yard 4th, which curves rightward along a lake to a tightly bunkered putting surface. Wilson's bunkering long ago lost its rougher-edged period styling, but this still represents higher-end public golf with a pedigree.

Redland Golf & Country Club - Homestead   ♦♦

Red Lawrence   www.redlandgolf.com
24451 Krome Ave, Homestead, FL 33030   (305) 247-8503
6,613 yds   Par 72   Rating: 71.1 / 122   (1947)

Still surrounded primarily by open agricultural acreage, the Redland Golf & Country Club was located very much in the middle of nowhere at the time of its postwar construction, making its 1947 debut with nine Red Lawrence-designed holes, with its second nine not being added until several years later. The original loop (today's front side) is the shorter, less interesting half, really only standing out at the 476-yard 9th, a short par 5 guarded front-left by a post-Lawrence pond. The newer, slightly longer inward half weighs in a little more heavily, offering the layout's two strongest par 4s at the demanding 451-yard 13th (a sharp dogleg right along the property line) and the 414-yard 18th (a sharp dogleg left around corner sand) as well as its best par 3 at the 193-yard 16th, whose green is fronted by a trio of bunkers. Not the sort of layout a serious golfer would travel for, but rather a better overall test than one might expect to find somewhat off the beaten track.

Briar Bay Golf Course - Miami ◆½

Robert von Hagge & Bruce Devlin   www.briarbaygolf.com
9399 SW 134th St, Miami, FL 33176   (305) 235-6754
1,802 yds   Par 31   Rating: 32.6 / 113   (1975)

A county-operated executive facility situated on a C-shaped tract northwest of the Falls Shopping Center, the Briar Bay Golf Course was built by Robert von Hagge and Bruce Devlin, who imbued it with enough character to rise above what one might expect from a 2,074-yard nine-hole muni. Featuring several narrow, tightly bunkered greens, it also includes a trio of engaging water-affected par 4s: the 243-yard 2nd (where a pond and left-side trees bother the drive), the 298-yard 3rd and the 323-yard 6th, comfortably the course's longest hole and one requiring a full approach over the corner of a pond.

BROWARD COUNTY

Adios Golf Club - Coconut Creek   ◆◆◆

Arnold Palmer   www.adiosgolfclub.org
7740 NW 39th Ave, Coconut Creek, FL 33073   (954) 429-0990
6,879 yds   Par 72   Rating: 74.3 / 141   (1985)

Bordering Florida's Turnpike just west of Deerfield Beach, the Adios Golf Club bears rather a different look from standard Arnold Palmer-designed fare, due largely to extensive landscaping between holes, less copious bunkering and the occasional use of open waste areas. The course is wedged into a compact rectangular site and, like most in South Florida, relies on water as its primary hazard. The layout is also notable, however, for the presence of several sharp doglegs (likely a necessity to make the routing work on limited acreage), with the 521-yard 13th – a 90-degree dogleg right, around a narrow pond – being the most forced. Another of the doglegs opens play, but the 518-yard 1st (which bends around an invasive waste bunker) is a very effective starter, setting the stage for a 3,445-yard front nine led by the 371-yard 5th (a sharp, watery dogleg left), the 552-yard pond-fronted 6th, and the 442-yard 9th, where water once again fronts the putting surface. The back's best come near the close, at the 328-yard 16th (a pond-crossed dogleg left), the 182-yard lakeside 17th and the 572-yard 18th, which plays across/ along a lake en route to a large, Y-shaped green. The proximity of the Turnpike is less than ideal, and though many are demanding, few holes can truly be considered strategic. But a set of well-contoured greens, plus the club's more rustic aesthetic, still add up to an interesting change from many more homogeneous facilities in the region.

Coral Ridge Country Club - Ft. Lauderdale   ◆◆◆

Robert Trent Jones   www.coralridgecc.com
3801 Bayview Dr, Ft. Lauderdale, FL 33308   (954) 449-4400
7,160 yds   Par 72   Rating: 75.0 / 133   (1956)

One of Ft. Lauderdale's more established golfing addresses, the Coral Ridge Country Club represented the South Florida debut of Robert Trent Jones, and occupies a narrow site less than half a mile inland from the Atlantic. Surely with an eye towards the region's burgeoning post-war market, Jones built a tough layout which, per his norm, challenges either with water (which meaningfully affects seven holes) or a combination of length and heavy bunkering. The outward half follows a narrow out-and-back routing into the property's northern reaches where, after opening with tightly bunkered par 4s of 444 and 431 yards, it peaks at the 550-yard well-bunkered 4th and the 177-yard 5th, whose greens wrap around opposite ends of the same lake. The 546-yard pond-guarded 7th is also notable, as is the 191-yard 8th, which plays to a narrow, hourglass-shaped green squeezed among four bunkers. The back nine is led early by the 565-yard 11th (water right) and the 196-yard 12th, an Eden-like one-shotter with two frontal bunkers and a steeply pitched putting surface. Not surprisingly, water is the driving factor among a trio of mid-size closers: the 355-yard 15th (a tricky dogleg left to a pond-guarded green), the 181-yard 16th (whose putting surface extends rightward, into the same hazard) and the straightaway 423-yard 18th. Classicists may not love the hazard-heavy, runway-tee aesthetic, but for Jones fans especially, this is a notably strong South Florida stop. The club added a nine-hole par 3 course built by Rees Jones (page 59) in 2015.

Ft. Lauderdale Country Club (South) - Plantation   ♦♦

Joseph Roseman   www.fortlauderdalecc.com
415 Country Club Circle, Plantation, FL 33317   (954) 587-4700
            6,661 yds   Par 72   Rating: 71.1 / 126   (1926)

The oldest private golf club still extant in South Florida, the Ft. Lauderdale Country Club
dates to 1926, when Chicago architect Joseph Roseman built today's South course on a
then-desolate inland site which is today surrounded by residential development, and
flanked to the west by Florida's Turnpike. Having enjoyed a brief moment in the spotlight
by hosting Henry Ciucci's 1931 victory in the one-time Fort Lauderdale Open, Roseman's
layout retains most of its original routing today, but all manner of sand and water have
been added, resulting in a shortish member-oriented track of somewhat hybridized style.
Perhaps surprisingly on a sub-6,700-yard layout, some of the best entries lie among the
course's four longest holes, including a pair of par 5s which are shortened to two-shot
status on an alternate "Championship" scorecard (the 460-yard pond-fronted 9th and the
489-yard 14th), as well as the 552-yard dogleg left 6th and the 521-yard 16th, one of
several holes marked by incongruously large bunkers dating to the 1980s. Among the par
4s, the out-of-bounds-lined 422-yard 2nd and the tightly bunkered 415-yard 18th rate the
strongest. Old to be sure, but not quite classic given its modern stylings.

Ft. Lauderdale Country Club (North) - Plantation   ♦♦½

Joseph Roseman / Red Lawrence   www.fortlauderdalecc.com
415 Country Club Circle, Plantation, FL 33317   (954) 587-4700
            6,888 yds   Par 72   Rating: 72.4 / 131   (1951)

The Fort Lauderdale Country Club's longer and more challenging North course was added
by Red Lawrence in 1951, six years before the then-municipally owned facility was sold
back into private hands. The North earned at least a modest footnote in professional
golfing history by hosting the 1965 Senior PGA Championship – a far less imposing event
in the decades before the Champions Tour, but one made relevant by Sam Snead's four-
shot victory. Like the South course, the North has also seen its share of updating, leaving
it today as a compact, well-bunkered track anchored by a variety of sturdy par 4s. On the
longer side, a quartet of strong two-shotters lead the way: the 438-yard 2nd (a gentle
dogleg left), the 433-yard dogleg right 9th (which does not return to the clubhouse), the
442-yard 13th (a sweeping dogleg right around a large ficus tree) and the tree-narrowed
427-yard 18th. Among the shorter entries, the 388-yard 5th and 368-yard 6th are nicely
bunkered dogleg rights, both of which can be shortened considerably via drives across
corner bunkers. And then there is the 387-yard 15th, an engaging entry which bends
leftward around a lake, daring longer hitters to carry both the water and another
incongruously large (and wildly shaped) bunker , the latter added in 2006.

Grande Oaks Golf Club - Ft. Lauderdale   ♦♦½

William Mitchell   www.grandeoaks.com
3201 West Rolling Hills Circle, Ft. Lauderdale, FL 33328   (954) 916-2900
          6,752 yds   Par 71   Rating: 72.6 / 138   (1959)

Originally known as the Rolling Hills Golf & Tennis Club, the Grande Oaks Golf Club began life as a strong William Mitchell-designed public facility which achieved timeless fame by doubling as the fictional Bushwood in the movie "Caddyshack." Redesigned by Raymond Floyd in 1999, it was the rare layout indeed to emerge from such alteration shorter and with a lower USGA rating. Redesigned again by Floyd in 2014, it became shorter still, but also a bit less stereotypically modern in appearance, with several wild bunkers removed, and a bit more contouring added to the putting surfaces. The 3,587-yard front nine is easily the longer half and offers stronger entries at the 269-yard par-3 5th, the 432-yard 6th (where both water and sand lie right of the green) and the 436-yard 9th, which bends dangerously rightward around a lake and which, in the initial Floyd redesign, included a sliver of alternate fairway to the right of the water (since removed). The inward half initially features shorter tests like the 395-yard 12th (played to a shallow, banana-shaped green) and the 305-yard 13th (driveable, but between trees right, and sand and water left) before closing with the 178-yard over-water 17th and the 419-yard 18th, which offers a pair of tree-separated greens, the left one requiring a long carry over water. The club also maintains a multi-hole practice facility to the east of the main layout.

Hollybrook Golf Club - Pembroke Pines   ♦♦

William Mitchell   www.hollybrook.com
900 Hollybrook Dr, Pembroke Pines, FL 33025   (561) 431-0600
          6,590 yds   Par 72   Rating: 71.9 / 134   (1969)

A seasonal private facility which, at present, accepts public play during the summer time, the Hollybrook Golf Club offers a shortish, compact William Mitchell-designed layout which manages to build a fair amount of challenge into its largely unchanged 6,590 yards. The 3,403-yard front nine fills the property's eastern half and follows a mostly back-and-forth routing which is led by three mid-size par 4s, the 399-yard 5th and the 420-yard 6th (located on opposite sides of a pair of lakes) as well as the 371-yard dogleg left 8th. The inward half lies west of Hollybrook Drive, where it circles a pair of large condominium complexes. Some 216 yards shorter, its par 4s average only 368 yards, with the best including the 379-yard pond-guarded 10th and the 396-yard 13th (where optimum tee shots flirt with left-side water) as well as the 297-yard drive-and-pitch 15th, a tempting entry whose angled green is bulkheaded above front-left water. If nothing else, this is a largely unaltered glimpse of basic 1960s Florida golf design. The club also offers an 18-hole par 3 course (page 60) located immediately north of the main layout.

Lago Mar Country Club - Plantation   ♦♦½

William Watts   www.lagomarcc.com
500 NW 127th Ave, Plantation, FL 33325   (954) 626-6544
        7,053 yds   Par 72   Rating: 74.1 / 139   (1970)

Originally designed by regional architect William Watts and renovated in 2009 by Kipp Schulties, the Lago Mar Country Club lies two miles from the edge of the Everglades, in the City of Plantation's western reaches. Fully encircled by houses, this has always been a tough, watery track whose network of interconnected lakes at least partially affects all 18 holes. Fortunately for the less skilled, the water is often only a flanking hazard, and then usually on the less-dangerous left side – though it is somewhat more invasive on front nine holes like the 568-yard dogleg left 4th, the 135-yard all-carry 5th and the 551-yard 7th, whose green angles along a front-left hazard. The back features a pair of par 5s upon which Schulties actually decreased the impact of water hazards, the 544-yard 10th (a dogleg left whose corner hazard was greatly reduced) and the 529-yard 13th, where a creek which menaced both lay-up zone and green was replaced by bunkering. But water remains central at incoming par 4s like the 440-yard 11th, the 373-yard 15th and especially the 414-yard 18th, which curls rightward along a lake which greatly threatens both drive and approach. Schulties' work did little to reduce the course's toughness but it did inject a notably higher degree of strategy, doing much to bring the layout into the modern age.

Parkland Golf Club - Parkland   ♦♦½

Greg Norman   www.parklandgcc.com
10001 Old Club Rd, Parkland, FL 33076   (954) 905-2120
        7,118 yds   Par 72   Rating: 74.5 / 135   (2004)

Another course built in the far western reaches of Southeast Florida civilization, barely a mile from the Everglades, the Parkland Golf Club is a residential development anchored by Greg Norman's first Southeast Florida design, a long, but not overwhelmingly difficult, 18. The course has been billed as carrying "a strong MacKenzie influence," but that was before a 2016 renovation which reduced the scale and frequency of its bunkering hugely, leaving a track that now appears almost sparsely hazarded, but which still offers a good number of engaging holes. Now especially, water is the name of the game, as it materially – if not too invasively – affects play on 16 holes. Going out, favorites include two entries with left-to-right angled lakeside greens, the 406-yard 3rd and the 202-yard 7th, the latter playing to one of the largest greens on a golf course dotted with several generously proportioned putting surfaces. But for many, the layout's best stretch comes late and includes the 422-yard 15th (with water left, and a centerline bunker dividing a notably wide fairway), the 485-yard par 4 17th (which sweeps leftward along a lake to a narrow bunkerless green) and the 557-yard 18th, a dogleg right around the same hazard played to a crescent-shaped, waterside putting surface.

Weston Hills Country Club (Tour) - Weston   ◆◆◆

Robert Trent Jones II   www.westonhillsgolfclub.com
2600 Country Club Way, Weston, FL 33332   (954) 384-4600
              7,069 yds   Par 72   Rating: 74.4 / 136   (1990)

Another club which lies close to the Everglades, this time in the far reaches of developed civilization west of Fort Lauderdale, the Weston Hills Country Club first came to national prominence while hosting the 1992 Honda Classic when Corey Pavin holed an 8-iron at the 72nd hole (the par-5 18th of the Tour course) to force a playoff, then beat Fred Couples on the first hole of sudden death. Also the site of Annika Sorenstam's victory in the LPGA's 1997 Tournament of Champions, the Tour course is notable for its difficult finish, which includes the 451-yard 15th (doglegging left around water), the 457-yard 16th (with water down the right) and the 215-yard 17th (ditto), all of which set up the 581-yard site of Pavin's heroics. The front nine, on the other hand, is slightly cramped out of the box, with holes 2-4 being fairly basic tests measuring only 329, 147 and 387 yards. The loop later features three stronger entries, however, the 207-yard 5th (whose green angles leftward, into a lake), the 545-yard 7th (a sweeping dogleg left around one more water hazard) and the 431-yard waterside 9th, which shares a slightly formulaic double green with the 18th. With housing flanking every fairway in some form or fashion, plentiful bunkering and water affecting play on 10 holes, this might appear to be generic, higher-end Florida golf. But with its dashes of history and fairly high degree of tactical challenge factored in, the Tour course actually measures up to a significantly higher level.

Weston Hills Country Club (Players) - Weston   ◆◆◆

Robert Trent Jones II   www.westonhillsgolfclub.com
2600 Country Club Way, Weston, FL 33332   (954) 384-4600
              7,256 yds   Par 72   Rating: 75.4 / 134   (1995)

The Weston Hills Country Club's newer Players course, which opened just about the time the PGA Tour's Honda Classic was moving on, is actually both longer and tougher than its older sibling, and in many places the more interesting test as well. Including several massive waste bunkers that are as much about giving the course a different look as anything hugely strategic, the Players opens with an outward nine highlighted by strong par 4s like the 441-yard 2nd (whose green angles beyond water and sand) and the watery 414-yard 9th. Additional outgoing favorites include tactically sound entries like the 423-yard split-fairway 3rd (which favors drives carrying right-side sand), the 440-yard smartly bunkered 6th and the 570-yard lakeside 7th. The back nine initially wanders out to the southwest, where it features a pair of well-bunkered dogleg rights (the 414-yard 10th and the 455-yard 12th) before looping around to the north of the clubhouse for a memorable four hole close. Highlights here include the 561-yard lakeside 16th (whose small green extends leftward, into the hazard), the dangerous 186-yard all-carry 17th and the 463-yard 18th, a gentle dogleg left which closely hugs left-side water from tee to green, and requires a particularly accurate tee shot. The historically minded may well prefer the Tour course but on balance, the Players provides the more strategically interesting golf.

Bonaventure Country Club - Weston   ◆◆½

Joe Lee   www.golfbonaventure.com
200 Bonaventure Blvd, Weston, FL 33326   (954) 389-2100
          7,064 yds   Par 72   Rating: 73.7 / 133   (1970)

A 36-hole facility for more than four decades, the Bonaventure Country Club averted financial trouble by selling its shorter and easier West course to a developer in 2011, leaving this, the former East course, as the club's sole golfing venue. Sitting on the edge of the Everglades, 10 miles inland from Fort Lauderdale, the challenging Joe Lee-designed layout entertains guests from an adjacent eponymous resort (among other neighborhood hostelries) and remains largely as Lee built it, with more than 75 bunkers present and water meaningfully affecting play on 11 holes. While several long and dry par 4s provide a bit of backbone (e.g., the 465-yard 4th is the number one stroke hole), it's the watery entries that tend to be most memorable, with the front nine featuring the 349-yard 2nd (which bends rightward along a lake), the 395-yard 5th (played to an island fairway and a waterside green) and the 549-yard 7th, a dogleg right with *agua* flanking its entire right side. The back opens with the 538-yard 10th (which dares a long, over-water second) before culminating in a strong homeward run composed of the 373-yard 15th (water left), the 581-yard 16th (water right), the 182-yard 17th (left again) and especially the 428-yard 18th, a tough, snake-like test with water down either side and a forced-carry approach.

Diplomat Golf Resort & Spa - Hallandale   ◆◆½

Joe Lee   www.diplomatgolf.com
501 Diplomat Pkwy, Hallandale, FL 33009   (954) 883-4444
          6,728 yds   Par 72   Rating: 71.6 / 137   (2000)

Though the main body of its resort sits nearly a mile distant on Hollywood Beach, the Diplomat Golf Club occupies a compact inland tract upon which golf has been played since a Red Lawrence-designed 18 first opened in 1957. While that layout was something of a period regional standout which offered a dash of history (Arnold Palmer won the 1969 Danny Thomas Diplomat Classic upon it), it was thoroughly overhauled by Joe Lee in 2000, with the result being a fairly challenging track offering a little more flavor than the average palm-and-lake-lined Gold Coast test. The front nine quickly comes alive at the 385-yard island-green 2nd before finding several of its best holes on the north side of Atlantic Shores Boulevard, where the 528-yard 4th provides a choice of water carries on one's second, and the 397-yard 8th bends leftward between lakes. The back nine begins calmly, with three of its first four holes being sub-400-yard par 4s, none of them too bothered by water. The four finishers, however, step up the challenge measurably and include water holes like the 160-yard 15th and the 162-yard 17th (both played to angled, bulkheaded greens) as well as the 410-yard twisting 18th – though also memorable is the 576-yard 16th, an awkward double dogleg closely flanked by high rises and a mini-mall.

Grand Palms Golf Resort - Pembroke Pines ◆◆

Ward Northrup   www.grandpalmsresort.com
110 Grand Palms Dr, Pembroke Pines, FL 33027   (954) 431-8800
        Grand/Royal: 6,881 yds   Par 72   Rating: 73.6 / 152   (1990)
        Sabal: 3,316 yds   Par 36   Rating: 36.2 / 134   (1990)

A lesser-known facility in a resort market dotted with heavyweights, the Grand Palms Golf Resort sits 10 miles inland, where it began playing golf over 36 housing-free holes of unrecorded origin in 1965. Enjoying a brief moment in the spotlight upon hosting the LPGA's Hollywood Lakes Open in 1968 (won by little-known Peggy Wilson), that facility was comprehensively overhauled by Ward Northrup in 1990, resulting in a housing-lined 27 holes whose calling card is the seemingly inexplicable 152 Slope that graces the pairings of its Grand and Royal nines. This is hardly to suggest that the pairing isn't challenging, however, as the Grand gets one's attention quickly at the 245-yard 2nd, then later builds around the 440-yard straightaway 5th, the 405-yard lake-fronted 8th and the 541-yard 9th, a sweeping dogleg left around houses. The Royal is easily the club's longest nine and features a menu mixed with quirk (back-to-back par 3s at the 7th and 8th), strong holes (the 411-yard 6th and the 537-yard lakeside 9th) and those less so, such as the 525-yard par-5 4th, whose fronting pond is large enough that those laying up must use little more than a wedge. The Sable nine fills the property's west side and is both shorter and marked by one or two slightly awkward entries. It does close solidly, however, with the 542-yard 8th having its lay-up zone pinched by right-side water, and the 425-yard 9th requiring a long second (or a short third?) to another water-fronted putting surface.

Heron Bay Golf Club - Coral Springs ◆◆½

Mark McCumber   www.heronbaygolfclub.net
11801 Heron Bay Blvd, Coral Springs, FL 33076   (954) 796-2000
                7,268 yds   Par 72   Rating: 74.9 / 133   (1996)

Known during its early, high-profile days as the TPC Heron Bay, today's Heron Bay Golf Club made its name by hosting the PGA Tour's Honda Classic from 1997-2002, listing names like Singh, Calcavecchia, Kuchar and Appleby among its winners. Never a favorite among the pros, however, it now operates in association with an on-site Marriott Hotel in a luxury real estate development on the edge of the Everglades, keeping its hand in the tournament ring by annually hosting the well-known Dixie Amateur. While canals line virtually every hole (as buffers for surrounding homes), water is seldom in play, leaving the nearly 100 enormous bunkers built by Mark McCumber to define the flat layout's character – a character which, alas, is rather more penal than strategic. From a tactical perspective, holes like the 408-yard 1st, the 357-yard 4th and the 431-yard 11th reward tee shots which flirt successfully with imposing sand, while the 222-yard 6th and 534-yard water-flanked 7th head up a brawny run which served as the finishers (prior to the nines being reversed) during the Honda days. But many a more discerning golfer may find too many holes to simply have sand *everywhere*, lessening playing interest and leaving Heron Bay's prime sales point to be the ever-alluring chance to walk in the footsteps of the pros.

Hollywood Beach Golf Resort - Hollywood   ♦♦

H.C. Tippett   www.hollywoodbeachgolfresort.com
1600 Johnson St, Hollywood, FL 33020   (954) 927-1751
            6,376 yds   Par 70   Rating: 70.8 / 124   (1923)

Long ago affiliated with the nearby Hollywood Beach Hotel, today's Hollywood Beach Golf Resort is a compact facility whose own on-site hostelry was built during the 1960s on a small patch of land to the right side of the 17th fairway. Designed by H.C. Tippett, the course has always been somewhat back-and-forth in nature, but it was good enough to host several Hollywood Opens during the 1930s, when it counted Byron Nelson and Vic Ghezzi among its champions. The club has witnessed some reconfiguring over the years, however, and today includes two sets of back-to-back par 3s (the 8th and 9th, then the 13th and 14th) as well as several par 4s where crossing water hazards that were once ornamental now require better ball-strikers to lay up. Among the stronger front nine tests are the 470-yard par-5 1st (whose green is fronted by a modern-era pond) and the 410-yard 7th, whose fairway is lined with bunkers added during the 1990s. The back is then anchored by a quartet of strong par 4s that includes the 415-yard lake-guarded 10th, the 440-yard 11th, the 440-yard dogleg left 17th and the 432-yard straightaway finisher.

Inverrary Resort (East) - Lauderhill   ♦♦♦

Robert Trent Jones   www.inverrary.com
3840 Inverrary Blvd, Lauderhill, FL 33319   (954) 733-7550
            7,196 yds   Par 72   Rating: 75.0 / 139   (1970)

A prominent residential development which includes an on-site resort hotel, Inverrary was one of the region's earlier clubs to inhabit a significantly inland site, its 36 Robert Trent Jones-designed holes sitting west of Florida's Turnpike, nearly eight miles away from the Atlantic. The club came to fame quickly as a tournament venue after opening in 1970, with the East course hosting (over reversed nines) the PGA Tour's Jackie Gleason Inverrary Classic from 1972-1983, the 1976 Players Championship (in the last of its three pre-Jacksonville editions) and the LPGA's Phar-Mor at Inverrary from 1990-1992. Thus counting no less than seven Hall-of-Famers among its champions, the East remains a challenging and fairly engaging test today, particularly within a set of watery par 3s that includes the 221-yard 3rd (whose narrow green angles rightward, beyond water and sand), the 202-yard 7th (familiar to older TV viewers as the old 16th), the 204-yard all-carry 12th and the heavily bunkered 210-yard 15th. Considered long in its tournament days (the PGA Tour played it at 7,128 yards), the East also draws strength from well-bunkered par 4s like the 467-yard 10th, the 448-yard 14th and the 438-yard 18th, though more engaging is the 417-yard 16th, which doglegs sharply right, around a lake. The historically minded will also enjoy the 399-yard dogleg right 8th (played to a very narrow green) and the 402-yard 9th, whose several dramatic finishes included the 1978 Inverrary, when Jack Nicklaus famously birdied the last five holes to edge Grier Jones by one.

Inverrary Resort (West) - Lauderhill   ♦♦½

Robert Trent Jones   www.inverrary.com
3840 Inverrary Blvd, Lauderhill, FL 33319   (954) 733-7550
              6,675 yds   Par 71   Rating: 71.7 / 131   (1971)

A lesser-known facility in a resort market dotted with heavyweights, the Grand Palms Golf Resort sits 10 miles inland, where it began playing golf over 36 housing-free holes of unrecorded origin in 1965. Enjoying a brief moment in the spotlight upon hosting the LPGA's Hollywood Lakes Open in 1968 (won by little-known Peggy Wilson), that facility was comprehensively overhauled by Ward Northrup in 1990, resulting in a housing-lined 27 holes whose calling card is the seemingly inexplicable 152 Slope that graces the pairings of its Grand and Royal nines. This is hardly to suggest that the pairing isn't challenging, however, as the Grand gets one's attention quickly at the 245-yard 2nd, then later builds around the 440-yard straightaway 5th, the 405-yard lake-fronted 8th and the 541-yard 9th, a sweeping dogleg left around houses. The Royal is easily the club's longest nine and features a menu mixed with quirk (back-to-back par 3s at the 7th and 8th), strong holes (the 411-yard 6th and the 537-yard lakeside 9th) and those less so, such as the 525-yard par-5 4th, whose fronting pond is large enough that those laying up must use little more than a wedge. The Sable nine fills the property's west side and is both shorter and marked by one or two slightly awkward entries. It does close solidly, however, with the 542-yard 8th having its lay-up zone pinched by right-side water, and the 425-yard 9th requiring a long second (or a short third?) to another water-fronted putting surface.

Jacaranda Golf Club (East) - Plantation   ♦♦½

Mark Mahannah   www.golfjacaranda.com
9200 West Broward Blvd, Plantation, FL 33324   (954) 472-5836
              7,245 yds   Par 71   Rating: 74.4 / 129   (1971)

Built just north of the Port Everglades Expressway, the Jacaranda Golf Club is another South Florida facility whose inland location was somewhat isolated at the time of its development, though today its 36 residence-lined holes serve multiple area hostelries including the adjacent Renaissance Fort Lauderdale-Plantation Hotel. Originally built by Mark Mahannah, both of the club's layouts received new millennium tune-ups from Bobby Weed, resulting in more aesthetically polished, tactically richer versions of 1970s Florida design. The older East course is much longer and more demanding, and is built around a collection of stiff par 4s, with the front nine including the 434-yard lake-guarded 1st, the 418-yard tree-narrowed 4th and the 444-yard 5th. The par-36 inward half then tops that with a particularly long trio: the 485-yard 12th (a tough, bunker-pinched dogleg right), the 483-yard 15th and the 468-yard 18th, where a prominent right-side fairway bunker dominates the landscape. The 257-yard par-3 8th and the 587-yard 14th (where left-side water bothers the lay-up zone) are similarly brutish, though equally noteworthy are a pair of short closers, the 338-yard 16th (where aggressive drives must carry a cluster of bunkers and avoid a right-side lake) and the watery 154-yard 17th.

Jacaranda Golf Club (West) - Plantation   ◆◆½

Mark Mahannah   www.golfjacaranda.com
9200 West Broward Blvd, Plantation, FL 33324   (954) 472-5836
           6,778 yds   Par 72   Rating: 72.8 / 130   (1975)

The Jacaranda Golf Club's shorter West course was created four years after the more demanding East and is truly a little brother, being very similar in style but considerably smaller of scale. Occupying the property's southwestern quadrant, the front nine opens in relatively staid fashion before picking up steam at the 501-yard 5th (where a large pond may force longer hitters to throttle down off the tee), the 403-yard dogleg left 7th, the stout (if basic) 204-yard 8th and the 555-yard 9th, a sweeping dogleg right and easily the layout's longest entry. The back nine is shorter (3,330 yards) but on the whole more engaging, and offers three of its strongest holes fairly quickly at the 514-yard 10th (which slithers among trees and left-side water), the 205-yard 11th and 421-yard 13th, a soundly bunkered dogleg right. The 519-yard 14th bends leftward between a pair of lakes and kicks off a fairly diminutive closing stretch that peaks at the 166-yard 17th (a bunkerless test played to a near-island green) and the 324-yard 18th, a thought-provoking par 4 requiring either a safe lay up or a dangerous blast slipped between sand and left-side water. Though certainly no match for the East course in terms of scale or pure difficulty, this does provide enough appealing golf to merit a visit in its own right.

Palm Aire Country Club (Palms) - Pompano Beach   ◆◆

William Mitchell   palmaire.clublink.com
2600 N. Palm Aire Dr, Pompano Beach, FL   33069   (954) 975-6225
           6,944 yds   Par 72   Rating: 73.0 / 128   (1959)

Dating to the late 1950s, the Palm Aire Country Club was one of Florida's earliest mega developments, eventually operating four regulation courses (plus a nine-hole executive track) on a huge, housing-lined property one mile west of Interstate 95. With the Dick Wilson-designed Pines course no longer active, guests of the club (and the immediately adjacent Wyndham resort) utilize three well-established Gold Coast layouts. The 1959 William Mitchell-designed Palms course occupies a Y-shaped tract on the property's east side and, despite being the club's longest layout, is actually rated its easiest. Having had much of its bunkering downsized or removed by Karl Litten in 1996, this is essentially just pleasant resort golf today - albeit on a somewhat brawny scale. Sand and water are left to affect play only sporadically, with outgoing favorites including the 511-yard creek-crossed 2nd and the 437-yard 9th, whose green is tucked behind a pair of large fronting bunkers. Coming home, the 525-yard 11th bends leftward around a pond before play later closes with the 395-yard 17th (a tricky driving hole flanked right by a pair of highrises) and the 420-yard 18th, a strong dogleg left with more right-side buildings in play.

Palm Aire Country Club (Oaks) - Pompano Beach   ♦♦½

George & Tom Fazio   palmaire.clublink.com
2600 N. Palm Aire Dr, Pompano Beach, FL 33069   (954) 975-6225
            6,910 yds   Par 71   Rating: 73.1 / 128   (1971)

The Palm Aire Country Club's second layout was the Oaks course, a 1971 George & Tom Fazio creation which was touched up by Tom (who removed or reduced many of his uncle's more relevant bunkers) just before the new millennium. Playing out of a separate clubhouse to the west, it far more resembles George's period stylings than Tom's current ones and, though challenging enough to be a former Nationwide Tour stop, is a relatively staid creation from beginning to end. Water is a frequent visual presence but has little meaningful affect on play (not once must it be carried), leaving the action to be anchored by a collection of longer par 4s that initially features the 454-yard 1st, the 457-yard 8th (which bends rightward, to a green angled leftward behind sand) and the 427-yard 9th, where a new millennium waste area flanks the right side. The par-36 inward half is much larger on the card, but much of this length is consumed by two long par 5s, with its strongest two shotters being the 438-yard 14th (a gentle dogleg right) and the 418-yard 15th, which bends leftward between flanking lakes. Noteworthy on the shorter side are the 345-yard dogleg right 2nd and the 356-yard 7th, a dogleg left which dares aggressive players to carry both the water and several trees that fill the corner.

Palm Aire Country Club (Cypress) - Pompano Beach   ♦♦

George & Tom Fazio   palmaire.clublink.com
2600 N. Palm Aire Dr, Pompano Beach, FL 33069   (954) 975-6225
            6,808 yds   Par 71   Rating: 73.3 / 132   (1972)

Playing out of the same clubhouse as its sister Oaks course, the Palm Aire Country Club's Cypress course is another early 1970s George and Tom Fazio design which, in its period, weighed in as a fairly demanding layout. Also like the Oaks, it has seen the great majority of its bunkering reduced dramatically in scale – though in something of an odd quirk, this does not apply to the final four holes, whose hazards remain almost exactly as initially constructed. The Cypress is routed between rows of condominiums and single-family homes and carries (narrowly) the club's highest rating and slope, and if the overall design is limited in its tactical scope, it remains reasonably challenging throughout. Solid par 4s are a frequent presence, their best including the tree-narrowed 404-yard 3rd, the 414-yard 9th (with water down its left side), the 461-yard 13th (a lake-guarded brute played to a now-bunkerless green) and the well-bunkered 417-yard 18th, where a tree in the left half of the fairway threatens the tee ball. The 586-yard 16th, easily the longest hole, is also notable, running along the club's western boundary before making a late right turn.

The Carolina Club - Margate

Robert von Hagge & Bruce Devlin   www.carolinagolfclub.com
3011 Rock Island Rd, Margate, FL 33063   (954) 753-4000
        6,735 yds   Par 71   Rating: 72.5 / 141   (1975)

Once a rustic, partially wooded von Hagge & Devlin design, The Carolina Club has evolved substantially over nearly five decades, with today's version retaining its original routing but including housing throughout its once-vacant interior, as well as more water and far blander bunkering – not to mention some renovative works by Karl Litten. The front nine forms a counter-clockwise loop to the south and is led by a trio of mid-size par 4s: the 415-yard dogleg right 2nd (where a lake lies just beyond the corner), the 385-yard lake-crossing 4th and the 420-yard 6th, the loop's longest two-shotter. Notably longer are the 470-yard 13th and the 445-yard 15th, though for many, the inward half's most engaging entries are the 535-yard water-crossing 14th and the 380-yard 16th, a gentle dogleg right around/across a narrow lake. Better/longer ball strikers will very quickly notice that the awkward positioning of water may require them to lay up on no less than eight holes – but in fairness to Messrs. Von Hagge & Devlin, nearly all of the offending hazards were constructed several years after their departure from the scene.

Colony West Country Club - Tamarac

Robert von Hagge & Bruce Devlin   www.colonywestgolfclub.com
6800 NW 88th Ave, Tamarac, FL 33321   (954) 721-7710
        7,258 yds   Par 71   Rating: 75.4 / 141   (1971)

Originally built with an eye towards hosting the Jackie Gleason Classic which, in the end, remained at Inverrary, Colony West's Championship course is one of the tougher ever produced by Robert von Hagge and Bruce Devlin – but not quite so tough as it was in the beginning, when 50+ additional bunkers (and 300 more yards) graced its fairways. Today a residence-lined facility which utilizes water as a primary hazard on nine holes, it opens with a 3,743-yard outward half swelled by the presence of the 588-yard dogleg right 1st and the 576-yard 7th, the latter a sweeping dogleg left around a lake. The loop is led by a run of three successive water-flanked par 4s: the 425-yard dogleg left 2nd, the 414-yard 3rd (a big dogleg right) and the stiff 434-yard 4th, which also turns significantly right, with a lake waiting beyond the corner. While the par-35 back is 228 yards shorter, it too is driven by its demanding two-shotters, especially the 443-yard 12th (a mean dogleg left around/across water), the dry, tree-narrowed 458-yard 15th and the 445-yard 18th, a water-crossing dogleg right. The story goes that Jack Nicklaus played the then-7,553-yard layout before its opening and declared it too tough for the PGA Tour. The resulting changes made Colony West a nationally prominent public test in the pre-"Upscale Daily Fee" era, and it certainly remains nobody's pushover today. The club also offers an 18-hole executive layout (page59) across the street, to the west of Pine Island Road.

Country Club of Coral Springs - Coral Springs   ♦♦

Ed Ault   www.ccofcs.com
10800 West Sample Rd, Coral Springs, FL 33065   (954) 752-4500
          6,779 yds   Par 71   Rating: 71.7 / 130   (1969)

Built near the western edges of South Florida civilization, just over a mile east of the Everglades, the Country Club of Coral Springs features a housing-encircled Ed Ault design routed around a central residential neighborhood and among numerous lakes, few of which affect play too significantly. Though several greens (particularly among the par 3s) offer little more than functional bunkering, Ault's layout finds some reasonable interest in its longer holes, including a trio of big par 5s: the 538-yard 3rd (whose second must contend with water and one of several incongruous modern waste bunkers), the 544-yard 14th (which bends gently between lakes) and the 565-yard dogleg left 16th. Longer par 4s like the 437-yard dogleg left 4th, the 450-yard 7th and the 430-yard 12th also add some challenge to the mix, but it is worth noting that the most invasive use of water is generally reserved for shorter entries like the 271-yard lakeside 1st, the 174-yard over-water 6th and the 189-yard all-carry 18th. Perhaps as a nod to the higher volumes of public course play, Coral Springs also includes some of the largest greens in the area.

Crystal Lake Country Club - Pompano Beach   ♦♦

Pat Pattison   www.crystallakecountryclub.com
3810 Crystal Lake Dr, Pompano Beach, FL 33064   (954) 943-2902
          6,798 yds   Par 72   Rating: 73.5 / 135   (1964)

A well-established facility located two-thirds of a mile west of Interstate 95, the Crystal Lake Country Club dates to 1964, but had its bunkering completely re-worked (and its back nine slightly reconfigured) by Rees Jones in 1981. With little room to expand within a compact, housing-encircled site, today's layout is of modest size and playing interest, particularly over a 3,560-yard front nine whose strength lies mostly in a trio of brawny (if somewhat basic) holes: the 450-yard dogleg left 4th, the 230-yard 5th (whose green is backed by a large horseshoe-like bunker) and the 605-yard tree-lined 7th. The shorter inward half follows a particularly tight, back-and-forth routing which, early on, is led by the driveable (but smartly bunkered) 315-yard 11th and the 228-yard bunker-ringed 12th. But the layout's most interesting run of golf is arguably to be found at its close, where the finishers include the 515-yard 15th (where sand tightly pinches the lay-up zone), the 160-yard 17th (played across one of several sandy waste areas) and the club's strongest overall test, the 575-yard 18th, whose green is button-hooked beyond a right-side pond.

Davie Golf Club - Davie   ◆◆½

William Watts   www.daviegolf.net
68201 SW 24th St, Davie, FL 33324   (954) 475-8200
        6,347 yds   Par 70   Rating: 71.1 / 135   (1969)

For decades a short and basic layout known as the Arrowhead Golf Club, today's Davie
Golf Club was significantly renovated by ex-Arnold Palmer associate Harrison Minchew in
2010 (in conjunction with a widening of the adjacent Interstate 595), then purchased by
the Town of Davie for operation as a municipal facility. Minchew's work involved a large-
scale expansion of water hazards and a complete rebunkering, resulting in a layout which
remains palpably short but also often interesting – even after the subsequent removal of
numerous Minchew bunkers. With nine holes sitting on either side of SW 24th Street, the
front follows something of an out-and-back routing on the northern side, with its most
engaging holes being a pair of shorter par 4s: the 323-yard 4th (where a tree, sand and
water all deter overly aggressive play) and the 303-yard 6th, whose narrow putting
surface is angled beyond front-left water and sand. The longer back nine finds its last
eight holes located on the south side of 24th Street, with early favorites including the 430-
yard 11th and the 437-yard dogleg left 13th. The action peaks at the close, however, with
the 577-yard 16th, the 158-yard 17th and the 424-yard 18th all playing to waterside greens
– though again, each has been softened a bit by the removal of relevant bunkering.

Deer Creek Golf Club - Deerfield Beach   ◆◆½

William Watts   www.deercreekflorida.com
2801 Deer Creek CC Blvd, Deerfield Beach, FL 33442   (954) 429-0006
        7,050 yds   Par 72   Rating: 75.3 / 137   (1971)

Located midway between Interstate 95 and Florida's Turnpike, the Deer Creek Golf Club
is a real estate-oriented facility whose William Watts-designed golf course opened in
1971 and hosted the LPGA from 1980-85, counting JoAnne Carner, Pat Bradley, Sandra
Palmer and Hollis Stacy (twice) among its winners. This layout was renovated during the
1990s by Arthur Hills, and while Hills had little choice but to retain the original routing, he
did add his standard quirky/interesting brand of shaping, resulting in a track less
bothered by water (which materially affects only six holes) than by some well-placed
sand and the occasional tree. The front nine is slightly the less-engaging half, and is led
both by its par 5s (the 529-yard canal-side 2nd and the straightaway 558-yard 6th) and a
pair of strong par 4s, the 432-yard 3rd (whose green is menaced by a small, left-side
bunker) and the 463-yard 5th, the number one stroke hole. The back is routed around a
central condominium complex and opens with the 339-yard 10th, a canal-crossed dogleg
right where trees all but rule out driving towards the green. Favorites thereafter include
the 191-yard 11th (all carry across a fronting pond), the 607-yard 16th (where a huge left-
side bunker threatens the lay-up zone) the 451-yard 18th, a tough, watery dogleg left.

Club at Emerald Hills - Hollywood   ♦♦½

Robert von Hagge & Bruce Devlin   www.theclubatemeraldhills.com
4100 North Hills Dr, Hollywood, FL 33021   (954) 961-4000
7,827 yds   Par 72   Rating: 78.6 / 148   (1969)

A relatively early player on the Gold Coast golf scene, the Club at Emerald Hills was built in 1969 by the then-prolific team of von Hagge & Devlin, though it was modernized (mostly through an extensive re-bunkering) by Charles Ankrom in 1989. The layout follows an expansive path through a range of Hollywood neighborhoods, with water – which materially affects 10 holes – being the most significant hazard. And while the normal back tees measure a stiff 7,368 yards, there are, as indicated, an additional set of markers stretching to an eye-popping 7,827. Of course, much of this muscle lies in a quartet of par 5s which *average* 633 yards (and thus consume one-third of the overall yardage by themselves), the best of which are the 643-yard 5th (a dogleg left to a very shallow green bulkheaded above a lake) and the 682-yard 18th, a brutal lake-flanked three-shotter whose green is perched dangerously beyond a canal. On balance, the front may be the more engaging half, offering the 434-yard 2nd (played to centerline-bunkered green), the 360-yard 4th (which features a quirky volcano-like target) and the 170- yard over-water 6th. Beyond the endless 18th, the longer back includes the 150-yard pond-fronted 11th and the tricky (and watery) 395-yard 15th, as well as the 473-yard 13th, a nasty par 4 where both drive and approach must carry a canal. The 7,368-yard tees carry a 75.9 rating, which is really all the golf course that a daily fee player could ever need.

Flamingo Lakes Golf & Country Club - Pembroke Pines   ♦♦

Ed Ramey   www.flamingolakescc.com
701 SW Flamingo West Dr, Pembroke Pines, FL 33027   (954) 435-6110
5,854 yds   Par 71   Rating: 68.5 / 122   (1984)

A slightly more demanding layout than it may at first appear, the Flamingo Lakes Golf & Country Club is a short, housing-oriented facility whose water-dotted property sits 12 miles inland from the Atlantic. Like many a diminutive layout, several of the strongest entries are drawn from a quintet of short par 3s, the most dangerous being a pair of all-carry tests, the 151-yard 14th and the 149-yard 16th. Less expected is a strong (if mostly short) set of par 5s which, though lightly bunkered, utilize water just enough to mount a challenge. Tops among these are the 556-yard 6th (a dogleg right along a narrow pond) and the 485-yard 10th, where a left-side lake edges in before the green. But while such entries do provide moments of interest, much of the layout is far more basic in nature, with only 22 bunkers present, five greens being hazard-free, and several more being flanked by largely irrelevant bunkers which do little more than frame targets. Not quite basic golf then, but this is definitely suited to newer or less-skilled players.

Orangebrook Golf & Country Club (East) - Hollywood   ♦½

Red Lawrence   www.orangebrook.com
400 Entrada Dr, Hollywood, FL 33021   (954) 967-4653
          6,574 yds   Par 72   Rating: 71.3 / 120   (1959)

The Orangebrook Golf & Country Club is a municipally owned facility which first opened its doors in 1933 with 18 holes designed by one A.J. Ewing, and it was that layout which first hosted the Women's International Four-Ball, a long-running event which saw names like Suggs, Zaharias and Rawls carved upon its trophy before finally leaving the club in 2012. Ewing's course was essentially torn up in 1959, however, when Red Lawrence expanded the facility to 36 holes, resulting in the East and West courses still in play today. The East course is the slightly easier of the pair, being a shortish, compact layout which partially abuts Interstate 95 along its eastern boundary. This is mostly basic golf save for a pair of more interesting par 4s, the 351-yard 13th (where water flanks the left side and angles before the green) and the 329-yard 15th, where drives must skirt both a left-side lake and an invasive fairway bunker. Among the other 16 holes, longer tests like the 221-yard 5th, the 592-yard 6th and the 547-yard 18th stand out the farthest.

Orangebrook Golf & Country Club (West) - Hollywood   ♦♦

Red Lawrence   www.orangebrook.com
400 Entrada Dr, Hollywood, FL 33021   (954) 967-4653
          6,626 yds   Par 71   Rating: 71.5 / 125   (1959)

The Orangebrook Golf & Country Club's West course is safely the facility's more engaging layout, its non-returning routing benefitting particularly from the construction of several modern-era ponds, as well as some bunkering added early in the new millennium. Still a fairly manageable layout by contemporary standards, It opens with a 3,404-yard front nine which includes stronger entries like the 409-yard 6th, the 200-yard pond-flanked 7th and the 381-yard 9th, whose fairway narrows between a pair of lakes before climbing gently to a shallow putting surface. But it is upon the 3,222-yard back that much of Orangebrook's best golf lies, beginning with the 534-yard 12th, a sweeping dogleg left which bends around corner bunkers and past a left-side pond. The 372-yard 13th includes water down the right side and before the green, while the 213-yard 14th plays to a putting surface set (not too dangerously) upon a large island. Most imposing by miles, however, is the 560-yard 18th, a huge closer which initially runs along Park Road before making a late right turn to a shallow pond-fronted green.

Oriole Golf Club - Margate   ♦½

William Dietsch   www.oriolegolfclub.com
8000 West Margate Blvd, Margate, FL 33063   (954) 972-8140
          6,460 yds   Par 72   Rating: 70.1 / 118   (1971)

One of several regional facilities built by ex-Robert Trent Jones sideman Bill Dietsch, the
Oriole Golf Club is a short, mid-range test whose lightly bunkered layout is routed amidst
a standard regional backdrop of multi-story condominiums and numerous lakes. As a
70.1 rating suggests, there won't be many major events contested here, but interesting
holes of various sizes do manage to appear. On the longer end are par 5s like the 520-
yard pond-fronted 9th (the number one stroke hole) and the 500-yard 17th, a quirky,
bunkerless test whose green is tucked beyond right-side trees. On the shorter side, the
195-yard 7th and the 140-yard 14th are both tightly bunkered one-shotters, while a pair of
diminutive front nine par 4s effectively utilize water, the 340-yard 2nd (where an angled
putting surfaces pushes ideal drives to flirt with a right-side lake) and the 320-yard 4th,
which tempts modern long-ballers to try and drive a green tucked beyond a left-side lake.

Pembroke Lakes Golf Club - Pembroke Pines   ♦♦½

Howard Watson   www.pembrokelakesgolf.com
10500 Taft St, Pembroke Pines, FL 33026   (954) 431-4144
          6,815 yds   Par 72   Rating: 73.3 / 140   (1974)

Originally built by Canadian architect Howard Watson in 1974, the Pembroke Lakes Golf
Club remained largely unaltered prior to undergoing a 2007 renovation by John Sanford,
an update which re-worked bunkering and built/re-shaped several lakes, but retained all
of Watson's original routing. Of course, there was relatively little choice in this regard as
the layout is residence flanked on all sides, particularly the front nine, which is squeezed
snugly around a large, multi-tower condominium complex. This is the shorter and less-
engaging half, with its best holes including the 373-yard pond-guarded 2nd, the 530-yard
6th (where an angled waste bunker – also doubling as a cart path – affects the second)
and the 400-yard 9th, a tricky, water-lined dogleg right. The back visits several residential
neighborhoods along the property's western half and makes use of water (plus additional
waste bunker/cart paths) more invasively, particularly at the 515-yard double dogleg
10th, the 370-yard dogleg right 12th (where longer hitters may be tempted to drive near
the green) and the 528-yard 14th, which dares a long water-carrying second. A trio of
par-4s led by the 424-yard pond-side 16th and the 403-yard 18th (a dogleg left whose
corner is filled by a waste bunker/cart path) eventually closes play in strong style.

Plantation Preserve Golf Club - Plantation ◆◆◆

Michael Smelek   www.plantation.org
7050 West Broward Blvd, Plantation, FL 33317   (954) 585-5020
         7,148 yds   Par 72   Rating: 72.9 / 134   (2006)

A long and challenging municipal facility owned and operated by the city, the Plantation Preserve Golf Club was built by Robert von Hagge partner Michael Smelek on a large triangular tract which formerly housed the Red Lawrence-designed Plantation Golf Club. Though some of the old corridors of play were retained, Smelek's long and frequently demanding creation is essentially a brand new layout. It is also, however, a layout which shows numerous signs of the von Hagge influence, first in the long, watery par 5s that begin each nine (a frequent von Hagge practice), then also in its wild, large-scale bunkering, and the double green shared by the 207-yard 15th and the 444-yard 17th. Of course, von Hagge's work was seldom dull, and Smelek also managed to recreate much of that playing interest here, with front nine favorites including the 383-yard 6th and 377-yard 7th (routed along opposite sides of the same lake) and especially the 335-yard 9th, which plays to a dangerously shallow island green backed by sand. The 3,712-yard back nine counters with the 189-yard over-water 12th, the 435-yard dogleg left 14th (which offers an alternate fairway pinched between more water and sand) and the 595-yard 18th, a gigantic dogleg left around both a lake and a near-300-yard-long bunker. The classically inclined may find it over-the-top in places, but there is more than enough interesting golf to make this one of Florida's strongest municipal layouts.

Pompano Beach Golf Course (Palms) - Pompano Beach ◆½

Robert von Hagge   www.pompanobeachfl.gov
1101 North Federal Hwy, Pompano Beach, FL 33060   (954) 781-0426
         6,280 yds   Par 71   Rating: 69.7 / 123   (1967)

Located less than a mile inland from the Atlantic, where its 36 holes are wedged between the Pompano Beach Airport and North Federal Highway, this municipally owned property first played golf over a Red Lawrence-designed 18 in 1954. But that layout was largely built over by Robert von Hagge in 1967 when he expanded the property to 36 holes, with the result being a facility which entertained the LPGA once in 1973, but which also shows little of the standard von Hagge tactical and aesthetic flair. Thus a short and relatively basic layout, the Palms course offers straight ahead golf whose most interesting holes are invariably those which incorporate water, specifically the 162-yard 6th, the 337-yard drive-and-pitch 8th (whose green angles along a front-right pond) the 320-yard 9th (where a lake lurks long and left of the green) and the 414-yard pond-guarded 16th. Among the dryer holes, strongest are the 357-yard dogleg left 12th (where sliced drives might still find water) and the 403-yard 18th, whose green sits behind front-right sand.

Pompano Beach Golf Course (Pines) - Pompano Beach ♦♦½

Robert von Hagge
1101 North Federal Hwy, Pompano Beach, FL 33060
7,119 yds   Par 72   Rating: 74.3 / 130   (1967)

www.pompanobeachfl.gov
(954) 781-0426

From the moment Robert von Hagge expanded Pompano Beach's municipal facility to 36 holes, its Pines course was the much longer and stronger half, with its non-returning routing mostly following a path around the property's perimeter. But feeling the Pines to be in need of an update, the city retained Greg Norman to perform a 2012 renovation, an operation which essentially retained von Hagge's routing while adding both length and bunkering, the latter configured to allow room for high-volume municipal play. The early holes lie flush to the airport and feature a pair of holes flanking a modern-era lake at runway's end, the 348-yard 2nd and the 212-yard 3rd. Thereafter, play is driven by a muscular mid-section led by the 443-yard 8th, the 575-yard 10th, the 473-yard par-4 11th and the 549-yard 12th, the number one stroke hole and one featuring centerline bunkers both in the lay-up zone and fronting the green. Norman also spruced up the finishing stretch, extending a lake to bring it greenside at the 373-yard 16th, adding a long right-side bunker at the 220-yard 17th and moving the putting surface adjacent to a long left-side lake at the 407-yard 18th. All told, one of the region's stronger municipal stops.

TPC Eagle Trace - Coral Springs

Arthur Hills
1111 Eagle Trace Blvd, Coral Springs, FL 33071
7,040 yds   Par 72   Rating: 75.4 / 147   (1983)

www.tpceagletrace.clublink.com
(954) 753-7222

The tide of architectural opinion has mostly greeted the PGA Tour's TPC franchise with a sort of vague indifference – and it can be argued that much of that ambivalence began right here. This is because as the Tour's second-ever TPC tournament venue, Eagle Trace drew inevitable comparison with the groundbreaking TPC Sawgrass, a tough measuring stick for any modern facility and one which may have prejudiced many opinions from the start. Built less than half a mile from the Everglades, Eagle Trace was created to host the PGA Tour's Honda Classic, a role it played (to some player dissatisfaction) nine times between 1984-1996. Thus counting names like Strange, Lietzke and Calcavecchia among its champions, the Arthur Hills-designed track is housing-flanked throughout but offers a solid dose of interesting golf within its lightly bunkered framework. Going out, notable entries include the 367-yard 4th (which bends leftward along water, and amidst several large bunkers), the 521-yard 5th (played to an shallow-but-very-wide near-island green) and the 193-yard water-crossing 7th. The back is led by the watery 391-yard 12th, the 452-yard canal-flanked 13th and – perhaps most familiar to TV viewers – the 406-yard 16th, whose bulkheaded putting surface extends outward into a lake. Conversely, a pair of long but basic closers (the 460-yard 9th and 470-yard 18th) linger less in the golfer's memory – but there remains enough history here to still make for an appealing stop.

Woodlands Country Club (East) - Tamarac   ♦♦

Robert von Hagge & Bruce Devlin   www.woodlandscountryclub.net
4600 Woodlands Blvd, Tamarac, FL 33319   (954) 731-2500
          6,785 yds   Par 72   Rating: 72.3 / 127   (1969)

Lying just across NW 44th Street from the more famous Inverrary Resort, the Woodlands Country Club features a pair of little-altered von Hagge and Devlin-designed 18s which, unlike their high-rise-dominated neighbor, play over a more tranquil landscape of single-family houses. The power line-crossed East course rates slightly easier but, like its sister, offers little that is flashy or spectacular, instead playing over a run of mid-sized, often heavily bunkered holes which occasionally touch on formulaic (e.g., the par-3 2nd and 6th sharing the then-obligatory von Hagge double green). Aside from these otherwise strong one-shotters, other outgoing favorites include the 488-yard par-5 5th (where water lurks left of the green) and the 447-yard 7th, a tough two-shotter which bends leftward along a canal. The back begins with the 566-yard dogleg left 10th (where a lake fills the corner) before being led by the 378-yard dogleg right 13th (where an aggressive over-water drive is tempting) and the 413-yard 18th, which bends rightward, past a prominent tree.

Woodlands Country Club (West) - Tamarac   ♦♦½

Robert von Hagge & Bruce Devlin   www.woodlandscountryclub.net
4600 Woodlands Blvd, Tamarac, FL 33319   (954) 731-2500
          6,811 yds   Par 72   Rating: 72.5 / 131   (1969)

The Woodlands Country Club's von Hagge & Devlin-designed West course is similar in size, style and challenge to its sister layout, but it does offer one genuinely differentiating feature: the use of deep, often extremely narrow greens throughout. From the 515-yard 1st, the 394-yard dogleg right 2nd and especially the 155-yard 4th (whose putting surface is little more than a sliver) onward, this offbeat component becomes the norm, requiring a higher degree of accuracy on one's mid- and short-iron approaches. It is again apparent at the strong 419-yard 5th, as well as at the 177-yard pond-guarded 8th, though it is less in evidence at the 559-yard 7th, which features a pond just before the green and is the course's number one stroke hole. The inward half commences with a typical von Hagge three-shot opener (a 513-yard dogleg right along a lake) before playing through a run of sub-400-yard par 4s at holes 13-15, providing a window for scoring. The 577-yard out-of-bounds-lined 16th is a full three-shotter for most, however, while the 442-yard 18th is a gentle dogleg left whose putting surface, in spots, is little more than a dozen paces wide. Due mostly to the playing interest generated by the slimness of its greens (as well as the lack of crossing power lines), this will likely be the choice for the one-round visitor.

Woodmont Country Club - Tamarac

Robert von Hagge & Bruce Devlin   www.woodmontcountryclub.net
7801 NW 80th Ave, Tamarac, FL 33321   (954) 722-4300
                    7,043 yds   Par 72   Rating: 73.6 / 137   (1976)

Originally built as another 36-hole von Hagge & Devlin-designed facility located towards the western end of the developed part of the Broward County, the Woodmont Country Club has been reduced to 18 holes since 2014, with its lesser Pines course closed and set to become 150+ private homes in the near future. Nominally a private club (but one that allows some public access), it now plays exclusively over its longer and tougher Cypress course, a residence-lined test which lacks some of the tactical elements often present in von Hagge & Devlin's best work. In modern terms, this is not a backbreakingly long layout, but it does include generously proportioned tests like the 602-yard pond-crossing 5th, the 570-yard 8th (a sharp, out-of-bounds-flanked dogleg right) and the 570-yard 10th, a sweeping dogleg left. Also broad-shouldered is a quintet of par 3s averaging 213 yards, the best of which include the 191-yard 3rd (all-carry across a lake), the 219-yard 7th and the 223-yard 16th, whose small, angled green sits behind front-right sand. Though water is present on more than half the holes, only rarely is it a major threat, with the 400-yard 11th, the 387-yard 12th and the 354-yard 18th being the most affected.

Colony West Country Club (Glades) - Tamarac   ♦

Robert von Hagge & Bruce Devlin   www.golfcolonywest.com
6800 NW 88th Ave, Tamarac, FL 33321   (954) 726-8430
        4,175 yds   Par 65   Rating: 61.0 / 107   (1974)

Sitting just across Pine Island Road from the Colony West Country Club's famously tough regulation 18, the club's executive Glades course is a far more basic par-65 layout routed among condominiums and single-family homes. A lightly bunkered track which also makes limited use of water, its most engaging entries are a pair of par 3s which share a large, horseshoe-shaped double green at the far end of a lake, the 124-yard 6th and the 135-yard 10th. Although the challenge is obviously limited, the layout's eight par 4s are of regulation size – though the 382-yard par-5 9th most obviously is not.

Cooper Colony Country Club - Cooper City   ♦½

Pat Pattison   www.coopercolonygolf.com
5050 SW 90th Ave, Cooper City, FL 33328   (954) 434-2181
        3,820 yds   Par 60   Rating: - / -   (1962)

In spots more ambitious than a typically humdrum executive layout, the Cooper Colony Country Club is an 18-hole track routed mostly among single-family homes and crossed by a lone (but prominent) water hazard, which at least somewhat affects more than half of its holes. Several of the strongest tests reside among the course's six par 4s, led by the 355-yard 1st and 335-yard 3rd (both crossed by the water), the 355-yard 10th (ditto) and the 313-yard 13th, a 90-degree dogleg left around one of the hazard's widest sections. The par 3s are a tad less engaging, but are fairly well bunkered throughout.

Coral Ridge Country Club (Rees) - Ft. Lauderdale   ♦½

Rees Jones   www.coralridgecc.com
3801 Bayview Dr, Ft. Lauderdale, FL 33308   (954) 449-4400
        1,399 yds   Par 27   Rating: - / -   (2015)

Located 600 yards west of Coral Ridge's clubhouse, the club's Rees Jones-designed par-3 nine lies on the site of the defunct (if grandly named) American Golfers Club, an 18-hole executive track built by Robert Trent Jones in 1958. Rees' far newer loop follows a clockwise path around a soon-to-be residential neighborhood and features holes ranging in length from 104-210 yards, many of which are well-bunkered and play to significantly contoured putting surfaces. Little here would stand out on a regulation course but the 158-yard centerline-bunkered 3rd, the 210-yard 5th and the 200-yard bunker-ringed 9th certainly offer something a notch or two above run-of-the-mill par-3 golf.

Eco Golf Club - Hollywood   ◆½

Unknown   www.ecogolfclub.com
1451 Taft St, Hollywood, FL 33020   (954) 927-1751
        2,259 yds   Par 32   Rating: - / -   (1982)

Affiliated with the Hollywood Beach Golf Resort, the municipally owned Eco Golf Club is something of a unique nine-hole executive loop, being routed around the city's water treatment facility. The plant's workings are mostly shielded from view by landscaping as the holes follow a clockwise routing, and while hazarding is limited, the combination of doglegs and greens more contoured than the muni norm does manage to create some challenge. The 362-yard 2nd (a sharp dogleg right which turns rather early) is a viable – if slightly awkward - test, while the 518-yard dogleg right 4th and the 381-yard pond-flanked 6th represent high-class executive course fare. Solid of this type.

Hillsboro Club Par 3 - Hillsboro Beach   ◆½

Unknown   www.hillsboroclub.org
901 Hillsboro Mile, Hillsboro Beach, FL 33062   (954) 941-2220

A back yard amenity to this exclusive seasonal residence club ideally situated on a point between the Atlantic Ocean and the Intracoastal Waterway, the Hillsboro Club's par-3 course has taken on multiple forms over the decades, with its present version being built during 2015. The club publishes no yardages or pars, nor has the layout been rated, but the holes are all of the short, pitch-and-putt variety and are routed among/around tennis courts, the club entrance road and a central lake. Several large bunkers affect play, while the lake allows for a showpiece at the 7th, whose green is a small bulkheaded peninsula which extends into the hazard's center. By any measure, this is high-end back yard golf.

Hollybrook Golf Club (Par 3) - Pembroke Pines   ◆

Unknown   www.hollybrook.com
900 Hollybrook Dr, Pembroke Pines, FL 33025   (561) 575-7891
        1,796 yds   Par 54   Rating: - / -   (1968)

In addition to its William Mitchell-designed regulation 18, the Hollybrook Golf Club also offers an 18-hole 1,796-yard par 3 course built among a sea of condominiums on the north side of Washington Boulevard. Tree-lined and frequently bunkered, it includes holes ranging from 72-142 yards in length, with nearly every entry being meaningfully bunkered and four having water at least somewhat realistically in play. A non-returning routing suggests 18 holes to be the norm but beyond that minor note, this too represents high quality back yard golf – particularly if one enjoys playing in view of their neighbors.

Lauderhill Golf Course - Ft. Lauderdale   ♦

Unknown   lauderhill-fl.gov
4141 NW 16th St, Ft. Lauderdale, FL 33313   (954) 730-2990
            1,212 yds   Par 30   Rating: - / -   (1968)

Squeezed into a tight track among condominiums, canals and mini-malls, the nine-hole Lauderhill Golf Course is a par-3 layout in disguise, its par of 30 only being achieved by classifying the 217-yard 2nd, the 160-yard 5th and the 200-yard 7th rather amusingly as par 4s. Twelve bunkers are very much in play while the canals are less so (save for the 110-yard 1st and 114-yard 9th), making for a decent practice site for irons, but little more.

Leisureville Community Association - Pompano Beach   ♦

Unknown
2921 West Golf Blvd, Pompano Beach, FL 33064   (954) 946-0350
            745 yds   Par 28   Rating: - / -   (1969)

The private facility of a retirement community built along the eastern flank of Interstate 95, Leisureville's 745-yard nine is a short, mostly open loop that forms a back yard for the two-story condominiums which encircle it. A central lake comes into play on two holes but with flat terrain, few trees and no bunkers, this is strictly golf of the most basic order.

Margate Executive Golf Course - Margate   ♦

William Dietsch   www.margategolf.com
7870 Margate Blvd, Margate, FL 33063   (954) 971-0807
            1,512 yds   Par 30   Rating: 27.0 / 90   (1982)

Located immediately south of the Oriole Golf Club, the Margate Executive Golf Course is a short and basic nine built into an oddly shaped, canal-crossed tract among rows of surrounding condominiums. There are only three bunkers in play and, while strictly speaking, the canal can be said to affect as many as five holes, it lies far enough off line to require a comprehensive miss to be found. Solid for beginners and the less-skilled.

Pine Island Ridge Country Club - Davie   ♦♦

Unknown   www.pircc.com
9400 Pine Ridge Dr, Davie, FL 33324   (954) 472-7600
          4,705 yds   Par 64   Rating: 62.7 / 111   (1976)

Renovated in the new millennium by Jeff Myers as a part of the same state-sponsored Interstate 595 expansion that affected neighbors Arrowhead and Lago Mar, Pine Island Ridge is a private facility boasting one of the longer, stronger executive layouts one is likely to encounter. Routed among a wide range of housing and an interconnected network of lakes, it is a heavily bunkered track whose holes frequently touch the water but seldom utilize it as a strategic hazard. Aside from the well-bunkered 288-yard 15th, the best golf falls in the course's mid-section and includes waterside par 3s at the 9th, 11th and 12th, as well as the 378-yard 10th, a dogleg right played to something of a peninsula green. Though there are few strategic questions, this is still top-shelf executive fare.

Seven Bridges at Springtree - Sunrise   ♦♦

William Dietsch   www.springtreegc.com
8150 Springtree Dr, Sunrise, FL 33351   (954) 572-2270
          4,042 yds   Par 62   Rating: 61.1 / 102   (1972)

Renovated in 2010 by Mark McCumber, the former Springtree Golf Course is owned by the Town of Sunrise and sports another of the region's high-end executive layouts. Routed among a mix of housing, lakes and commercial development, its front nine features three holes built around the same central lake: the difficult 209-yard 3rd, the 109-yard all-carry 4th and the 312-yard 6th, a drive-and-pitch across the water. The back is led by the water-flanked 344-yard 14th before reaching two shortish closers, the 124-yard 16th (where water lurks behind the green) and the 328-yard 18th, which bends awkwardly right, between the maintenance yard and a neighboring mall.

Sunrise Lakes Phase 3 Golf Course - Sunrise   ♦

Unknown   www.sunriselakesfl.com
9361 Sunrise Lakes Blvd, Sunrise, FL 33322   (954) 741-8352
          1,675 yds   Par 31   Rating: - / -   (1981)

Another private facility set within a veritable stadium of surrounding condos, Sunrise Lakes Phase 3 is a shortish executive nine divided in half by a central canal. Though not of an advanced design standard, it does offer a reasonably high level of backyard golf, with water occasionally creeping in at the edges, and a trio of short par 4s – the 267-yard 1st, the 263-yard 5th and the 310-yard dogleg right 9th – offering a bit more than exercise.

Sunrise Lakes Phase 4 Golf Course - Sunrise ♦

Unknown   www.sunriselakesfl.com
10102 Sunrise Lakes Blvd, Sunrise, FL 33322   (954) 748-4567

Located across Nob Hill Road to the west, Sunrise Lakes Phase 4 follows the formula of its sister Phase 3, though here the development is larger, which in turn mandated a more expansive routing among the buildings. The club doesn't publish yardages and has not been rated but it is of the same style and caliber of Phase 3, save for the par-4 7th, a slightly awkward dogleg right whose drive is threatened by water and a left-side tree.

Wynmoor Golf Course - Coconut Creek ♦♦

Unknown   www.wynmoor.com
1310 Ave of the Stars, Coconut Creek, FL 33066   (954) 978-2677
              3,432 yds   Par 60   Rating: 58.2 / 84   (1974)

Lying just west of Florida's Turnpike, the Wynmoor Golf Course is a challenging executive layout occupying lake-dominated ribbon of land within a veritable sea of condominiums. Though flanking numerous holes, this seemingly endless central water hazard only materially affects perhaps nine of them – though in several cases, its presence is quite invasive. The most engaging holes by far, these all feature water very much in play down their right sides and include the 318-yard 1st, the 213-yard par-4 7th, the 286-yard 16th (whose green angles along the shoreline) and the 247-yard 18th, another sub-regulation par 4, this time driveable over water to a bulkheaded green.

PALM BEACH COUNTY

Aberdeen Golf & Country Club - Boynton Beach   ◆◆◆

Desmond Muirhead   www.aberdeencountryclub.com
8251 Aberdeen Dr, Boynton Beach, FL 33437   (561) 738-4903
            7,016 yds   Par 72   Rating: 74.5 / 137   (1987)

Things are very much up in the air at the Aberdeen Golf & Country Club as, at the time of this writing, Jim Fazio is in the process of performing a major renovation. Aberdeen, of course, has long stood immortal as the place where the late Desmond Muirhead dove off the golf design deep end, building holes that resembled mermaids (the 393-yard 11th), bunkers shaped like "grasping hands" (at the 169-yard 3rd), a watery par-3 17th which was "a combination of Pine Valley and the Bolshoi" and an "existential" 18th hole built in homage to Kierkegaard and Sartre. Indeed, the contrived nature of such things is rather more obvious than how Muirhead continued to find work in their aftermath, but perhaps the answer lies in this: Beyond its search for the meaning of life (and aesthetics which draw cringes from many), there actually was a unique and strategically challenging golf course here. It is difficult to say whether Muirhead went this bizarre route because he thought it would get him publicity (it did) or because he hoped it might cast him as an historical innovator (less so). But regardless, whether one fully grasped number 18's "stimulation of spatial flow" or not, Aberdeen has certainly represented memorable, often engaging golf. Fazio's project is slated to homogenize things considerably, not only removing Muirhead's many museum pieces but replacing them with more generic cape-and-bay-style bunkering, as well as large sand beaches that descend into water hazards. This Collectability Rating, then, is in homage to what was – bizarre as it may have been.

Addison Reserve - Delray Beach   ◆◆½

Arthur Hills   www.addisonreserve.cc
7201 Addison Reserve Blvd, Delray Beach, FL 33446   (561) 637-4004
        Salvation/Trepidation: 6,808 yds   Par 72   Rating: 73.1 / 143   (1995)
        Redemption: 3,239 yds   Par 72   Rating: 35.9 / 136   (1995)

Set within a patchwork of golf courses just east of Florida's Turnpike (its neighbors being the faraway-sounding St. Andrews and Gleneagles), Addison Reserve offers 27 Arthur Hills-designed holes which wend their way through a seemingly endless maze of single-family homes. Renovations have added numerous bunkers over the years (most protecting fairways), leaving a facility whose strongest 18 pairs the Salvation and Trepidation nines. Of these, the Salvation is the slightly longer, but aside from the 558-yard pond-fronted 9th, it is anchored by a group of fairly similar shorter par 4s like the 378-yard 1st (which bends leftward, around a lake), the 390-yard 2nd (ditto, but to the right), the 371-yard 5th (back to the left) and the 371-yard 8th (ditto). The Trepidation is both shorter and a shade less engaging, at least until a closing stretch that begins with the driveable (but dry) 317-yard 6th and the 185-yard 7th, a lake-crossing par 3 which, fully encircled by some 50 homes, gives the phrase "stadium golf" real meaning. The 432-yard 9th (a bunkerless dogleg right along a lake) is a suitably strong finisher. The shorter Redemption nine fills the property's narrower eastern half, and opens and closes with short, water-affected par 4s, the 360-yard 1st (a tricky dogleg left) and the 329-yard 9th, which squeezes between front-right water and left-side homes. The 171-over-water yard 4th is another notable on a layout which also requires some long cart rides between holes.

Club at Admiral's Cove (East) - Jupiter   ◆◆◆

Robert von Hagge   www.admiralscove.net
200 Admiral's Cove Blvd, Jupiter, FL 33477   (561) 744-1700
        6,827 yds   Par 70   Rating: 73.2 / 147   (1987)

The Club at Admiral's Cove is a real estate-oriented development which squeezes an impressive 45 Robert von Hagge-designed holes (plus countless homes) into a compact site bordered to the east by the Intracoastal Waterway. Von Hagge's first work here was the East course, a modern, challenging layout routed around (and occasionally across) several inlets off the Intracoastal. A track marked both by its often-wild bunkering and some expansive cart rides, it opens in the property's northern half, where a pair of par 3s (the 205-yard 3rd and the 175-yard 5th) play to greens protected my massive swaths of sand. However, the outer half's strongest golf falls within a trio of pond-fronted par 4s: the 424-yard 6th, the 431-yard 7th and the dangerous 390-yard 9th. The back is shorter and at times slightly cramped, particularly early on where the 173-yard over-water 10th and potentially driveable 337-yard 13th lead the way. The remainder of the loop then makes an out-and-back journey to the property's southwest corner and includes the 411-yard 15th (with its long, over-water second), the 216-yard lakeside 16th, the 648-yard 17th (an endless dogleg right around a huge bunker) and the 465-yard 18th, whose inlet-jumping approach is borderline impossible for the less-skilled. Though wedged tightly among the housing, and being of only moderate size on the scorecard, the East course remains one of the tougher tracks built by the intrepid von Hagge.

Club at Admiral's Cove (Golf Village) - Jupiter   ◆◆½

Robert von Hagge   www.admiralscove.net
200 Admiral's Cove Blvd, Jupiter, FL 33477   (561) 744-1700
        West/North: 6,508 yds   Par 71   Rating: 72.4 / 141   (1988)
        South: 2,983 yds   Par 35   Rating: 34.6 / 141   (1988)

In 1988, the Club at Admiral's Cove retained Robert von Hagge to add their 27-hole "Golf Village," which plays out of a separate clubhouse west of Alternate A1A where, lacking the labyrinth of inlets that mark the East course, things are more tightly (and cohesively) routed. The highest-rated combination pairs the West and North nines, with the West being led by a trio of water holes: the 367-yard 2nd (played to a railroad-tie buttressed green angled along front-right water), the 208-yard all-carry 6th and the narrow 583-yard 9th, a sweeping dogleg left along a large lake. Despite measuring only 3,309 yards, the North is the longest of the Village nines and features back-to-back par 5s at the 564-yard 3rd and the 505-yard 4th, as well as the tightly bunkered 207-yard 5th and the 360-yard lake-flanked 9th. Most engaging, however, is the 342-yard dogleg left 6th, which bends around a pond and dares the longer hitter to have a go at the putting surface. The sub-3,000-yard South nine includes several less memorable holes, but it also offers three watery par 4s which, despite their limited size, inject a dose of difficulty: the 370-yard 6th (which curls rightward, along a pond), the 361-yard drive-and-pitch 7th and the 370-yard 8th, a dogleg left to a near-island green. The compact nature of these nines is obvious, but while their shortness makes them somewhat less difficult than the East course, all three pack enough challenge to at least keep better players on their toes.

BallenIsles Country Club (East) - Palm Beach Gardens   ♦♦♦

Dick Wilson & Joe Lee   www.ballenisles.com
100 BallenIsles Circle, Palm Beach Gardens, FL 33418   (561) 622-0220
7,189 yds   Par 72   Rating: 75.0 / 143   (1964)

One of the Palm Beach area's earlier inland developments, this 54-hole Ballenisles
Country Club has, since its 1964 opening, been alternately known as the PGA National
Golf Club (while serving as the PGA of America's home during the 1960s and '70s) and the
JDM Country Club. Its marquee entry is the Dick Wilson-designed East course, site of the
1971 PGA Championship (won by Jack Nicklaus) and World Cup (claimed by Nicklaus and
Lee Trevino), and for many years a staple in *Golf Digest*'s national Top 100. A significantly
altered track that has lost much of Wilson's most imposing period bunkering, it is today a
housing-ringed test which, despite its lustrous tournament pedigree, no longer truly
stands out among so many newer entries within the region – though as its 75.0 rating
suggests, it certainly remains challenging. Most noteworthy here is the 463-yard 18th,
whose original dual-fairway configuration (the left option requiring a long water carry)
has long since been narrowed to a single target – though little real advantage was ever
gained by taking the bold route anyway. Additional favorites include the 443-yard lake-
flanked 2nd, the 368-yard pond-guarded 9th, the 515-yard 12th (which turns left, around/
across a lake) and the 392-yard 13th, a dogleg right which curls around the same hazard.
Not what it once was, then, but as one of only two South Florida courses ever to host a
Major championship, this remains a challenging and historically important stop.

BallenIsles Country Club (North) - Palm Beach Gardens   ♦♦½

Dick Wilson & Joe Lee   www.ballenisles.com
100 BallenIsles Circle, Palm Beach Gardens, FL 33418   (561) 622-0220
6,865 yds   Par 72   Rating: 73.4 / 138   (1964)

Both the North and South courses at the BallenIsles Country Club contain Dick Wilson-
designed holes dating to 1964, as Wilson's second layout for what was initially a 36-hole
facility (then known as the West) was divided up by Joe Lee while creating a third course
in 1969. Renovated in 2013 by Kipp Schulties, the modernized North (which lies in the
property's northwest corner) is rated as the club' easiest, its playing corridors being fairly
wide, its use of water seldom too threatening. Further (and rather progressively), it was
among the first courses in the region to includes a set of short course tees (measuring
3,943 yards) to accommodate seniors or the less-skilled. Among the North's strongest
front nine entries are the 443-yard lake-flanked 2nd (the number one stroke hole), the
477-yard 3rd (a reachable par 5 which curves rightward, around more water) and the 380-
yard dogleg right 9th, whose green lies far afield. Coming home, the 424-yard lake-
fronted 10th kicks off the action, with remaining favorites including a trio of outlying tests:
the 438-yard dogleg right 12th, the 167-yard lakeside 13th and the 359-yard 14th, which
curls leftward around the same hazard. Though still retaining its pre-Schulties routing,
stylistically, this has morphed somewhat from the stylings of Dick Wilson and Joe Lee.

BallenIsles Country Club (South) - Palm Beach Gardens   ♦♦½

Dick Wilson & Joe Lee   www.ballenisles.com
100 BallenIsles Circle, Palm Beach Gardens, FL 33418   (561) 622-0220
                6,875 yds   Par 72   Rating: 74.0 / 138   (1969)

Like its North course, the BallenIsles Country Club's South course dates in part to 1964, but the early stylings of both Dick Wilson and Joe Lee (who reconfigured holes in 1969) were largely paved over during a 2000 renovation performed by Florida-based architect Gene Bates. Now offering a more modernized look (particularly in its bunkering), the South is not quite a regional standout but it does feature several strong and engaging par 5s, including the 553-yard 7th (where water lines the entirety of the left side), the 536-yard 9th (a tempting double-dogleg which dares long water carries on both the drive and second) and the 531-yard 17th, whose green angles leftward, behind a lake. Strong mid-size par 4s like the 434-yard water-crossing 5th and the 415-yard 8th (where a lake borders the left side) help to carry the non-returning routing to the property's southwestern reaches, where the 176-yard over-water 11th and the driveable (but heavily bunkered) 315-yard 13th begin the long road back. Among the closers, the well-bunkered 415-yard 15th and the aforementioned 17th stand out the furthest, while the 385-yard 18th plays to a wildly shaped waterside putting surface. Bates significantly advanced things here, but most one-round visitors will, understandably, opt to play the East.

Banyan Golf Club - West Palm Beach   ♦♦♦

Joe Lee   www.banyangolfclub.com
1393 Lyons Rd, West Palm Beach, FL 33411   (561) 793-2800
                7,150 yds   Par 72   Rating: 74.7 / 139   (1973)

An imposing, very much under-the-radar Joe Lee design dating to 1973, the Banyan Golf Club lies a short drive west of Florida's Turnpike, where it has long managed to keep its fine golf-only site secluded even as the once-desolate neighborhood has grown up around it. One of Lee's strongest efforts, Banyan stands apart from many regional facilities by virtue of the thick flora that separates many fairways – trees rather creatively transplanted from the oncoming path of Interstate 95 as it eminent domained its way across the Palm Beach landscape. The design itself is vintage Lee, featuring heavy, mostly penal bunkering and plenty of water – though these hazards are usually more angular than of the forced-carry variety, resulting in a layout which is quite challenging but not quite overwhelming. Consequently, while strong tests like the 230-yard bunker-fronted 13th, the 453-yard 15th and the 450-yard bunker-narrowed 18th abound, it is the water holes that linger longest in the memory. Going out, these include the 189-yard 3rd, plus a pair of shorter, lake-flanked par 4s, the 389-yard 4th and the 354-yard 7th. Coming home, the 415-yard dogleg left 11th is a standout while the 516-yard dogleg left 14th and the 415-yard 17th (where a lake flanks first the right, then the left sides) also rate highly. Lying distant from the heart of Palm Beach and having never hosted a major professional event, Banyan remains one of the region's least-seen (and least-altered) facilities.

Bear Lakes Country Club (Lakes) - West Palm Beach   ♦♦♦

Jack Nicklaus   www.bearlakes.org
1901 Village Blvd, West Palm Beach, FL 33409   (561) 478-0001
            7,439 yds   Par 72   Rating: 75.9 / 150   (1984)

Located on a long, rectangular tract just west of Interstate 95, the Bear Lakes Country Club was among the earliest of Jack Nicklaus's solo projects in his adopted South Florida, its Lakes course (1984) following only his 1972 co-design (with Desmond Muirhead) of nearby Mayacoo Lakes. Lying on the north side of Village Boulevard, the Lakes was renovated by Nicklaus in 2003 and is the more demanding of the club's two 18s, being routed over generally flat terrain and relying on a typical Florida mix of water and sand for playing interest. Though the double green that serves holes 9 and 18 is formulaic, the rest really isn't, particularly since the removal of several large waste bunkers that were a large part of the original design. The 3,691-yard front nine throws in one smaller entry at the 174-yard 8th (whose green complex extends forward, into a lake) but the loop is better represented by a trio of strong par 4s: the 473-yard centerline-bunkered 5th, the 435-yard 7th (the number one stroke hole, with narrow green lying just at water's edge), and the 471-yard pond-fronted 9th. The back nine is even longer (3,748 yards) and, after initially featuring the 189-yard over-water 11th and the 482-yard lake-flanked 13th, peaks over a closing run that includes the 435-yard 15th (a demanding dogleg left over more water) and the 573-yard 17th, whose small green is tucked rightward, behind a stand of trees. And lastly, there is the 429-yard 18th, a lake-divided split fairway test daring an enormous left-side carry in order to open up an unimpeded approach.

Bear Lakes Country Club (Links) - West Palm Beach   ♦♦♦

Jack Nicklaus   www.bearlakes.org
1901 Village Blvd, West Palm Beach, FL 33409   (561) 478-0001
            7,392 yds   Par 72   Rating: 75.9 / 140   (1987)

The Bear Lakes Country Club's newer Links course (which Jack Nicklaus renovated in 2007) sits south of Village Boulevard where it has been marketed as a "Scottish-style" design – and while such pitches always miss the mark, this is at least something different from the standard regional fare. Actually, in its initial form, the Links was a schizophrenic sort of test, alternately interpreting "Scottish" to mean either vast stretches of open sand (unlike anything seen at St Andrews) or the occasional cluster of small, round bunkers, with lots of artificial mounding (and the odd double fairway) thrown in. And while its renovated form is not exactly a transportive experience, it does offer a more open, less overtly tropical appearance amidst its typically engaging golf. Once again, many of the centerpieces tend to be on the longer side, with the front nine offering a pair of parallel lakeside par 5s (the 595-yard 2nd and the water-fronted 573-yard 6th) plus the layout's number one stroke hole, the 467-yard straightaway 5th, and the 484-yard par-4 9th. The back opens with 397-yard lake-flanked 10th before featuring the 476-yard 12th (whose once-bunkerless elevated green now sports a single fronting hazard), the watery 447-yard 14th and the 376-yard, split-fairway 15th. Thus while it hardly resembles Scotland, the Links is certainly more interesting than if Nicklaus had simply built a second 18 identical to the first. Also notable: Though I-95 does indeed border the property, its impact is minimized by a housing buffer (some quite substantial) on all but three holes.

The Bear's Club - Jupiter   ◆◆◆½

Jack Nicklaus   www.thebearsclub.com
250 Bear's Club Dr, Jupiter, FL 33447   (561) 626-2327
                7,153 yds   Par 72   Rating: 75.2 / 153   (1999)

Occupying a fairly spacious site just a long par 4 inland from the Intracoastal Waterway, The Bear's Club clearly got a lot of Jack Nicklaus's attention during the design process, particularly as the great man himself is known to spend some of his personal time here. The overall design plan takes advantage of this generous acreage, allowing for housing to be limited to the perimeter and large chunks of native landscape to remain intact, giving many holes a feeling of rustic seclusion that completely belies the club's well-developed surroundings. Even more importantly, there is little architectural trickery here, and a fair amount of creativity in evidence; how many high-end Florida courses, for example, can claim four par 3s with green complexes completely unaffected by water? Notable early holes include a trio routed among a northern section of lakes and wetlands: the 240-yard 2nd (with plenty of fairway for those missing short), the 433-yard lakeside 3rd and the 375-yard 5th, a drive-and-pitch to a narrow green bulkheaded above a marsh. Additional strong two-shotters are plentiful, including the 419-yard dogleg left 9th, the 439-yard water-lined 11th and the tightly bunkered 465-yard 17th. Yet more impressive still is a collection of par 5s led by the 540-yard sand-lined 8th, the 525-yard 10th (which double doglegs to a pond-guarded green) and the semi-gimmicky 18th, which offers the option of being played as either a 551-yard three-shotter or a 414-yard par 4 – with trees, sand, a semi-split fairway and a waterside putting surface making either choice something of an adventure. Less flashy than much of Jack's period work, this is one of the stronger pre-2000 layouts in the extensive Nicklaus portfolio. **(GD: #8 State GW: #142 Modern)**

Boca Grove Golf & Tennis Club - Boca Raton   ◆◆½

Karl Litten   www.bocagrove.org
21351 Whitaker Dr, Boca Raton, FL 33433   (561) 487-5300
                6,808 yds   Par 72   Rating: 73.5 / 151   (1982)

Initially designed in 1982 by the globetrotting Karl Litten, the Boca Grove Golf & Tennis Club gained a quick dash of fame by hosting the Champions Tour from 1983-85 – and being lucky enough to celebrate Arnold Palmer (twice) and Gary Player as its champions. The layout is routed through rows of (mostly) single-family homes on a large rectangular tract just east of Florida's Turnpike, where it underwent a 2011 renovation at the hands of Jim Fazio. With corridors of play pretty well carved in stone, Fazio's work focused primarily on bunkering and greens, with the result being a track with a somewhat more restrained and polished feel. Like many in the region, most of its more memorable moments lie within holes defined by water, with the front nine's best including the 171-yard 3rd, the 438-yard 4th (where a pond hugs the left side before crossing the fairway) and the 422-yard lake-guarded 9th. The back is initially led by the 379-yard dogleg right 10th (which dares a drive across a corner waste area) and the 508-yard pond-fronted 12th before closing with trio of semi-awkward finishers: the 365-yard dogleg left 16th (a forced lay-up hole), the 551-yard 17th (a sharp dogleg left around a lake – with the daring, over-water tee shot blocked by a five-story condominium) and the 360-yard lake-fronted 18th.

Boca Lago Country Club - Boca Raton   ♦♦

Robert von Hagge & Bruce Devlin   www.bocalago.com
8665 Juego Way, Boca Raton, FL 33433   (561) 482-5000
    South/East: 6,496 yds   Par 72   Rating: 70.3 / 142   (1975)
    West: 3,098 yds   Par 35   Rating: 35.5 / 135   (1975)

Located just across Florida's Turnpike from Boca Grove, the Boca Lago Country Club was for several decades a sprawling 36-hole von Hagge & Devlin-designed facility, before the new millennium closing of its southwestern-most nine left the club with 27. Real estate development clearly took initial priority here (witness several tight 90-degree doglegs around housing), leaving the architects to squeeze in their holes as best they could. The former East course remains largely intact as today's South and East nines, a short but fairly challenging pairing which mixes mid-range holes with a handful of much tougher watery ones. The 3,176-yard South offers its strongest golf in two of its three par 5s, the 546-yard 3rd (where a left-side lake affects both the second and the third) and the 505-yard 9th, a tricky driving hole upon which interceding water may force longer hitters to lay up. The East features another imposing three-shotter at its 542-yard 1st (where water must be carried twice) as well as the 468-yard 8th (easily the club's longest par 4), but it also includes a pair of awkward holes with overly sharp doglegs, the 428-yard 3rd and the 363-yard 5th. The 3,098-yard West nine quickly incorporates two more such doglegs (at the 422-yard 2nd and the 515-yard 4th) while being led by the 517-yard 6th (a lake-flanked dogleg left) and the 193-yard 9th, whose narrow green is squeezed by sand and water.

Club at Boca Pointe- Boca Raton   ♦♦

Bob Cupp   www.bocapointecc.com
7144 Boca Pointe Dr, Boca Raton, FL 33433   (561) 864-8500
    6,876 yds   Par 72   Rating: 72.6 / 139   (1982)

Another Turnpike-adjacent property, the Club at Boca Pointe was laid out by Bob Cupp (under the Nicklaus Design masthead) in 1982 on a heavily developed site filled with both single-family homes and high-rise condominiums. Far less tactically engaging than one might anticipate from a period Nicklaus production, this at times borders on functional golf, particularly over a 3,504-yard front nine which gains length from the 585-yard creek-crossed 6th and the 462-yard 9th, but offers only one really notable test, the 397-yard dogleg left 7th. The shorter back utilizes more frequent water hazards to pump up the interest level, first at the 388-yard 12th (whose green sits flush against a right-side lake), then later over a finishing stretch kicked off by the 404-yard 15th, which bends leftward around another invasive hazard. Play closes with a pair of demanding (though formulaic) finishers, the 192-yard 17th and, more impressively, the 528-yard 18th, where water borders the entire left side en route to a green tucked left, beyond the end of the hazard.

Boca Rio Golf Club - Boca Raton   ♦♦♦½

Robert von Hagge   www.bocariogolfclub.com
22041 Boca Rio Rd, Boca Raton, FL 33433   (561) 482-3300
              7,116 yds   Par 72   Rating: 74.6 / 138   (1967)

Located just west of Florida's Turnpike, the Boca Rio Golf Club is a small, men-only facility which for four decades has maintained one of the region's best – if least publicized – golf courses. Built by Robert von Hagge just prior to his prolific partnership with Bruce Devlin, it is a mostly unspectacular design which relies far less on water (which seriously affects only five holes) than almost any top Florida course of its era. It is also a richly landscaped facility, with native flora backing most greens and dividing many fairways, often giving the compact property a secluded feeling despite its relatively central location. On this occasion at least, von Hagge's bunkering is colorful but seldom over the top – save, perhaps, for the giant hazard (with two trees in its middle) that fronts the double green that serves the 9th and 18th. Front nine standouts include the 495-yard par-5 1st (where water hugs the front-left of the green), the 410-yard dogleg left 5th and the 541-yard 8th, which twists between stands of trees to a small, attractive greenside. Coming home, nearly all of the closers are notable, including the 413-yard 14th (a sharp dogleg left), the engaging 539-yard double dogleg 16th and the 180-yard 17th, whose massive, water-fronted green (easily the club's largest) features several nasty pin positions. And then there is the lake-flanked 425-yard 18th; a fine par 4 whose double green was rather more cutting edge (and a von Hagge trademark) at the time of its construction. Long absent from any list major tournament venues and largely overlooked on the national level, Boca Rio rates among the best of an admittedly weak architectural period.

Boca West Country Club (Palmer I) - Boca Raton   ♦♦½

Desmond Muirhead   www.bocawest.com
20583 Boca West Dr, Boca Raton, FL 33434   (561) 488-6924
              7,220 yds   Par 72   Rating: 75.0 / 143   (1970)

A sprawling 1970s development that counts 54 separate residential "villages" amidst and around its 72 holes, the Boca West Country Club spent the first several years of the new millennium undergoing a complete renovation of its entire golfing facility. Its Palmer I (née No. 1) course, originally built by the incomparable Desmond Muirhead in 1970, was also the first to be overhauled, with Arnold Palmer & Co. doing the job (and thus getting his name on the masthead) in 1997. Occupying the property's southwestern quadrant, it is easily the club's longest layout but, for the most part, offers typical South Florida fare, with bunkering being less prolific than the Palmer norm and water serving as the primary hazard on at least 10 holes. The 399-yard dogleg right 11th – with water-divided split fairways – stands out the farthest here, with the front nine's supporting cast including the 545-yard 3rd (where right-side water affects both lay up and approach), the 401-yard lakeside 4th and the 620-yard 6th, whose mermaid-like fairway is a holdover from the Muirhead era. In addition to the thought-provoking 11th, the back later closes strongly with the watery 414-yard 15th (a sweeping dogleg left), a pair of bunkerless entries at the 196-yard over-water 16th and the 436-yard 17th, plus the watery, reachable 506-yard 18th.

Boca West Country Club (Fazio II) - Boca Raton   ♦♦½

Desmond Muirhead   www.bocawest.com
20583 Boca West Dr, Boca Raton, FL   33434   (561) 488-6924
         6,811 yds   Par 71   Rating: 73.4 / 146   (1971)

The Boca West Country Club's Fazio II (née No. 2) course was the second to be built within this huge development, with Desmond Muirhead again doing the honors, this time in 1971. Occupying the property's southeastern section, it would later be renovated in 2005 by the regionally prominent Jim Fazio, a job which largely maintained Muirhead's corridors of play but shifted around several holes, while also downscaling the bunkering and, surprisingly, lessening the impact of water as well. Thus, the present layout is a relatively a low-key work by both Muirhead's and Fazio's standards, with its much shorter front nine being led by the 559-yard 2nd (where a grassy depression guards the green front-left), the 205-yard water-flanked 6th and the 400-yard 9th, a solid, bunker-narrowed two-shotter. At 3,568 yards, the back nine is a different story, beginning with the 550-yard 10th (where a pair of centerline bunkers front the green) and the 195-yard sand-narrowed 12th. The 566-yard 13th (a sharp dogleg left around water - and houses) is an attention-getter, while the 470-yard par-4 18th, a gentle dogleg right, is a robust closer. Gone, unfortunately, is Muirhead's old 128-yard 16th, whose slim peninsula green stuck dangerously out into a canal where the present (heavily reshaped) 17th tee now stands; it would certainly still rank as the layout's most intriguing feature.

Boca West Country Club (Palmer III) - Boca Raton   ♦♦½

Robert von Hagge & Bruce Devlin   www.bocawest.com
20583 Boca West Dr, Boca Raton, FL 33434   (561) 488-6924
         6,753 yds   Par 71   Rating: 72.4 / 139   (1974)

The Boca West Country Club's Palmer III (née No.3) course occupies the property's northeastern section where it began life in 1974 as a relatively staid von Hagge & Devlin design. Its renovation would come in 1999 at the hands of Arnold Palmer, a rebuild that would largely maintain the layout's original corridors of play (but reversing holes 3-5) while altering most of the bunkering and adding several water hazards. Following a somewhat attenuated routing that touches four separate segments of the property, it is shorter than Palmer's No.1 course but possesses at least as many interesting holes. Early on these include the 516-yard 2nd (where water forces a major second-shot decision), the 443-yard dogleg left 3rd and the 410-yard lakeside 5th – all of which originally played second fiddle to the watery 556-yard 9th prior to that hole's recent shortening to a par 4, presumably due to safety issues with the adjacent driving range. Following a cart ride over a long bridge to the 10th tee, the inward half initially offers the 401-yard water-menaced 12th as well as the 185-yard 14th, whose green curls rightward, along a pond. The homestretch is headed by a pair of somewhat varied par 5s, the 579-yard 15th (a sharp dogleg left with water lurking beyond the corner) and the 504-yard 18th, a reachable test with out-of-bounds right, a lake left and a waterfall backing the green.

Boca West Country Club (Dye IV) - Boca Raton   ◆◆◆

Joe Lee   www.bocawest.com
20583 Boca West Dr, Boca Raton, FL 33434   (561) 488-6924
                6,954 yds   Par 71   Rating: 74.3 / 133   (1982)

Situated by itself in the property's northwestern corner, Boca West's Dye IV (née No.4) course was originally a 1982 Joe Lee design before eventually becoming the last of the club's four layouts to be overhauled, in this case by Pete Dye in 2007. Though without a doubt a softer Dye design (being nearly devoid of extra-deep bunkering and railroad ties, and including only one par 4 in excess of 430 yards), it does offer a predictably large menu of strong holes and, in addition to several long cart rides, features the narrow, almost rectangular bunkers that Dye was employing in the later 2000s. The 3,396-yard front nine is the less-engaging half, with its strongest entries including the 584-yard 3rd (which passes a large right-side waste area en route to a pond-guarded green), the 400-yard 7th, the stiff (though fairly basic) 230-yard 8th and the 420-yard bunker-narrowed 9th. After opening with the 562-yard dogleg right 10th, the longer inward half is led by the 187-yard 12th (played to a putting surface ringed by sand) and two strong par-4 finishers, the 451-yard 17th (which bends leftward along a narrow lake) and the 420-yard 18th, where water angles in short-right of the putting surface. Those expecting the TPC Sawgrass surely be disappointed, but even in this lighter form, Dye's signature stylings make for a nice alternative upon the club's 72-hole landscape.

Boca Woods Country Club (Woods) - Boca Raton   ◆◆

Joe Lee   www.bocaratongolfandcountryclub.com
10471 Boca Woods Ln, Boca Raton, FL 33428   (561) 487-2800
                6,647 yds   Par 72   Rating: 72.7 / 141   (1981)

The westernmost of Boca Raton's private clubs, the Boca Woods Country Club is a large, lake-dotted facility offering a pair of shortish, housing-lined courses built during the early 1980s. The Woods (née South) course was a 1981 Joe Lee design which, despite being a tad blander than Lee's period norm, will rate for many as the more engaging test. This is particularly true of its power line-crossed front nine which measures only 3,281 yards but includes a pair of strong par 5s, the 546-yard 2nd (where several fingers of an adjacent lake pinch the fairway) and the slightly awkward 534-yard 5th, which doglegs 90 degrees left around a residential neighborhood. Also notable here are the loop's closing par 4s, the 380-yard 8th (a tree-bothered dogleg right) and the 424-yard 9th, which curls along a right-side lake. The inward half is steady but somewhat staid in its hazarding, leaving its most engaging entries to be a pair of varied par 5s: the 512-yard tree- and bunker-dotted 11th and the 548-yard 18th, which dares a long second over water to a shallow green.

Boca Woods Country Club (Lakes) - Boca Raton   ♦♦

Karl Litten   www.bocaratongolfandcountryclub.com
10471 Boca Woods Ln, Boca Raton, FL 33428   (561) 487-2800
                6,816 yds   Par 72   Rating: 73.8 / 143   (1984)

The Boca Woods Country Club's Lakes course (née the North) is three years newer than
the Woods, and is both the longer and slightly tougher layout. It is also a track whose
routing clearly made major concessions to real estate planning, for it includes numerous
cart rides among residences to travel from hole to hole and, more tellingly, multiple
entries whose scale (and semi-awkward doglegs) indicate their being wedged into
whatever acreage was available. Though Karl Litten's bunkering has been altered a bit
over the years, the more engaging holes lie among the 14 which are water-affected. On a
front nine which also works around the power lines, these include a pair of short, pond-
guarded dogleg rights (the 386-yard 4th and 360-yard 5th), a much longer dogleg right (the
90-degree 412-yard 7th) and the 326-yard drive-and-pitch 9th. As with the Woods course,
the back is again the less exciting half, with highlights including the 184-yard over-water
12th and the 581-yard pond-guarded 13th, as well as a pair of solid mid-size closers, the
420-yard lake-flanked 17th and the 395-yard finisher.

Bocaire Country Club - Boca Raton   ♦♦½

Joe Lee   www.bocairecc.com
4989 Bocaire Blvd, Boca Raton, FL 33487   (561) 997-6556
                6,795 yds   Par 72   Rating: 73.3 / 139   (1984)

Built (and later renovated) by Joe Lee in 1984, the Bocaire Country Club is a compact,
facility routed among rows of single-family homes on a site which sits between North
Military Trail and the off-site Country Club course of the nearby Boca Raton Resort. To be
sure, Bocaire is a shortish layout which doesn't rate among Lee's elite designs, a fact
magnified by a reduction in both the number (modestly) and scale (significantly) of his
bunkering over time. Still, as one might expect of his work, there is a fair amount of
challenging golf here. Relatively little of it appears on the front nine, however, as this
3,374-yard loop offers five sub-400-yard par 4s (none of them special) and is thus led by
the 189-yard over-water 3rd. But the back measures up somewhat more impressively,
particularly over a four-hole run which includes the 512-yard 11th (a tree-pinched dogleg
right), the tactically engaging 415-yard 12th (which twists between two lakes), the
driveable (but smartly bunkered) 333-yard 13th and the 446-yard 14th, where out-of-
bounds lines the right side. Toss in the 202-yard 16th and the 546-yard 17th (where a
post-Lee centerline bunker menaces the second) and it all adds up to reliable period fare.

Broken Sound Club (Old) - Boca Raton   ◆◆◆

Joe Lee   www.brokensoundclub.org
1401 Northwest 51st St, Boca Raton, FL 33431   (561) 994-8505
          6,906 yds   Par 72   Rating: 74.6 / 142   (1976)

The Broken Sound Club boats two Joe Lee-designed courses occupying adjacent sites on either side of North Military Trail and, despite both being renovated by Gene Bates, they are actually of widely differing characters. The Old course (which has gained a measure of attention by serving as a Champions Tour stop since 2007) sits on the eastern side and is golf-only, its holes buffered by trees and considerable outside corporate development, but no internal housing. Lee's period bunker styling has all been re-worked now (as have several central water hazards) and while the layout is flat and "Floridian" in nature, it does offer several interesting tests including front nine favorites like the difficult 568-yard 6th (which makes a late left turn around a lake), the 290-yard driveable 7th (whose bulkheaded green is flanked left and long by water) and a pair of mirror-image lake-guarded par 3s, the 172-yard 3rd and the 169-yard 8th. The back's most engaging entries come early, first at the 401-yard lake-flanked 10th (where two small trees complicate the drive), then at the 207-yard 12th (whose plateau green sits above a deep left-side bunker) and the 453-yard 13th, which plays to a Bates-era peninsula green jutting rightward, into a pond. The 535-yard 18th is particularly well-suited to the Champions, being eminently reachable but also bothered by four bunkers angling along the right-center of the fairway. A solid regional track – but one boosted greatly by the presence of the pros.

Broken Sound Club (Club) - Boca Raton   ◆◆½

Joe Lee   www.brokensoundclub.org
1401 Northwest 51st St, Boca Raton, FL 33431   (561) 994-8505
          6,868 yds   Par 72   Rating: 73.5 / 141   (1985)

Joe Lee reportedly received input from Johnny Miller when designing the Broken Sound Club's newer Club course, which lies two blocks to the west of the Old course and is more of a typical, housing-squeezed South Florida layout (i.e., only the 385-yard 6th fails to be flanked by homes on at least one side). Renovated by Gene Bates in 2002, it is rated just over a full stroke easier than the Old course but still possesses several notably difficult holes, with the front nine being anchored by the 6th (a Cape-like design with water left) and the 537-yard 9th, a reachable par 5 with a lagoon crossing the fairway and a narrow, bulkheaded green angling behind more front-left water. The inward half initially features the 188-yard 12th (mostly for playing to an island green complex – albeit a well-buffered, unthreatening one) as well as a pair of watery dogleg lefts: the 539-yard 13th and the 398-yard 16th, which requires a lake carry on approach. Most memorable, however, is the 405-yard 18th, a gentle dogleg left played to a far less forgiving island green complex set beneath the clubhouse; there is no good bailout option here.

Delaire Country Club - Delray Beach   ♦♦½

Joe Lee   www.delaire.org
4645 White Cedar Ln, Delray Beach, FL 33445   (561) 499-9090
         Lakes/Woods: 6,635 yds   Par 72   Rating: 72.8 / 140   (1979)
         Hills: 3,348 yds   Par 36   Rating: 36.0 / 129   (1979)

Located just north of the canal which divides Boca Raton and Delray Beach, the Delaire Country Club is another area facility which twice engaged the ever-popular Joe Lee, first to build it in 1979, then to perform a renovation in 2002 – though a more recent 2016 update was also noteworthy as it downsized Lee's trademark bunkering considerably. What exists today, then, is a 27-hole facility routed over a typically flat, housing-dotted property, with the Lakes and Woods nine (formerly known as the Blue and Brown) narrowly forming the highest-rated 18-hole combination. The Lakes runs out to the east and, per its name, is a water-heavy loop, offering strong entries like the 534-yard 2nd (a sweeping dogleg left around a narrow lake), the 358-yard 5th (played to a railroad-tied green jutting leftward into a pond) and two more water-guarded tests, the 369-yard 8th and the 421-yard 9th. The 3,296-yard Woods nine runs along the club's northern boundary where, after the stiff 451-yard 1st and the 150-yard 3rd (played to a large green bulkheaded above a pond), it features a pair of quirky par 4s (the 384-yard 6th and the 340-yard pond-narrowed 8th) as well as a strong closer at the 420-yard 9th. The Hills (née Orange) nine is the club's longest but is highlighted by its tiny 316-yard 4th, a short dogleg right offering a direct route across water. The loop also closes strongly with the 427-yard 6th followed by a trio of pond-guarded tests measuring 404, 363 and 398 yards.

Delray Dunes Golf & Country Club - Boynton Beach   ♦♦♦

Pete Dye   www.delraydunes.org
12005 Dunes Rd, Boynton Beach, FL 33436   (561) 732-1600
         6,843 yds   Par 71   Rating: 73.3 / 138   (1969)

Though modified several times in later years by Pete Dye himself (including a complete reconfiguration of the 10th hole to accommodate a late 1990s driving range expansion), the Delray Dunes Golf & Country Club was Dye's first Florida design, and came early enough in his storied career that it lacks most of the unique retro/modern stylings that would ultimately come to define him. Unfortunately it also lacks a degree of strategic interest comparable with his strongest works, with its bunkering only moderately thought-provoking and water materially effecting play on only four occasions. A trio of longer par 4s (the 483-yard dogleg right 6th, the 440-yard into-the-wind 13th and the 470-yard 16th) add muscle, and holes like the 550-yard pond-guarded 4th and the 183-yard 17th (whose green sits above a tiny-but-prominent front-left bunker) require some thought. But for many, the most lingering impressions will be made by a pair of par 4s guarded by railroad tie-buttressed water hazards, the 320-yard 8th (whose fronting pond discourages too much aggressiveness) and the 393-yard 18th, which bends gently rightward to an enormous triangular putting surface. Delray Dunes will never be confused with the TPC Sawgrass, but with housing set well back from the corridors of play, this is more tranquil than many of the region's more famous layouts – and for Dye fans in particular, an interesting look at his pre-Harbour Town style.

Eastpointe Country Club (East) - Palm Beach Gardens ◆◆½

George Fazio www.eastpointe-cc.com
13535 Eastpointe Blvd, Palm Beach Gardens, FL 33418 (561) 626-6863
7,011 yds   Par 72   Rating: 74.4 / 136   (1974)

Built by George Fazio in the northwestern reaches of Palm Beach Gardens, the Eastpointe Country Club is one of the former PGA Tour player's longer and tougher creations, and one which remains mostly unchanged from its 1970s infancy. Though the competent ball striker will only find water meaningfully in play on seven holes, Fazio's bunkering is both strategic in its positioning and aesthetically different from his round-and-basic norm, these hazards having shown a more modern "Florida" look from their inception. The housing-lined routing is shaped loosely like a W, with the front nine lying to the east, where it is led by a trio of water-affected holes: the 416-yard 3rd (whose green angles rightward above a pond), the 414-yard dogleg right 5th (the number one stroke hole) and the 205-yard all-carry 8th. The 446-yard 9th is a demanding closer and sets the stage for an inward half led by more strong par 4s, including the 432-yard 10th, the 404-yard dogleg right 11th and the 447-yard pond-flanked 13th. Most imposing, however, is the 463-yard 18th, a nasty closer which bends right, along a lake, en route to a bunkerless, bulkheaded island green complex situated directly behind the clubhouse.

Eastpointe Country Club (West) - Palm Beach Gardens ◆◆½

Tom Fazio www.eastpointe-cc.com
13462 Crosspointe Dr, Palm Beach Gardens, FL 33418 (561) 626-6863
6,388 yds   Par 70   Rating: 71.9 / 134   (1982)

Originally a separate private facility located between the Eastpointe Country Club and Pete Dye's famed Old Marsh Golf Club, this, the former Eastpointe Golf & Racquet Club, was absorbed into the Country Club via a 2015 merger, resulting in the two-generations-of-Fazios 36-hole facility in play today. Operating out of its own clubhouse, this is a decidedly short track whose housing-lined holes are dotted with the quasi-basic bunker stylings of Tom Fazio's earlier years, as well as enough water to create a handful of genuinely challenging holes. Among these are a quartet of testing par 4s which includes the 458-yard lake-flanked 2nd and a trio of closers: the 402-yard 16th (a dogleg left around two ponds), the 451-yard creek-fronted 17th and the 384-yard 18th, which demands a long (but sand- and rough-buffered) lake carry on approach. Shorter favorites include the 316-yard dogleg left 6th (potentially driveable, but across trees and neighboring houses) and two watery par 3s, the 183-yard 7th and the 159-yard 10th. Solid enough stuff, and a kinder and gentler alternative to Uncle George's tougher East course - but this should not to be confused with the younger Fazio's more ambitious work of later years.

Emerald Dunes Golf Club - West Palm Beach   ◆◆◆

Tom Fazio   www.edgclub.com
2100 Emerald Dunes Dr, West Palm Beach, FL 33411   (561) 687-1700
         7,218 yds   Par 72   Rating: 75.4 / 146   (1989)

Situated just west of Florida's Turnpike, the Emerald Dunes Golf Club is another Tom Fazio design completed before his primary emphasis became aesthetics – though unlike some of those early works (whose bunkering could be round and quasi-geometric), it exudes much of the attractive polish that would come to exemplify his later work. It is also a strong test with a fairly high degree of tactical interest, water frequently in play and all manner of bunkering, large and small, sprinkled throughout. Though seldom rated among the regional elite, Emerald Dunes does offer numerous strong holes, initially including the 602-yard 5th (with green tucked leftward, behind a lake), the 453-yard dogleg left 7th and the 464-yard 9th, a sharp, demanding dogleg right around water. Equally notable is a back nine finishing stretch that opens with the 211-yard uphill 14th and the 422-yard 15th, a lake-flanked dogleg right whose green is angled above a right-side depression. Play then turns for home with the 179-yard 16th (whose large green extends into a front-left pond), the 585-yard 17th (where trees and sand pinch the lay-up zone) and the 442-yard 18th, a heavily bunkered dogleg-left with likely the closest one will find to a truly rectangular green in modern golf. Though built around two residential neighborhoods (with a third destined to press in along the layout's eastern edge), there is enough of a rustic flavor here to make for a strong and attractive stop.

The Everglades Club - Palm Beach   ◆◆◆

Brian Silva
356 Worth Ave, Palm Beach, FL 33480   (561) 820-2662
         6,017 yds   Par 70   Rating: 71.0 / 140   (2003)

The Everglades Club has long been synonymous with Palm Beach society, its affairs central to the goings-on of the wintering elite, its Addison Mizner-designed clubhouse having introduced the Mediterranean architectural style that would come to define much of the region. Yet despite its social cachet, plus a splendid location on the shores of Lake Worth, the Club's original Seth Raynor-designed golf course was a far cry from Ranyor's best – and thus the subject of numerous changes prior to Brian Silva's comprehensive 2003 renovation. Smartly, Silva made no attempt to restore Raynor's work, but instead crafted a brand new course in the distinctive Raynor fashion, squeezing 18 diminutive holes into this thimble-sized site, all the while trying to duplicate the great engineer's unique bunker and green stylings. The result is actually rather impressive in this regard, with a laundry list of *faux* Raynor features being boosted by plenty of water and regular Atlantic sea breezes; indeed, this is one of the tougher short courses a golfer is likely to encounter. Though small on the card, holes like the 364-yard 2nd, the 162-yard 4th, the dangerous 341-yard 5th and the 363-yard 13th are all water-menaced to a degree that would scare Pete Dye. But while interesting holes are frequent and the occasional replica appears (e.g., the 198-yard Biarritz 14th), the numerous greens bulkheaded with railroad ties are a constant reminder that none of this is genuine Raynor – and thus, while plenty engaging, not quite a Seminole or Gulf Stream for the classically minded.

The Falls Club - Lake Worth

◆◆◆

Joe Lee
6455 Jog Rd, Lake Worth, FL 33467

www.thefallsclub.com
(561) 964-5700

6,806 yds   Par 72   Rating: 73.6 / 139   (1988)

Filling a compact, inland site that once served as a cattle farm, the housing-free Falls Golf Club was a later Joe Lee design and, in addition to thus being one of his most modern, is also quite tactically engaging. A great deal of shaping was required to transform the pancake-flat terrain, with countless sprawling bunkers and one waterfall-covered mini-mountain (left of the 16th green) dominating the landscape. But in addition to the bells and whistles, there are plenty of strong holes here, the most memorable of which are nearly all anchored by water. On the outward half, these include the 535-yard 8th (a heavily bunkered par 5 which bends sharply right, around a lake) as well as a trio of pond-flanked two-shotters: the 389-yard dogleg left 5th, the 371-yard 6th (whose fairway slips between a pair of lakes) and the 401-yard 9th. The back commences with the 401-yard 10th (a sharp – but this time dry – dogleg left) before playing its way clockwise around the northern perimeter to the 315-yard 15th, a predictably narrow entry which is readily driveable via a long left-side water carry. The remaining finishers then circumnavigate a central lake behind the clubhouse, with the aforementioned 164-yard 16th playing to a putting surface which extends forward, off the front of a waterfall-adorned island, and the 535-yard 18th actually turning more than 90 degrees left around the water, daring a long and gutsy carry for those attempting to get home in two.

Country Club of Florida - Village of Golf

◆◆◆

Robert Bruce Harris
22 Country Rd, Village of Golf, FL 33436

www.ccfgolf.com
(561) 732-9771

7,002 yds   Par 72   Rating: 74.1 / 141   (1957)

Located two miles inland from Boynton Beach, the ambitiously named Country Club of Florida is a postwar Robert Bruce Harris design which, though never well-known outside of its immediate region, was well thought of enough early on to host the 1963 U.S. Senior Women's Amateur. Harris's layout was renovated by Arthur Hills in 1987 who, with three decades worth of low-density flanking homes already in place, had little choice but to retain the original routing while reconfiguring the bunkering comprehensively – an approach repeated by Lester George when he followed a similar renovative pattern in 2006. The end result of this maneuvering was a tactically improved track which, owing to its older lineage and revised bunkering, also offers a quasi-classic feel that differs a bit from most in the region. The front nine is led early by the 463-yard 3rd (a soundly bunkered dogleg left) and the 175-yard, reverse Redan 4th, then later by the 531-yard 6th, another dogleg left whose driving zone is divided by a pair of centerline bunkers. The inward half opens strongly with the lake-menaced 461-yard 10th (a monster of a par 4) and the twisting 564-yard 11th, then adds the watery, 142-yard 13th and the 372-yard 14th, where a long, left-side water carry off the tee leaves an open pitch to a small, angled green. Toss in long (but dry) par 4s at the 446-yard 9th (a sweeping dogleg left) and the 451-yard 18th and it all adds up to a strong, established golf course – and the exceedingly rare track to have actually been improved by a modern makeover. **(GW: #141 Classic)**

Fountains Country Club (South) - Lake Worth   ♦♦½

Robert von Hagge & Bruce Devlin   www.fountainscc.com
4476 Fountains Dr, Lake Worth, FL 33467   (561) 642-2700
            6,783 yds   Par 72   Rating: 72.8 / 139   (1972)

A sprawling facility routed through a residential development one mile east of Florida's Turnpike, The Fountains Country Club spent more than three decades utilizing a trio of von Hagge & Devlin-designed courses (playing out of dual clubhouses) before fending off economic troubles by selling its North course to a developer in 2016. What remains then is a pair of 18s of relatively similar challenge and style, with the South course actually offering more new holes despite its earliest version being nearly a decade older. The front nine is the less-engaging half here, though it opens nicely with the 530-yard lake-flanked 1st, and later includes solid entries like the 416-yard lake-and-tree-narrowed 4th and the 543-yard 5th, which makes a late left turn to a sand- and pond-fronted green. Following the slightly awkward 371-yard dogleg right 10th, the longer inward half is highlighted by a run of four straight water holes: the 560-yard 12th (a double-dogleg daring a long second over water), the 170-yard 13th, the 422-yard 14th (a sweeping dogleg left around a lake) and the 528-yard 15th, which bends significantly rightward en route to a bunkerless green whose left side is flanked closely by a pond.

Fountains Country Club (West) - Lake Worth   ♦♦½

Robert von Hagge & Bruce Devlin   www.fountainscc.com
4476 Fountains Dr, Lake Worth, FL 33467   (561) 642-2700
            6,789 yds   Par 71   Rating: 73.2 / 139   (1981)

Mostly the older half of the well-established Fountains Country Club's remaining 36 holes, the von Hagge & Devlin-designed West course bears the odd distinction of both beginning and ending at the property's original northern clubhouse while having its 9th green lie adjacent to the newer southern one. The West's 3,244-yard, par-35 front nine is the property's shortest and initially follows a slightly disjointed routing southward, covering a great deal of ground at the 575-yard 3rd (a sharp dogleg left which turns slightly early) before playing through a run of four consecutive sub-400-yard par 4s and culminating with the 207-yard 9th, whose green sits beyond a front-right bunker with a lone palm tree in its center. The back opens with the lake-fronted 376-yard 10th before making most of its return trek north via the 519-yard 11th (where one picks their line across water on the second) and the 563-yard straightaway 12th. But the West's best golf is saved for a strong finishing run that includes the 479-yard par-4 15th, the 218-yard 16th (whose narrow green is flanked left by water and right by sand) and the 450-yard 18th, a dogleg right played around/across water to a narrow, heavily bunkered putting surface.

Frenchman's Creek (South) - Palm Beach Gardens   ♦♦½

Gardner Dickinson   www.frenchmanscreek.com
13495 Tournament Dr, Palm Beach Gardens, FL 33410   (561) 622-8300
            7,034 yds   Par 72   Rating: 75.1 / 147   (1973)

Though altered in later years by Bob Cupp, Jim Fazio and Jay Morrish (among others), both courses at the 36-hole Frenchman's Creek Beach & Country Club were originally designed by the late Gardner Dickinson – a seven-time PGA Tour winner and noted Ben Hogan disciple, and one of the game's more insightfully independent thinkers. Though Dickinson's routings have been largely retained, water is slightly more prevalent today, particularly on the longer South course, which for many may narrowly rate as the more interesting layout. The front nine is the longer half and circumnavigates a residential neighborhood in the property's southwestern quadrant, where it initially finds strength at the 595-yard 4th (played through a canal-crossed lay-up zone), the 202-yard 5th, which requires a long water carry. Also notable, however, are the 465-yard 8th (where slices will find more water down the right side) and one more lake-crossing par 3, the 174-yard 9th. The shorter (but stronger) inward half then kicks off with two more watery tests, the 177-yard island-green 11th and the 392-yard pond-fronted 12th, before powering through a strapping homestretch which includes the 510-yard 15th (whose green angles rightward along a pond), the 565-yard 17th (water left) and the 428-yard 18th, a soundly bunkered test played to a narrow green angling along one final water hazard.

Frenchman's Creek (North) - Palm Beach Gardens   ♦♦♦

Gardner Dickinson   www.frenchmanscreek.com
13495 Tournament Dr, Palm Beach Gardens, FL 33410   (561) 622-8300
            6,938 yds   Par 72   Rating: 75.1 / 144   (1973)

Every bit as challenging as its sister South layout, Frenchman's Creek's Gardner Dickinson-designed North course was renovated in 2004 by Jim Fazio, who made some significant changes to Dickinson's routing; indeed, the back nine could well be considered a Fazio original creation today. Water is now in play – often quite invasively – on no less than 15 holes, with a meandering creek affecting play on three of the front nine's best: the 435-yard 4th, the 223-yard 6th and the 400-yard 7th, the latter pair featuring greens angled closely along the water. The revised inward half then follows an exceedingly compact (and highly complex) routing which, in addition to making water a continuing central presence, creates some long cart rides and the occasional close angle of play. It also features several scary waterside putting surfaces, including those of the 555-yard 12th (whose back tee drives very nearly must carry the 14th green), the 177-yard bunkerless 15th (with green bulkheaded above a left-side lake) and the 416-yard 17th, a testing dogleg left. The 537-yard 14th (played to a green angling rightward along both sand and water) is another tough entry, as is the 423-yard 18th, another watery dogleg left. Gardner Dickinson's footprints have grown increasingly less visible over the years but if one likes a challenge, few clubs in Southeast Florida offer two such difficult layouts.

Frenchman's Reserve - Palm Beach Gardens   ◆◆◆

Arnold Palmer   www.frenchmansreservecc.com
3370 Grande Corniche, Palm Beach Gardens, FL 33410   (561) 630-0333
            6,867 yds   Par 72   Rating: 72.8 / 139   (2002)

Built surprisingly close to the ocean for a new millennium facility, Frenchman's Reserve lies a mile and a half directly west of famed Seminole, and just south of Frenchman's Creek, on a site which manages to retain a few patches of native overgrowth amidst rows of single-family houses. Despite these homes bordering most fairways (generally at a respectable distance), the course offers a somewhat less manufactured aesthetic than many an Arnold Palmer design, particularly after recently having its bunkers reshaped into a less flashy, more classic look. The 3,476-yard outward half first plays across a large grass-dotted bunker at the 155-yard 2nd before being anchored by a trio of mid-size par 4s: the 434-yard 6th (flanked by water left, and the number one stroke hole), the 418-yard 7th (water right, and close to the putting surface) and the 410-yard 9th, a sharp, tricky dogleg right. The back then opens with the 538-yard lake-flanked 10th but doesn't peak until a watery close headed by the driveable 325-yard 15th, whose stonewall-buttressed green sits above a left-side lake. Most memorable, however, are the 17th and 18th, the former being a 395-yard sharp dogleg left which, with a huge over-water carry (and a favorable breeze), might just be driveable by longer hitters, while the latter is a solid 447-yard dogleg right to a narrow green wedged tightly between water and sand.

Gleneagles Country Club (Legends) - Delray Beach

Karl Litten   www.gleneagles.cc
7667 Victory Ln, Delray Beach, FL 33446   (561) 498-3606
            7,047 yds   Par 72   Rating: 74.3 / 141   (1984)

A real estate-oriented facility situated just east of Florida's Turnpike, the Gleneagles Country Club offers a pair of 1984 Karl Litten designs which vary considerably in size and challenge – a discrepancy which widened even further following a major 2011 renovation of the bigger Legends course by Kipp Schulties. Having hosted a Bruce Crampton victory during a one-off 1986 visit by the Champions Tour, the Legends now stretches beyond 7,000 yards, and while surrounding housing necessitated that Litten's original corridors of play be retained, Schulties did reverse the course of three back nine holes, enhancing the challenge considerably. Most notable here is a quartet of solid par 5s, the strongest of which include the 555-yard 7th (a gentle dogleg right routed along left-side water), the 637-yard 12th (which bends rightward along a lake to a stonewall-bulkheaded green) and the 573-yard 18th, where well-placed bunkering (more than a right-side pond) requires thought on the second. Holes 14-16 are the reversed trio, with the changes making the 14th a tricky, water-laden 356-yarder and the 15th a 160-yard short iron to a narrow green angling leftward into a lake. Though still not quite among the South Florida elite, the renovated Legends is certainly a much stronger and more engaging track.

Gleneagles Country Club (Victory) - Delray Beach   ◆◆

Karl Litten   www.gleneagles.cc
7667 Victory Ln, Delray Beach, FL 33446   (561) 498-3606
           6,043 yds   Par 71   Rating: 69.7 / 129   (1984)

The Gleneagles Country Club's much shorter Victory course fills the property's eastern half where it retains all of Karl Litten's original, highly compact (and somewhat complex) routing but has seen its bunkering modified into a more restrained style in the new millennium. Stretching little more than 6,000 yards, it is an obviously diminutive track – so much so, in fact, that only a single par 4 measures in excess of 385 yards. There are, however, a handful of interesting holes present, with the front nine featuring a nice pair at the 491-yard 7th (which bends sharply rightward around a lake) and the 181-yard 8th, whose green angles rightward along another water hazard. The inward half quickly offers the layout's best sustained run of golf, a trio composed of the 226-yard 11th (whose narrow green curls along a large front-right bunker), 353-yard lakeside 12th and the 404-yard 13th, where left-side water affects both drive and approach. The 110-yard over-water 14th (played to a railroad tie-buttressed target) then kicks off a homeward run that culminates with the 368-yard pond-guarded 18th. A solid (if short) "second" course.

Gulf Stream Golf Club - Gulf Stream   ◆◆◆½

Donald Ross   www.gsgcfl.com
2401 North Ocean Blvd, Gulf Stream, FL 33483   (561) 278-0392
           6,835 yds   Par 72   Rating: 73.8 / 138   (1923)

One of the Gold Coast's most established facilities, the Gulf Stream Golf Club is situated in an affluent residential neighborhood just north of Delray Beach, admirably positioned on a narrow island between the Atlantic Ocean and the Intracoastal waterway. A much-publicized facility during the Golden Age, it long existed as a quiet, under-the-radar sort of club boasting a short but quite engaging Donald Ross-designed layout bathed in Old Florida ambience. But in a surprising move, the club engaged member Pete Dye to perform a 2013 renovation, a job which retained all of Ross's routing but rebuilt/shifted numerous greens and tees, and re-cast the layout in Dye's own modern bunkering style. A great deal of length has also been added, extending play well beyond 6,800 yards (some reports cite a total approaching 7,000) - though much of this lay in extending the 10th hole from a 419-yard par 4 to a three-shotter in excess of 500. Aside from several man-made lakes, the layout's distinguishing feature is a central ridge which bisects the property, affecting holes like the 322-yard 8th (a tricky drive-and-pitch to an elevated green) and the 455-yard 13th, which runs southward atop its spine. Among the holes most greatly altered by Dye are the 177-yard lake-fronted 4th (whose slim green is now rock wall bulkheaded), the expanded 10th, the par-3 11th (shortened by 30 yards but now more watery) and the 320-yard 15th, a pond-guarded drive-and-pitch whose green has been completely reshaped. The most memorable entry, however, is surely the 425-yard 18th, which sits by itself on the beach side of Ocean Boulevard, and now includes an impressive Dye-designed alternative version pressed flush against the Atlantic.

High Ridge Country Club - Lantana   ◆◆◆

Joe Lee   www.highridgecc.com
2400 Hypoluxo Rd, Lantana, FL 33462   (561) 586-3333
              6,928 yds   Par 72   Rating: 75.4 / 142   (1982)

A rare housing-free facility in a Gold Coast region where golf's main raison d'être is to sell real estate, the High Ridge Country Club lies surprisingly close to the ocean (just half a mile west of Interstate 95) for a course built in the 1980s, and features a strong Joe Lee layout renovated in the new millennium by Kipp Schulties. Though its contouring was largely manufactured by Lee, the course is naturally wooded and utilizes a wide range of water hazards, particularly over an outbound run that includes the 429-yard 3rd (a demanding dogleg left with water inside the corner), the 181-yard all-carry 4th, and two holes which Schulties reconfigured, the 410-yard 5th (a dogleg right along an expanded lake) and the twisting 556-yard 6th. The inward half's clear standouts are its par 5s, the 540-yard 13th (where lakes flank both sides of the fairway and the right edge of the green) and especially the 508-yard 15th, an enticing dogleg left where a lake filling the corner also extends before the putting surface. The closers begin with a shortish pair requiring real accuracy, the 388-yard, bunker-narrowed 16th and the 389-yard tree-narrowed 17th. The revised 435-yard 18th, meanwhile, plays to a shallow green angled beyond a front-right lake – a notably strong finish to a layout which has long stood among the most overlooked along Florida's very crowded and deep Gold Coast.

Hunters Run (South) - Boynton Beach   ◆◆◆

Robert von Hagge & Bruce Devlin   www.huntersrun.net
3500 Clubhouse Lane, Boynton Beach, FL 33436   (561) 737-2582
              7,008 yds   Par 72   Rating: 75.5 / 143   (1979)

An enormous residential community situated half a mile west of Interstate 95, Hunters Run features a trio of housing-lined von Hagge & Devlin-designed courses, all of which, though somewhat re-bunkered, retain a good deal of their original challenge and style. Highest-rated is the South course, a 7,008-yard test whose outward half opens with a twisting 570-yard par 5 before playing through a run of solid, if not terribly memorable holes. More noteworthy, however, are a pair entries falling late in the loop, the 392-yard 7th (a sharp dogleg right around a corner bunker and trees) and the 586-yard 9th, a water-flanked test which makes a late rightward jog to a typically small putting surface. The back nine also opens in solid-but-unspectacular style before picking up markedly in the property's housing-free southeastern corner. The keystone here is the 548-yard 14th, an imposing dogleg right which can be shortened considerably via a long over-water second to a peninsula green which juts forward into the hazard. The 431-yard 15th and the lake-crossing 189-yard 16th continue a strong march home which concludes with the 404-yard pond-fronted 17th and the 424-yard 18th, a challenging dogleg left.

Hunters Run (North) - Boynton Beach   ♦♦½

Robert von Hagge & Bruce Devlin   www.huntersrun.net
3500 Clubhouse Lane, Boynton Beach, FL 33436   (561) 737-2582
6,764 yds   Par 71   Rating: 74.2 / 143   (1979)

Hunters Run's von Hagge & Devlin-designed North course weighs in at nearly 250 yards less than the adjacent South and is rated more than a full stroke easier – though more significantly, it will, for most, be the 54-hole facility's least interesting entry. The par-35 front nine opens on a difficult note with the 406-yard 1st, a thorny dogleg right made particularly testing by a prominent left-side tree and front-left water. The action slows a bit thereafter, though the loop does include the 423-yard 5th (where water crosses the fairway – forcing some to lay up off the tee - then guards the green front-right), the 571-yard 8th and the 400-yard 9th, which curls gently rightward to a putting surface angled along a pond. The back nine requires several significant cart rides within its routing and initially features a pair of short, watery par 4s, the 353-yard 11th and the 383-yard 13th, the latter a 90-degree dogleg left around a lake. The 174-yard 15th plays across a fronting pond and sets up an entirely dry closing led by the 190-yard 17th (whose green has shrunken away from its surrounding bunkers over the years) and the stout 450-yard 18th.

Hunters Run (East) - Boynton Beach   ♦♦½

Robert von Hagge & Bruce Devlin   www.huntersrun.net
3500 Clubhouse Lane, Boynton Beach, FL 33436   (561) 737-2582
6,553 yds   Par 71   Rating: 73.2 / 139   (1979)

The East course at Hunters Run, though comfortably the club's smallest, is in many ways also its most interesting, particularly after being renovated in 2008 by Kipp Schulties, who had previously done work on both the South and North as well. With water now meaningfully in play on 16 holes, the reconfigured layout may not be overwhelmingly tough overall but it does provide several clear opportunities to post big numbers. Among the more challenging tests, the front nine includes the 178-yard 5th (whose bunkerless green extends rightward into a lake), the 420-yard 6th (which bends leftward around a pond) and the 385-yard 9th (ditto). But the really dangerous holes lie mostly on the back, specifically at the 590-yard 12th (with putting surface angled along invasive water), the 330-yard 14th (whose green juts leftward into a lake) and especially the 215-yard 15th, whose tightly bunkered green complex is itself a narrow peninsula extending far outward into the same hazard. Additional favorites include the 390-yard 3rd (which requires a slightly tricky drive across water) and the 565-yard 18th, where a right-side pond can threaten both the lay-up zone and the left-to-right-angled putting surface.

The Club At Ibis (Legend) - West Palm Beach   ♦♦♦

Jack Nicklaus   www.clubatibis.com
8225 Ibis Blvd, West Palm Beach, FL 33412   (561) 625-8500
                7,187 yds   Par 72   Rating: 75.4 / 144   (1991)

If nothing else, the 54-hole Club at Ibis serves to demonstrate that Jack Nicklaus really is the great family man he has long been portrayed as; with two Nicklaus sons building their own layouts here, had there been more land available, perhaps even wife Barbara might have gotten into the act. But while the younger generation was indeed afforded some time in the limelight, the centerpiece of this far-inland residential development is clearly Jack's own Legend course, a big, broad-shouldered design which hosted the LPGA during the late 1990s (with Karrie Webb winning twice) and features massive waste bunkering on more holes than not. There is, of course, the usual parade of long, often interesting par 4s, such as the 460-yard 2nd (which bends leftward, around a huge bunker), the 429-yard 14th and the 445-yard water-lined 18th. Also present is the occasional smaller two-shotter of note, such as the 392-yard 6th (where drives which carry right-side sand avoid flirting with water on the approach) and the 390-yard centerline bunkered 12th. Par 5s are well represented as well, first at the 576-yard 8th (where a tiny centerline bunker 30 yards shy of the green has far more impact than any of the larger hazards), then at the wild 549-yard, lake-divided 11th. But most memorable, by miles, is the 159-yard 13th, whose angled, TPC-Sawgrass-type island green provides absolutely no bailout options. One wonders how many less-talented members have emptied their bags here.

The Club At Ibis (Heritage) - West Palm Beach   ♦♦½

Jack Nicklaus II   www.clubatibis.com
8225 Ibis Blvd, West Palm Beach, FL 33412   (561) 625-8500
                7,062 yds   Par 72   Rating: 74.2 / 145   (1991)

The Club at Ibis' Heritage course was laid out by Jack Nicklaus II and might be considered a kinder and gentler version of its flagship Legend layout – but only just. Indeed, there is more than enough sand and water present to keep the challenge level high, though tactical considerations tend to be somewhat fewer and further between than on Papa Bear's layout. The front nine is characterized by several more gigantic waste bunkers, with the 387-yard 2nd and the 535-yard 8th (a gentle dogleg left) especially feeling their presence. Rather more dangerous, however, are the 166-yard 3rd (whose bulkheaded green pushes leftward, into a pond) and the 438-yard 9th, a tough lakeside dogleg right made marginally easier by the large bunker which separates the putting surface from water. The back nine then offers several truly imposing holes, the centerpieces of which include the 550-yard 12th (whose pear-shaped green extends dangerously rightward, into a lake), the 364-yard 17th (ditto, only the putting surface extends directly forward) and the 447-yard 18th, were a right-side lake affects both the drive and the approach to a narrow bulkheaded target. The overall challenge here may be less than on the Legend, but there are still plenty of places where one can quickly ring up big numbers.

The Club At Ibis (Tradition) - West Palm Beach   ♦♦½

Steve Nicklaus   www.clubatibis.com
8225 Ibis Blvd, West Palm Beach, FL 33412   (561) 625-8500
         7,130 yds   Par 72   Rating: 74.7 / 139   (2001)

The Club at Ibis' Tradition course was built in 2001 by ex-Florida State football player (and number two son) Steve Nicklaus and, being a decade newer than both the Legend and Heritage, was forced to follow a non-returning routing through the property's southern third. Squeezed more tightly among housing and lakes than its siblings, it offers plenty of muscle and challenge (its 74.7 rating is half a stroke tougher than the Heritage) but water, while ever-present, is seldom terribly invasive; indeed, only at the 169-yard 17th is a forced carry ever truly required. Overall, the level of tactical interest may rate a bit less than on the other two layouts, and several holes are actually fairly basic in their design. But a number of stronger entries are also present, with the front nine featuring the 442-yard lake-guarded 3rd, the tactically bunkered 592-yard 4th and the 447-yard 7th, which plays to a small, tightly bunkered green. The back nine is led by the 521-yard 12th (a sweeping dogleg left with a small centerline bunker complicating the second) and the demanding 462-yard 18th, which bends rightward, around one final lake. For the serious visitor, the Legend and Heritage (in that order) will be preferred options

Indian Spring Country Club (East) - Boynton Beach   ♦♦½

Robert von Hagge & Bruce Devlin   www.indianspringcc.com
11501 El Clair Ranch Rd, Boynton Beach, FL 33437   (561) 737-5544
         7,070 yds   Par 72   Rating: 75.3 / 143   (1975)

A 36-hole facility built in two phases (1975 and 1980) by period regional stars Robert von Hagge and Bruce Devlin, the Indian Spring Country Club was renovated by Kipp Schulties beginning in 2004 – with flanking housing once again mandating the retention of nearly all of the East course's original routing. This, the older layout, is both longer and tougher, and has also seen one more wave of more recent change, as a number of larger, more wildly shaped bunkers were reduced/reshaped during 2015. Despite its current 75.3 rating, this was not one of von Hagge & Devlin's tougher designs originally, and with five par 4s measuring between 350-385 yards, and water being frequent but seldom too invasive, it still offers a fair degree of playability today. The front nine is led by a trio of solid par 4s – the 439-yard 3rd, the 374-yard lakeside 5th and the 404-yard dogleg left 6th – as well as the 202-yard 9th, which angles across a pond. The back is built around a robust (if rather basic) finishing stretch that includes the 449-yard lake-flanked 14th, the 571-yard 16th, the brutish 243-yard 17th and the 441-yard 18th, a gentle dogleg right.

Indian Spring Country Club (West) - Boynton Beach   ♦♦

Robert von Hagge & Bruce Devlin   www.indianspringcc.com
11501 El Clair Ranch Rd, Boynton Beach, FL 33437   (561) 737-5544
                6,555 yds   Par 71   Rating: 72.4 / 138   (1980)

The Indian Spring Country Club's West course is the shorter half of this 36-hole inland facility which lies exactly halfway between the Atlantic Ocean and the eastern edge of the Everglades. The West sits entirely across El Clair Ranch Road from the club's older East course, where its nines form a pair of clockwise loops around neighborhoods of single-family homes and condominiums. The 3,187-yard outward half was materially altered by Kipp Schulties new millennium renovation, beginning with the 497-yard par-5 1st, whose green complex now juts leftward, into a lake after decades of lying 150 yards right, near the 2nd tee. Holes 4 and 5 were entirely new, while lengthened noticeably was the 439-yard 9th, a tough par 4 whose green angles along a right-side lake. The back nine saw significant changes made to holes 13 and 16, and today features a pair of engaging and watery opening and closing par 5s, the 528-yard 10th (where Schulties extended a pond to protect the front-left of the green) and the 563-yard 18th, a genuinely strong hole whose putting surface is buttonhooked left, around the tip of a large lake.

Jonathan's Landing Golf Club (Village) - Jupiter   ♦♦½

George & Tom Fazio   www.jonathanslanding.com
16823 Captain Kirle Dr, Jupiter, FL 33477   (561) 744-4321
                6,701 yds   Par 71   Rating: 73.5 / 131   (1978)

The Jonathan's Landing Golf Club is a 54-hole development whose courses operate at multiple addresses, with an initial 18 holes built within the club's original residential center and 36 newer ones situated seven miles to the northwest, in Martin County. The Village course is the original 18, and is a George & Tom Fazio design built among houses and a network of canals along the Intracoastal Waterway, a mile from the Atlantic. Demonstrating far more of George's rather staid period stylings than Tom's flashier future ones, the layout is largely basic in scope and makes surprisingly limited use of water, particularly on a front nine led by the 494-yard pond-fronted 7th (the loop's sole water hole) and the 443-yard straightaway 9th. For the most part, the back represents more of the same - that is, until it reaches a trio of somewhat memorable finishers which begins with the 184-yard 16th (an all-carry test played diagonally across a wide inlet) and the unique 526-yard 17th, a distinctive dogleg right involving two water crossings, an island fairway and, rather uniquely, a ferry ride after one's second. And then there is the 18th, whose green sits just beyond another sizeable inlet and which is a drive-and-pitch for most – unless one has stepped back to the 468-yard championship tee.

Jonathan's Landing Golf Club (Fazio) - Jupiter   ◆◆◆

Tom Fazio   www.jonathanslanding.com
18505 SE Clubhouse Dr, Jupiter, FL 33477   (561) 744-8200
           6,904 yds   Par 72   Rating: 73.8 / 139   (1987)

Jonathan's Landing's 36-hole inland facility, which is known as Old Trail, is a very different proposition from its original Village course, the biggest distinction being a lack of interior housing – an aesthetic plus which also allows it to shoehorn 36 compact holes within roughly the same acreage as the entire 18-hole Village development. Lying west of Interstate 95, some six miles from the ocean, the facility's older and stronger course is the Fazio, built by Tom in 1987 over a landscape dotted by woods, wetlands and man-made lakes. Though not among the Fazio elite, it is a fairly strong, often interesting track whose shorter front nine is led by the 186-yard 3rd (whose narrow green is hugged closely by a long right-side bunker), the 314-yard dogleg left 7th (potentially driveable across water) and a pair of longer entries at the close, the 430-yard 8th and the 553-yard bunker-lined 9th. The back opens with the 421-yard 10th (played to a deep, very narrow green) before being powered by its finishers, a quartet made up of the 539-yard 15th (where aggressive seconds must angle across a right-side pond), the 156-yard well-bunkered 16th and a pair of longer par 4s with water down their right flanks, the 432-yard 17th and the 455-yard straightaway 18th. Being 600 yards longer than the adjacent Hills course (and rated nearly three shots tougher), this will be the first choice for most visitors to Old Trail.

Jonathan's Landing Golf Club (Hills) - Jupiter   ◆◆

Arthur Hills   www.jonathanslanding.com
18505 SE Clubhouse Dr, Jupiter, FL 33477   (561) 744-8200
           6,301 yds   Par 71   Rating: 70.9 / 130   (1989)

Squeezed tightly into the property's northern half, the Jonathan's Landing Golf Club's much shorter Hills course perhaps did not give Arthur the acreage necessary to produce his most inspired work, with the result being a 6,301-yard layout which, given its slight proportion, seems quite well suited to the reasonably skilled senior golfer. The front nine is comfortably the longer half but also the less interesting, with notable entries including the twisting 560-yard 2nd (the number one stroke hole), the 305-yard pond-fronted 3rd and the 500-yard 4th, where drives flirt with left-side water and the green is tucked beyond right-side sand. The back then measures a scant 3,039 yards but opens with the 542-yard pond-fronted 10th, an obviously full-size test. Play then makes a brief foray into the wetlands for a pair of short back-to-back par 3s, the 166-yard 12th (where a long, fairly deep bunker flanks, then curls behind the putting surface) and the 138-yard 13th. The routing re-emerges at the 512-yard 14th (which bends gently leftward around a lake) before closing with a pair of mid-size, water-flanked par 4s, the tough 406-yard pond-guarded 17th and the 414-yard 18th, where a man-made pond can affect bigger drives.

Jupiter Country Club - Jupiter   ◆◆◆

Greg Norman   www.jupitercountryclub.com
126 Rosala Ct, Jupiter, FL 33478   (561) 746-3950
             7,259 yds   Par 72   Rating: 75.2 / 136   (2010)

One might assume that short of building a brand new course on the site of an older one, it would be impossible in the year 2010 to find enough land to develop a new facility on the east side of Interstate 95. The Greg Norman-designed Jupiter Country Club proves that assumption correct – but just barely. Indeed, the golf course is surprisingly well located, sitting just west of both the Interstate and Florida's Turnpike on a surprisingly large tract ribbed with rows of upscale residential development. Norman's routing follows a mostly east-west path (in deference to the housing) and despite being long by all but touring professional standards, is reasonably manageable for average players due mostly to a near-complete absence of water carries. The lone exception to this is the 140-yard 2nd (played downhill and across a pond), a diminutive entry which is more than offset by stout par 4s like the 430-yard 5th, the 458-yard 7th, the 442-yard 8th and the 453-yard 15th, where a pair of centerline bunkers affect the tee ball. Centerline sand is also the defining hazard (for both drive and second) at the 514-yard lake-flanked 4th, perhaps the most engaging test prior to a big finish that includes the 555-yard waterside 16th, the 227-yard 17th (whose elevated putting surface angles above left-side sand) and the 456-yard uphill 18th, a long and demanding finisher. Still, despite its overall scale, as the 136 slope suggests, this is somewhat more playable than it may at first appear.

Lost City Golf Club - Atlantis   ◆◆

William Mitchell   www.atlantisgolf.org
301 Orange Tree Dr, Atlantis, FL 33462   (561) 966-7600
        South/North: 6,892 yds   Par 72   Rating: 73.2 / 135   (1960)
        East: 3,453 yds   Par 36   Rating: 36.7 / 132   (1964)

Located just west of Palm Beach County Park Airport, just over three miles inland from the Atlantic, the Lost City (née Atlantis) Golf Club began its life as a sprawling residential development in 1960, when William Mitchell-designed an initial 18 holes, today's South and North nines. Though somewhat the longer half, the South is fairly basic in style, following an out-and-back routing through a neighborhood of single-family homes. Anchored by a steady diet of simple, mid-size par 4s, it also offers the 526-yard 1st (which twists past a small right-side water hazard) and the 504-yard pond-flanked 5th. The North features three of its best holes early: the 430-yard tree-narrowed 1st, the 430-yard dogleg right 2nd (whose green sits above a right-side creek) and the 527-yard pond-guarded 3rd. The loop also includes the 405-yard 6th (a sharp dogleg left around an invasive corner bunker) and the stiff 216-yard 8th. Mitchell returned to design the East nine four years after its siblings, routing it around two lakes across Orange Tree Drive from the initial 18. These lakes meaningfully affect play on four holes, the highlights of which are the 390-yard dogleg right 2nd (where one chooses just how much water to attempt to carry), the 349-yard 3rd and the 540-yard 4th, where it flanks the right side before cutting in just in front of the green. Though far dryer, both the 244-yard tightly bunkered 5th (a difficult one-shotter on any layout) and the 451-yard straightaway 6th (flanked by left-side out-of-bounds) likely represent the club's most demanding back-to-back challenges.

Lost Tree Club - North Palm Beach   ◆◆◆

Mark Mahannah   www.losttreeclub.com
11520 Lost Tree Way, North Palm Beach, FL 33408   (561) 626-1501
6,849 yds   Par 72   Rating: 73.7 / 140   (1964)

Located half a mile south of the legendary Seminole Golf Club, the Lost Tree Club was one of South Florida's first high-end residential golf developments, occupying a splendid coastal stretch between the northern reaches of Lake Worth and the Atlantic. Greg Norman and Dr. Cary Middlecoff are among the notables who have resided here, though the community's number one resident has, since 1970, been one J.W. Nicklaus, who did his part for the club by renovating its aging Mark Mahannah-designed golf course in 2002. As a result, Lost Tree is now a far tougher test, with expanded and re-positioned bunkers, several lakes added or enlarged, and multiple greens moved closer to these hazards. Water is the primary design feature, affecting play on 13 holes but with varying degrees of invasiveness; indeed, on the front nine's two strongest holes, it will only catch a bad hook at the strong 203-yard 4th, and is absent altogether at the 425-yard 9th. Coming home, *agua* is more of a factor at the 200-yard 11th and the 181-yard 14th (which sit on opposite banks of the same lake) as well as within a trio of strong closers: the 460-yard 16th (where it sits left of the green), the potentially driveable 341-yard 17th (ditto) and the 507-yard 18th, a reachable finisher whose fairway sweeps leftward, around a long pond. As with other area courses built on oceanfront sites, there is no actual seaside golf here – that land instead being reserved for some of the most expensive homes in Florida. But the presence of the Golden Bear alone makes Lost Tree a stop of significance.

Loxahatchee Club - Jupiter   ◆◆◆

Jack Nicklaus   www.theloxahatcheeclub.org
1350 Echo Dr, Jupiter, FL 33458   (561) 744-6168
7,240 yds   Par 72   Rating: 75.9 / 153   (1985)

The Loxahatchee Club made a major splash upon its mid-1980s arrival, partly due to its encouragement of walking (a rarity in cart-dependent South Florida) but also because of the course's over-the-top mounding, which resembled grass-covered Swiss mountain ranges more than anything natural or golf-like. The mounding has since been softened, however, leaving a layout which, like many period Jack Nicklaus designs, is something of a love/hate proposition. For fans of this style it works well, with water and oversized bunkering seemingly everywhere, and tactical considerations being a regular presence throughout. For the more classically oriented, it is contrived and predictable (e.g., the obligatory double green the used to serve the 13th and 15th, the island green at the exciting 601-yard 16th, etc.). But there are, as ever, numerous engaging holes, including a trio of front nine entries whose putting surfaces are perched dangerously above water: the 167-yard all-carry 5th, the 388-yard 6th (a watery lay up-and-pitch, and one of the shorter number one stroke holes in existence) and the 551-yard lake-flanked 8th. The inward half first offers the 399-yard 11th (a slightly awkward test where drives carrying left-side sand yield a water-free approach) before being led by the aforementioned island-green 16th (something of a template hole in the Nicklaus portfolio) as well as the 451-yard water-lined 18th. Loxahatchee was ranked 81st in the U.S. by *Golf Digest*'s in 1989, but today fails to crack the top 30 in Florida – so, in the end, still a matter of taste.

Mayacoo Lakes Country Club - West Palm Beach   ◆◆◆

Desmond Muirhead & Jack Nicklaus   www.mayacoo.com
9697 Mayacoo Club Dr, West Palm Beach, FL 33411   (561) 793-1703
         6,906 yds   Par 71   Rating: 74.2 / 150   (1972)

Jack Nicklaus's first-ever South Florida design, Mayacoo Lakes was completed during the Golden Bear's short-lived partnership with the iconoclastic Desmond Muirhead and drew great initial publicity, mostly due to what was then considered its frightfully high degree of difficulty. Subsequent Nicklaus tinkerings (plus the effective shortening of its 6,906 yards by modern equipment) have since softened things, though plenty of water and some narrow, tree-lined playing corridors still keep the challenge high – as a 150 slope clearly indicates. The two nines follow narrow out-and-back routings at a 90-degree angle to one another, with the less-engaging outward half being led by the 208-yard lakeside 3rd, the tree-narrowed 455-yard 4th and the 528-yard pond-guarded 9th. The par-35 back nine offers a deeper menu of notables, including strong two-shotters like the 409-yard 12th (which plays to a narrow green angled behind a lake), the 456-yard lake-flanked 15th, the watery 395-yard 16th and especially the 441-yard finisher, whose very large putting surface bends rightward, around a fronting pond. Though it seems like a million years ago, Mayacoo spent much of the 1980s ranked within *Golf Digest*'s national top 100 – which, once again, squares somewhat oddly with the same publication not rating it among Florida's top 30 today. (Aside: The goofy two-greens-on-an-island 6th must be one of golf's prophetic holes, foreshadowing both the gimmickry that touched some of Nicklaus's later work and the patent silliness of most of Muirhead's.)

Country Club at Mirasol (Sunset) - Palm Beach Gardens   ◆◆◆

Arthur Hills   www.mirasolcc.com
11600 Mirasol Blvd, Palm Beach Gardens, FL 33418   (561) 776-4949
         7,192 yds   Par 72   Rating: 75.2 / 153   (2002)

Much like at Jonathan's Landing up the coast in Jupiter, Arthur Hills was again forced to play second fiddle to Tom Fazio at the Country Club at Mirasol, his Sunset course coming first chronologically, but being wedged into a far more confined section of the property, forcing his routing to largely run back-and-forth among double rows of housing. Hills still managed to produce a strong and varied layout, however, a course which (perhaps not surprisingly) peaks during a three-hole, housing-free run through wetlands composed of the 572-yard double dogleg 15th (where a marsh crossing is required on the second), the 187-yard 16th and the 515-yard dogleg right 17th, which dares a long wetlands-jumping shortcut for those hoping to reach the green in two. The housing-lined holes, meanwhile, may be less aesthetically appealing but they do include a number of tests marked by strategic bunkering and/or water hazards, including the 415-yard 3rd (featuring a long wetlands carry off the tee), the well-bunkered 544-yard 9th, a pair of stiff par 4s at the 438-yard 12th and the 442-yard 13th, and the intimidating 218-yard 14th, where anything pulled even slightly left splashes down. At 7,192 yards, and carrying a 75.2 rating, this would be the number one layout at many clubs, but beyond the housing, it has also lacked the big-stage PGA Tour exposure of its younger and tougher sibling.

Country Club at Mirasol (Sunrise) - Palm Beach Gardens ◆◆◆

Tom Fazio   www.mirasolcc.com
11600 Mirasol Blvd, Palm Beach Gardens, FL 33418   (561) 776-4949
          7,332 yds   Par 72   Rating: 76.1 / 144   (2003)

As host to the PGA Tour's Honda Classic from 2003-2006, the Country Club at Mirasol's Tom Fazio-designed Sunrise course drew much attention for its crowned, elevated greens and closely cut fallaways – Fazio's response to the great success found by several "minimalist" architects in reintroducing the ground game to modern design. Though housing-lined in spots, the Sunrise is less confined than the Sunset, particularly during a development-free excursion into the wetlands that comes at holes 11-15. The front nine forms a counter-clockwise loop around the property's southern expanse where, though the less exciting half, it includes the 246-yard 3rd (whose green sits above several deep left-side bunkers), the 562-yard dogleg left 5th and the 445-yard 9th, which skirts left-side water en route to an elevated, bunkerless and very shallow putting surface. The action picks up quickly upon entering the wetlands, however, where the well-bunkered fairways are reasonably wide but big misses will usually require a re-load. The 221-yard 11th sets the pace here, but the real standouts are a pair of demanding dogleg rights, the 473-yard 13th and the 470-yard 14th – an obviously testing twosome quickly backed by the 486-yard lake-flanked 16th. For those who believe that quality golf courses identify quality winners, the Sunrise produced Major champions Justin Leonard, Padraig Harrington and Todd Hamilton, as well as 2011 world number one Luke Donald – a pretty decent haul.

Mizner Country Club - Delray Beach   ◆◆½

Arnold Palmer & Ed Seay   www.miznercc.org
16104 Mizner Club Dr, Delray Beach, FL 33446   (561) 638-5600
          6,909 yds   Par 72   Rating: 74.2 / 142   (1999)

Named for Addison Mizner, the famed Golden Age architect who made his name in Palm Beach and his short-lived fortune (wiped out by the Depression) in Boca Raton, the Mizner Country Club features a heavily shaped Arnold Palmer layout whose large-scale, flowery-shaped bunkering was recently fully renovated by the ubiquitous Kipp Schulties. With every hole flanked by water, rows of single-family homes or both, Schulties could make precious few changes to Palmer's routing, leaving this a shortish track but one quite capable of holding its own with many of the region's tougher tests. The club's most memorable entry, easily, comes at the 184-yard 9th, a dangerous, island-green test which would surely have worked better were it built in front of the dining room rather than between Lyons Road and the club parking lot. Somewhat better geographically situated are favorites like the 358-yard smartly bunkered 4th, a pair of strong back-to-back par 4s at the 470-yard 11th and the 428-yard pond-guarded 12th, and a pair of tough finishers at the 223-yard over-water 16th and the 362-yard 17th, whose bulkheaded green is perched above a left-side pond. For most, the recent renovation will be viewed in a positive light.

Old Marsh Golf Club - Palm Beach Gardens   ♦♦♦♦

Pete Dye   www.oldmarshgolf.com
7500 Old Marsh Rd, Palm Beach Gardens, FL 33418   (561) 626-7400
                7,215 yds   Par 72   Rating: 75.8 / 152   (1987)

Pete Dye's design for the Old Marsh Golf Club holds an important – if rarely noticed – place in the history of golf course architecture, for it set new environmental standards for water retention by essentially sloping the outer edges of the perimeter holes towards the property's center, thus channeling irrigation water (not to mention chemicals) into an internal recycling system, keeping the adjoining Everglades pesticide-free. Such a radical approach was surely needed just to get the project permitted, for Old Marsh is rather uniquely situated, its acreage jutting westward into the glades, with vast wetlands thus flanking it on three sides. This has long served to give the club an isolated, quiet feel in region where such is nearly unheard off – undeniably an enormous plus in terms of aesthetics and ambience - but it also made its development a bit more of an adventure. Limited amounts of usable land existed within the site, and much of that was utilized for the 125+ single family homes that were included in the master plan. As a result, Dye was left with approximately 75 acres of *terra firma* upon which to construct his 18 holes, essentially making it inevitable that forced carries and invasive water hazards would be commonplace. The result, then, was one very demanding golf course, a layout full of exciting and interesting holes, but also one which had little choice but to bring water and/or wetlands into play on all 18 of them. Following a reasonably tame opener, a taste of things to come is offered at the 545-yard nicely bunkered 2nd, the first of numerous holes which require at least some wetlands carry off the tee. The layout's most famous test falls relatively early at the 430-yard 5th, Dye's slightly controversial approximation of the Alps hole at Prestwick wherein an enormous mound makes the approach to the small, water-flanked green entirely blind. This is followed immediately by the tough 485-yard 6th (with water and sand right, and a narrow driving area), leaving the remainder of the front nine to be highlighted by the 185-yard 8th (whose angled green is bulkheaded above water both right and long) and the 463-yard 9th, which pairs with the parallel 460-yard 18th in one of the earliest examples of what would become a Dye staple: closing holes being routed along the opposite banks of a central lake. The back nine opens with the 313-yard 10th, a quirky, driveable test which from its back tees requires nearly a full carry across angling wetlands if the green is to be reached. The 399-yard dogleg left 11th (played along wetlands, fairway narrowing as it goes) is similarly engaging, while the 525-yard 12th dares a long second to a green which is tucked leftward beyond both wetlands and sand. The challenge then amps up considerably at the 223-yard wetlands-hugging 14th before peaking at the 15th, a daunting 501-yard par-4 which makes a near-90-degree left turn after first requiring a massive carry from an island tee set far out in a marsh. In its aftermath, the 573-yard 17th (with green guarded right by sand and water) and the aforementioned 18th seem almost tame by comparison. With climate change and water management practices leading to a rise in the waters surrounding the club, a major renovation was undertaken in 2016 to raise every green and fairway several feet – the synchronicity of which was important as Dye has long noted the Old World way in which Old Marsh's greens generally lie at fairway level. As an environmental trend setter and a uniquely secluded, highly demanding venue amidst the South Florida sprawl, Old Marsh is, undeniably, one of the region's most desirable stops. **(GD**: #30 State)

1	2	3	4	5	6	7	8	9	Out
374	545	200	401	430	485	556	185	463	3639
4	5	3	4	4	4	5	3	4	36
10	11	12	13	14	15	16	17	18	In
313	399	525	406	223	501	176	573	460	3576
4	4	5	4	3	5	3	5	4	36

Old Palm Golf Club - Palm Beach Gardens   ◆◆◆½

Raymond Floyd   www.oldpalmgolfclub.com
11089 Old Palm Dr, Palm Beach Gardens, FL 33418   (561) 472-5100
                7,401 yds   Par 72   Rating: 76.1 / 146   (2004)

Wedged between Florida's Turnpike and Interstate 95, a mile south of where they run together at Donald Ross Road, the Old Palm Golf Club is a modern, highly demanding Raymond Floyd design routed among woods, native sandy terrain and lots of expensive real estate. Though hardly subtle in its challenge or classic in its stylings, the course certainly appeals to the modern professional, for in addition to designer Floyd, overseas stars Lee Westwood, Louis Oosthuizen and Charl Schwartzel are among those who have recently resided here. The far shorter 3,601-yard front nine makes a narrow out-and-back journey to the south and saves its best entries for the return leg, namely the 172-yard 6th (played over water to a very shallow green), the 418-yard 7th and the 537-yard 9th, which includes an over-water drive, then second and third shots menaced by a man-made creek. The back stretches a gargantuan 3,800 yards and is loaded with long par 4s, the best of which include the 470-yard lake-flanked 10th, the 478-yard tree-narrowed 14th, the 452-yard 16th (played to a very narrow green) and especially the 486-yard 18th, where sand flanks the entire left side and the same custom-made creek that crosses the 9th angles before the putting surface. Also notable are the 609-yard 12th (with driving zone squeezed by several massive bunkers), and the 402-yard 13th, whose big centerline bunker (with limited fairway on either side) resembles the one that Floyd re-shaped on the (since-remodeled) 11th hole at Doral's Blue Monster in 1996. On the whole, tough, sometimes-engaging stuff - but much of its Collectability lies in the club's A-list clientele.

Palm Beach Country Club - Palm Beach   ◆◆◆

Donald Ross   www.palmbeachcountryclub.org
760 North Ocean Dr, Palm Beach, FL 33480   (561) 844-3501
                6,155 yds   Par 72   Rating: 70.4 / 132   (1917)

Much like its neighbors the Everglades Club and The Breakers Resort, the Palm Beach Country Club occupies a not-quite-large-enough (though hugely valuable) property, in this case a squarish expanse stretching across the narrow island's entire width, from the Atlantic Ocean to Lake Worth. As such, this tight, tree-lined layout is among the more shoehorned one will encounter; indeed the site is so confined (the 10th fairway has long doubled as the practice range) that despite numerous renovations, there has been little choice but to retain virtually all of Donald Ross's original 1917 routing. The addition of numerous bunkers (particularly during a 2010 renovation) plus the ever-present sea breeze provide moments of challenge, and holes like the 425-yard 6th (a sharp, narrow dogleg right), the 180-yard pond-guarded 12th, the 418-yard into-the-wind 15th and the neatly bunkered 335-yard 18th (which shares a double green with the 15th) can all hold their own. In truth, the course doesn't play anywhere near as short as its 6,155 yards might suggest, for that total is dragged down significantly by the presence of six par 3s, three of which are strong tests extending beyond 200 yards. Sadly, long gone are the vast sandy expanses which gave Ross's original design a wildly natural feel; were these still intact, this would stand among the region's more unique tests. But instead, we are left with the not-uncommon circumstance of a club's considerable social prominence driving its Collectability at least a little more than the pure caliber of its golf.

Palm Beach Polo Club (Dunes) - West Palm Beach   ♦♦½

Ron Garl & Jerry Pate   www.palmbeachpolo.com
11199 Polo Club Rd, West Palm Beach, FL 33414   (561) 798-7405
          7,066 yds   Par 72   Rating: 74.2 / 138   (1984)

An expansive residential community located more than 10 miles inland from the Atlantic, the Palm Beach Polo Club features a pair of 1980s courses routed through rows of single-family homes, both of which are fairly challenging, but neither of which quite rank among the area's best. The older Ron Garl and Jerry Pate-designed Dunes course is billed as a links-style test which, as always, misses that mark widely. It is, however, an occasionally interesting layout which does not overuse water and features a variety of sand hazards, from tiny pot bunkers to vast, open waste areas. Of course, where water is employed, it has a significant impact, particularly on the front nine's two par 3s, the 198-yard 5th (laid neatly into a triangular plot along the property boundary) and the 180-yard 8th, another all-carry test. While stronger par 4s like the 450-yard 6th and the 415-yard 9th fill out the front nine, it is another watery entry, the 544-yard 11th (whose green is closely guarded by a lake) that kicks off the more imposing back nine, which weighs in at 3,605 yards. Tops here are the 455-yard 12th and the 234-yard 13th, as well as the 531-yard 17th (whose green sits behind a huge front-right bunker) and the 441-yard 18th.

Palm Beach Polo Club (Cypress) - West Palm Beach   ♦♦♦

Pete & P.B. Dye   www.palmbeachpolo.com
11199 Polo Club Rd, West Palm Beach, FL 33414   (561) 798-7405
          7,116 yds   Par 72   Rating: 75.1 / 145   (1989)

Built in 1989 by Pete and P.B. Dye, the Palm Beach Polo Club's Cypress course is arguably a bit more engaging than the older Dunes course – though some of its quasi-geometric shaping suggests that perhaps P.B.'s name should sit alone atop the design masthead. Transversing large wetlands and requiring some even larger cart rides over the course of its non-returning routing, the Cypress begins with an outward half that includes multiple waterside greens (at the 532-yard 2nd, the 382-yard 3rd and the 421-yard 9th) as well as several holes built around oversized bunkering, led by the 428-yard 4th, the 427-yard 5th and the 513-yard 7th. But if few of these stand especially tall in the overall Dye pantheon, the 3,694-yard back nine steps the action up a notch, initially featuring the 182-yard 11th (its peninsula green jutting dangerously leftward, into a pond) and the 462-yard, water-guarded 13th. But even more imposing is a demanding closing stretch composed of the 442-yard 15th (where water lines the entire right side en route to a massive green), the 231-yard bunkerless 16th (water right and a tiny target), the 641-yard 17th (water left, with the green angled along the end of the hazard) and the 450-yard 18th, a straightish variation on the template watery Dye par-4 closer with a lake marking the entirety of the left side. For most, the Cypress course will be the choice if playing only one round here.

Pine Tree Golf Club - Boynton Beach   ◆◆◆◆

Dick Wilson   www.pinetreegolfclub.com
10600 Pine Tree Terrace, Boynton Beach, FL 33436   (561) 732-6404
            7,301 yds   Par 71   Rating: 75.3 / 138   (1962)

If the legendary Seminole is the unquestioned Golden Age giant of South Florida golf, its postwar counterpart must surely be the Pine Tree Golf Club, a track which garnered universal national acclaim upon its 1962 opening. How much acclaim, exactly? Frequent visitor Ben Hogan called it "the greatest flat course in the country," and Sam Snead is reported to have rated it "the best golf course in the South." *Golf Digest* placed it among the nation's top 10 in its inaugural 1966 ranking of "America's 100 Most Testing Courses" and, following the magazine's retooling the ranking as "America's 100 Greatest Golf Courses," it retained a spot among the top 20 through the 1970s. Both the course's designer of record Dick Wilson and a major contributor in its planning, his partner Joe Lee, were initial club members, inspiring the pair to produce a layout which in some ways is more impressive today than in its infancy. Indeed, measuring 7,116 yards in 1966, Pine Tree could rely heavily upon length to guarantee its challenge in those early years – a luxury which its current 7,301-yard edition is largely not afforded relative to the skilled, equipment-enhanced modern player. And in real terms these numbers are somewhat inflated anyway, as the course boasts but a single par 4 over 460 yards (the 474-yard 7th) and has roughly 18% of its total length consumed by a pair of huge par 5s, the 603-yard 5th and the famous 666-yard 16th. Yet Pine Tree remains a challenging test today, largely because of Wilson's generous use of sand, with nearly 130 bunkers in play, ranging from very small hazards to vast, waste-like expanses dotted with grass islands. Seldom flashy or spectacular, Pine Tree presents a succession of strong, interesting holes, with nearly every putting surface featuring narrow, sand-guarded corners ripe with demanding pin placements. Many may consider the front nine to be the less-exciting half, though two of its par 4s are worthy of note: the 437-yard 4th (whose green angles beyond copious sand) and the aforementioned 7th, a long and dangerous test which sweeps rightward along a lake. The back then kicks off with the 507-yard 10th (today a monster par 4 after decades as a friendly three-shotter) before offering a fine run of golf at the 456-yard pond-fronted 12th, the 158-yard 13th (played across a sea of grass-dotted sand to an angled, hourglass-like green) and the 378-yard 14th, which doglegs leftward around a lake and dares the skilled player to take a more aggressive line. In truth, the endless 16th is limited from a tactical perspective (though its green is fronted by a centerline bunker) but it ably sets up a pair of strong par-4 finishers, the 430-yard 17th and the 458-yard 18th, the latter marked by four bunkers guarding the preferred left side of the fairway and an approach played across another fronting pond. Some critics argue that Pine Tree was merely among the best courses of a very poor architectural era, and it must fairly be noted that the club no longer occupies a spot among most national top 100s. Part of this, however, is surely due to its reticence towards venturing into the national tournament spotlight, with its most prominent past events being only the 1978 U.S. Senior Amateur and a one-off visit from the LPGA (won by Kathy Whitworth) in 1968. But there is lots of history and ambience to go with the golf at Pine Tree (Hogan and Snead didn't reach their conclusions by *not* spending time here) and following a 2005 restoration by Bobby Weed, today's course greatly resembles Wilson's original – all of which continues to make it one of the region's cornerstone stops.   **(GD:** #190 USA, #15 State **GW:** #125 Modern**)**

1	2	3	4	5	6	7	8	9	Out
413	186	416	437	603	218	474	395	521	3663
4	3	4	4	5	3	4	4	5	36
10	11	12	13	14	15	16	17	18	In
507	227	456	158	378	358	666	430	458	3638
4	3	4	3	4	4	5	4	4	35

Polo Club of Boca Raton (Equestrian) - Boca Raton   ♦♦½

Karl Litten   www.poloclub.net
5400 Champion Blvd, Boca Raton, FL 33496   (561) 995-1200
            7,012 yds   Par 72   Rating: 74.9 / 145   (1986)

A 36-hole real estate-oriented development built upon a sprawling, oddly configured site three miles inland from the Atlantic, the Polo Club of Boca Raton features two Karl Litten-designed 18s, each of which has been updated in the new millennium by Tim Freeland. The more significant player here is the Equestrian course, a tough, watery test whose expansive routing visits distant residential neighborhoods, requires several huge cart rides and utilizes enough railroad ties to lay track halfway to Canada. Upgraded by Freeland in 2006, it is led – at least aesthetically – by its par 3s, which include the 147-yard 3rd (played over water to a bulkheaded green), the 184-yard 11th (ditto, but with a framing waterfall) and the stiff 213-yard 15th. Beyond these one-shotters, the somewhat blander front nine is built around a trio of shortish lake-guarded par 4s, the 370-yard 4th, the 421-yard 8th and the 414-yard 9th. The 3,738-yard par-37 back nine, by contrast, is led by a pair of long back-to-back par 5s, the 573-yard 13th (which twists past a left-side pond to a bunkerless green) and the 588-yard 14th, where a single tree and a long swath of rough divide the lay-up zone and a centerline bunker fronts the wide putting surface. Though contrived in every respect, there is no shortage of challenge here.

Polo Club of Boca Raton (Club) - Boca Raton   ♦♦½

Karl Litten   www.poloclub.net
5400 Champion Blvd, Boca Raton, FL 33496   (561) 995-1200
            6,829 yds   Par 72   Rating: 73.7 / 144   (1986)

The Polo Club of Boca Raton's shorter Club course is squeezed into tight acreage on the property's east side, where housing considerations obviously took frequent priority, resulting in the presence of several sharp doglegs, particularly within the 3,527-yard front nine. The layout was renovated by Tim Freeland at the dawn of the new millennium and while he was thus forced to retain Karl Litten's original routing, a fair amount of change/modernization did take place, resulting in a track which is rated more than a full stroke easier than the Equestrian course but which carries nearly an identical slope. Outbound favorites include the 223-yard 2nd (where two trees and a prominent waste bunker define play), the 592-yard 6th (a sharp dogleg left to a lake-guarded green) and watery par 4s like the 413-yard 3rd and the 403-yard dogleg right 9th. The shorter inward half (which, like the Equestrian, includes several notable cart rides) is also led by its par 4s, the strongest being the 403-yard dogleg right 11th, the pond-narrowed 354-yard 14th and the 424-yard lake- and oversized bunker-lined 15th. By contrast, the 18th is an early turning 360-yard dogleg left wedged between houses and Champion Boulevard – a very fitting close.

Preserve At Ironhorse - West Palm Beach   ◆◆◆

Arthur Hills   www.preserveatironhorse.com
8055 Ironhorse Blvd, West Palm Beach, FL 33412   (561) 624-5550
7,060 yds   Par 72   Rating: 74.4 / 144   (1989)

Built within the Everglades a quarter-mile west of Florida's Turnpike, this, the former Ironhorse Golf & Country Club was made famous as the subject of the book *Driving The Green*, which chronicled the many environmental and logistical challenges faced during its late 1980s development. Designed by Arthur Hills, and later touched up by regional star Kipp Schulties in 2006, it is a challenging, mid-size design routed among wetlands, lakes and multiple residential neighborhoods whose single-family homes are often set well back from the line of play. The longer front side lies north of the clubhouse, where two of its holes parallel the tracks of the old Seaboard Railroad (including the pond-flanked 562-yard 6th) and the most engaging tests include the 410-yard 4th (whose fairway bends along a left-side lake) and the 220-yard 7th, an all-carry over-water par 3 offering a variety of angled tees. Save for a marathon cart ride from the 203-yard lake-fronted 11th to the 402-yard 12th, the back nine is most memorable for the 184-yard 13th (whose slim green is pinched between left-side water and right-side sand), the 434-yard 17th (a lake-flanked dogleg right) and especially the 533-yard 18th, something of a double dogleg and a hole requiring a pair of big water carries for those aiming to get home in two. Not Hills' most strategically rich design, perhaps, but it puts up a strong challenge – and besides, a good deal of its fame lies in its literary aspects.

Royal Palm Yacht & Country Club - Boca Raton   ◆◆◆

Jack Nicklaus   www.rpycc.org
2425 Maya Palm Dr, Boca Raton, FL 33432   (561) 395-2200
7,046 yds   Par 72   Rating: 75.1 / 141   (2003)

The Royal Palm Yacht & Country Club bears the distinction of sitting on real estate once occupied by one of America's great Golden Age designs, William Flynn's South course of the neighboring Boca Raton Resort & Club. A casualty of World War II, Flynn's layout was long gone by the time Robert Trent Jones built a new facility here in 1959, and that track has since been updated both by Joe Lee in 1988 and, quite comprehensively, Jack Nicklaus in 2003. Though still utilizing most of Jones's original routing, Nicklaus's residence-lined layout is considerably more interesting, particularly within its par 5s, a strategic and watery bunch which include the 552-yard 1st (whose green is buttonhooked behind a front-right pond), the 543-yard 13th (which makes a late left turn around more water) and the 560-yard pond-guarded finisher. Waste bunkers are also a regular presence, notably at the 180-yard all-carry 5th, the 446-yard 6th (which largely occupies the site of Flynn's original 18th hole) and the 634-yard 8th, whose green is tucked behind right-side sand. Far less imposing in magnitude is the single pot bunker which guards the angled green at the 175-yard 17th – but one would rather try to escape from one of the waste bunkers anytime. Factor in several demanding mid-size two-shotters within the back nine and Royal Palm measures up nicely in the Boca Raton market – suffering only by comparison to the splendid Golden Age layout buried beneath it.

St. Andrews Country Club (Palmer) - Boca Raton   ♦♦½

Ted McAnlis   www.standrewscc.com
17557 Claridge Oval West, Boca Raton, FL 33496   (561) 451-4900
                6,526 yds   Par 72   Rating: 73.5 / 140   (1982)

Another multi-course residential facility situated in the shadow of Florida's Turnpike, the St. Andrews Country Club offers 36 modern holes routed among countless lakes and rows of single-family homes. The domiciles long ago locked in the courses' playing corridors but not Ted McAnlis's original 1982 stylings, with the older Palmer course (née the East) being renovated by Arnold Palmer in 2003. A short, lake-dotted design, it is also the more player-friendly, with generally wide fairways and much of its greenside water set back at a reasonable distance. The front nine follows a counter-clockwise path in the property's southeastern section and features both a pair of short-but-watery par 4s (the 347-yard 2nd – which plays to a peninsula green – and the 373-yard 5th) as well as two solid par 5s, the 522-yard 3rd (which bends rightward along a lake) and the 503-yard 9th, where better players will surely try to reach in two since most of the lay-up zone has been consumed by a huge left-side bunker. Back nine entries of note include the 415-yard 10th (whose green angles along a left-side lake) and the 335-yard 17th, an iron-and-pitch to a smallish putting surface situated beyond both water and sand.

St. Andrews Country Club (Fazio II) - Boca Raton   ♦♦½

Ted McAnlis   www.standrewscc.com
17557 Claridge Oval West, Boca Raton, FL 33496   (561) 451-4900
                7,000 yds   Par 72   Rating: 75.1 / 144   (1985)

The St. Andrews Country Club's longer and tougher Fazio II (née Olde) course initially debuted three years after its sister Palmer layout as a similarly proportioned (and watery) Ted McAnlis design, and that track was renovated by Gene Bates in 1995. But Bates' version too has now gone under the knife via a 2016 Tommy Fazio project, the result of which is a longer, stronger and watery track which retains its original routing but has had the majority of its bunkering rebuilt or moved. The water is particularly apparent late in each nine, the front closing with a pair of varied-but-interesting par 4s, the 340-yard 8th (where a lake, a tree and a centerline bunker complicate attempts at driving the green) and the 405-yard 9th, where right-side water greatly threatens both tee shot and approach. On the back nine, the 165-yard 16th plays to a green bulkheaded above front-right water, the 405-yard tactically strong 17th requires the negotiation of two lakes, and the 455-yard 18th is something of a mirror image of the famously tough 18th at Doral's Blue Monster, in Miami. Also notable are the 445-yard out-of-bounds-lined 5th, the 470-yard par-4 10th and the 560-yard 13th, where two left-side lakes affect all three shots.

Seminole Golf Club - Juno Beach ◆◆◆◆½

Donald Ross
901 Seminole Blvd, Juno Beach, FL 33408   (561) 626-0280
             6,836 yds   Par 72   Rating: 73.8 / 145   (1929)

It has been written that the Seminole Golf Club was the lone design commission that the legendary Golden Age architect Donald Ross ever actively campaigned for and, if those words are true, it's easy to understand why. For here, just north of the Palm Beaches, is that most uncommon of Florida properties, a seaside tract blessed with two large dune ridges – a regional geographic anomaly which Ross skillfully managed to incorporate into the design of some 13 holes. Alas, Ross's work is not 100% intact, for the club hired Dick Wilson in 1947 to move the 18th green onto the ridge which separates the golf course from the beach, and it has been widely speculated that Wilson rebuilt many putting surfaces and bunkers thereafter. But regardless of the precise nature of its pedigree, Seminole offers a deep roster of classic holes, relying upon some impressive bunkering, one central lake, the unique natural terrain and the constant ocean breeze to present one of America's finest, most aesthetically appealing tests. Play opens with a pair of short par 4s that hint at things to come on the uphill approach to the 387-yard 2nd, whose green is attractively situated within the inland dune. The 504-yard dogleg right 3rd then descends to lower ground before climbing to another elevated green, leaving the 450-yard 4th and the heavily bunkered 207-yard 5th to run back and forth across the ridgetop. Seminole's most significant hole is the 388-yard 6th, a strategic bunker-laden beauty which annual spring visitor Ben Hogan once famously cited as "the finest par four in America." While such may represent unachievable praise, the hole – which includes an angled line of bunkers severely narrowing its fairway - certainly has few equals. The downhill, pond-fronted 432-yard 7th and the stiff 235-yard 8th then see the golfer off to a back nine which commences with the 390-yard lakeside 10th, then begins to show its full charm at the 170-yard 13th, whose bunker-ringed green backed up against the seaside dunes has long been a favorite of both players and photographers. Seminole's second world-class entry (and the closest thing one will find to "spectacular" here) is the 497-yard 15th, a sweeping, split-fairway dogleg right whose shorter option is pinched between sand (as well as a line of palm trees) and the central lake. But aside from its own distinctive greatness, the 15th also kicks off one of American golf's more memorable closing stretches, a run which next offers the 410-yard dogleg right 16th, which dares an aggressive drive across right-side sand en route to another green nestled against the seaside dunes. The 175-yard 17th then tees off from atop the dunes and plays to an exposed, windblown target surrounded by deep bunkers, while the 417-yard 18th, a slight dogleg left, follows a similar pattern, culminating in Wilson's narrow, elevated putting surface, which lies just paces from the beach. Seminole has forever shunned the big event spotlight, though the club's famed pro-am was once big enough to count names like Arnold Palmer, Lloyd Mangrum and Sam Snead among it its winners - and Mangrum also won the PGA Tour's lone official visit, the 1942 Seminole Victory Open. Despite its myriad charms, there is the occasional dissenting opinion which suggests Seminole to be at least somewhat overrated. But even if such heretics are in any way correct, the club's mix of great golf, rich history and splendid Gold Coast ambience make it a national golfing treasure – and, by a comfortably wide margin, Southeast Florida's most desirable golfing stop. **(G:** #14 USA, #23 World **GD:** #13 USA, #1 State **GW:** #13 Classic)

1	2	3	4	5	6	7	8	9	Out
375	387	504	450	207	388	432	235	500	3478
4	4	5	4	3	4	4	3	5	36
10	11	12	13	14	15	16	17	18	In
390	420	367	170	512	497	410	175	417	3358
4	4	4	3	5	5	4	3	4	36

Stonebridge Country Club - Boca Raton

Karl Litten
10343 Stonebridge Blvd, Boca Raton, FL 33498
7,006 yds   Par 72   Rating: 74.8 / 147   (1985)

www.stonebridgefl.com
(561) 488-0800

Located in Boca Raton's far western reaches, little more than half a mile from the Loxahatchee Wildlife Refuge, the Stonebridge Country Club's Karl Litten-designed layout initially established itself by hosting the LPGA from 1986-1989, counting Nancy Lopez and Dottie Pepper among its champions. Unfortunately, Stonebridge is also demonstrative of two trends in modern Southeast Florida golf, for it seems that nary a Karl Litten course in the region has escaped new millennium redesign – and, as took place here in 2015, it also seems that few non-elite area facilities select a renovating architect not named Kipp Schulties. Of course, as with most housing-centric facilities, Litten's routing was mostly unchangeable, leaving Schulties to perform his standard menu of toning down wild period bunkering while adding a bit of length, in this case creating a bigger and better layout overall. Front nine favorites here include a pair of watery par 4s, the 389-yard dogleg left 5th and the dogleg left 420-yard 6th, before the back kicks off with the 525-yard 10th (which dares a long lake-crossing second) and the similarly watery 185-yard 11th. Also strong is the 418-yard 18th, whose green is nearly surrounded by sand.

Tequesta Country Club - Tequesta

Dick Wilson
201 Country Club Dr, Tequesta, FL 33469
6,845 yds   Par 71   Rating: 73.6 / 132   (1957)

www.tequestacountryclub.net
(561) 746-4501

Occupying a housing-encircled site that sits above a fork in the Loxahatchee River, flush against the Martin County line and two miles inland from the Atlantic, the Tequesta Country Club was the first residential layout ever built by the prolific Dick Wilson. Though several swaths of "native" sand added in recent years by club member Tommy Fazio have affected the course's aesthetics, the great majority of Wilson's work remains intact, resulting in a layout carrying a bit more old-fashioned charm than many newer facilities in the region. The outward half is by far the tamer, initially offering the 295-yard 2nd (driveable, but to a green flanked by a recently expanded pond) before peaking with a pair of back-to-back par 5s, the 511-yard dogleg left 6th and the 555-yard lake-guarded 7th. The par-35 back nine, on the other hand, is rather more testing, led by a collection of five longer par 4s, the best of which include the 432-yard 15th and 429-yard 16th (both sharp dogleg rights), and especially the 452-yard 18th, which bends rightward, around a narrow lake. For those wondering how many original Wilson bunkers are missing, the answer is relatively few, as this was never one of his more prolifically bunkered creations.

Trump International Golf Club - West Palm Beach   ♦♦♦½

Jim Fazio   www.trumpinternationalpalmbeaches.com
3505 Summit Blvd, West Palm Beach, FL 33406   (561) 682-0700
              7,326 yds   Par 72   Rating: 76.3 / 155   (1999)

After "using his familiar sue-and-negotiate tactics" (– the Palm Beach Post) to convince Palm Beach County to lease him the necessary land, Donald Trump reportedly spent $40 million to construct Trump International's Championship course, creating his version of tropical golfing paradise and the flagship entry in the Trump golfing fleet. While some of that money surely went to creating an effective jungle buffer around the otherwise open property, the rest, one can assume, went into the Disneyland-like waterfall that backs the 17th green, and towards building several additional hills that serve as a relief to the pancake-flat landscape. The course received much early publicity by hosting the final eight playings of the LPGA's season-ending ADT Championship (counting Webb, Mallon, Sorenstam and Ochoa among its winners), allowing TV viewers to see that designer Jim Fazio did manage to create something *different* here – which, given his client's emphasis on marketing flash, was likely just what the doctor ordered. The shorter front nine mostly represents basic Florida golf of the highest variety, led by the 335-yard dogleg right 6th (driveable over water), the demanding 473-yard 8th and a pair of water-guarded par 5s, the 539-yard 3rd and the 553-yard 9th. The 3,731-yard back then steps it up a notch, first at the 419-yard 10th (which sweeps rightward, around water), then with closers like the 550-yard creek-divided 15th, the watery 406-yard 16th and the Mt. Vesuvius-backed 215-yard 17th which, despite its utterly contrived green complex, is actually a rather engaging entry.   (GD: #156 USA, #9 State)

Trump Intn'l Golf Club (Trump) - West Palm Beach   ♦♦

Jim Fazio   www.trumpinternationalpalmbeaches.com
3505 Summit Blvd, West Palm Beach, FL 33406   (561) 682-0700
              3,605 yds   Par 36   Rating: 37.7 / 147   (2006)

The Trump International Golf Club's modestly named Trump nine was added by Jim Fazio seven years after his work on the main course and was carved from jungle within a small tract across a tributary of the West Palm Beach Canal. At 3,605 yards, it offers a decent amount of size, but from a design perspective, this was clearly a less-ambitious undertaking. Notable early are a pair of arrow-straight (and fairly basic) long par 5s, the 575-yard 1st and the 625-yard 3rd. But the action picks up somewhat at the sand-narrowed 235-yard 5th, then peaks over a trio of closers composed of the 431-yard 7th (a 90-degree dogleg left around a central lake), the 153-yard 8th (played to a TPC-Sawgrass island-green knockoff) and the 465-yard dogleg right 9th, whose approach passes two very large right-side bunkers. Although there is a fair amount of challenge present here, this extra loop still offers far less charm and strategy than the original 18.

Trump National Golf Club - Jupiter   ♦♦♦

Jack Nicklaus
106 Ritz-Carlton Club Dr, Jupiter, FL 33477
7,531 yds   Par 72   Rating: 76.4 / 149   (2002)

www.trumpnationaljupiter.com
(407) 345-6150

Sharing its A1A-adjacent site with Jack Nicklaus's Bear's Club, Trump National - Jupiter began life as Ritz-Carlton's initial entry into the private golf club field (even if the course was managed by Marriott) before the hotel chain sold it to The Donald in late 2012. Like the Bear's Club, Trump National's fairways are flanked by scrub-filled waste areas, giving it a pleasantly rustic feel. Unlike its highly ranked neighbor, however, Trump National includes several large residential neighborhoods within its interior, affecting the layout's ambience and aesthetics adversely. Notable in terms of design are bunkers which are quite small (though plentiful) and greens which are both small and generally fairly narrow, placing a real premium on iron play. And there is, without question, plenty of interesting golf here, with the front nine being led by a trio of strong par 4s: the 422-yard centerline-bunkered 3rd, the 491-yard 5th (played to a typically narrow target) and the 402-yard 9th, which culminates in a none-too-natural-looking bunker-fronted peninsula green. The back nine's initial standouts are its two par 3s, the 168-yard island-green 11th (which offers no real bailout option) and the 230-yard Redan-like 14th. At least equally engaging, however, is the finishing trio, with the 345-yard 16th daring a water-cheating drive towards a narrow, bulkheaded green, the 546-yard 17th curling along a left-side lake, and the 451-yard 18th requiring a long second to a bunkerless putting surface angled behind still another pond. One of the stronger entries in the Trump portfolio.

Via Mizner Golf Club - Boca Raton   ♦♦

Robert von Hagge & Bruce Devlin
6200 Boca del Mar Dr, Boca Raton, FL 33433
6,222 yds   Par 70   Rating: 69.2 / 131   (1972)

www.viamiznergcc.com
(561) 392-7990

Its relatively early construction allowing it to be built somewhat closer to the ocean than many future area developments, the Via Mizner Golf Club (née the Country Club at Boca Raton) is a von Hagge & Devlin design which was later touched up (mostly in its bunkering) by Charles Ankrom. A short, moderately challenging layout whose nines follow narrow out-and-back paths amidst housing, it makes little more than scenic use of most of the lakes and canals that dot the property, with the most invasive of water appearing on the 2,985-yard front nine. Striking out to the west, this tiny loop is led by the 326-yard driveable 3rd and the imposing 432-yard lake-bothered 6th, though less appealing is the 475-yard dogleg left 2nd, a tree-lined, early turning par 5. The back then runs eastward where it is led by two more lake-bordered entries (the 418-yard 11th and the 426-yard 13th) as well as the 415-yard 16th, a tricky driving hole affected by water, sand and trees. A newly private facility, this is, for the present, mid-range Florida golf.

Wanderers Club - Wellington ♦♦½

Ted McAnlis   www.wc.coth.com
1900 Aero Club Dr, Wellington, FL 33414   (561) 795-3501
         7,052 yds   Par 72   Rating: 74.0 / 135   (1984)

Formerly the public-access Wellington Golf Club, the revamped Wanderers Club joins its neighbor Wellington National as the western-most courses on the coastal side of Palm Beach County, and is now a private facility whose equestrian theme includes the practice range doubling as an undersized polo field. The golf course was originally built by Florida-based designer Ted McAnlis in 1984. Renovated in 2007 by Peter Jacobsen and Jim Hardy, it has followed the regional norm of retaining an original housing-defined routing, but it today possesses considerably more bunker-oriented playing interest – though an adjacent nine-hole executive loop was abandoned as a part of the reconfiguring. Not overly long in total, the new layout does offer several muscular holes of distinction, particularly on a front nine which includes two tactically hazarded par 5s (the 579-yard 2nd and the 552-yard watery 7th) and two strong par 4s, the 453-yard 4th (a sand-narrowed dogleg right) and the 449-yard lake-flanked 6th. The inward half, if slightly weaker, still features several notable entries including a pair of long, sandy par 3s (the 222-yard 11th and the 219-yard 15th) as well as the 566-yard 12th (where a centerline bunker complicates the second) and the 427-yard pond-guarded 18th.

Wellington National Golf Club - Wellington ♦♦½

Gene Bates & Johnny Miller   www.wellingtonnationalgolfclub.com
400 Binks Forest Dr, Wellington, FL 33414   (561) 333-5731
         7,253 yds   Par 72   Rating: 74.7 / 136   (1989)

Joining its southern neighbor the Wanderers Club as the western-most courses in the coastal section of Palm Beach County, the Wellington National (née Binks Forest) Golf Club has endured a tumultuous existence since 1989, actually closing for five years prior to re-opening in 2007 following a Gene Bates renovation. As its original name suggests, the course was indeed built within a wooded setting, a somewhat unique attribute in the region, but also one mitigated by both the endless rows of housing also built therein and the long stretch of power lines which slice across the property. Much of the layout's challenge lies simply in its size, particularly over a front nine which includes solid par 5s like the 574-yard creek-bothered 2nd and the 525-yard 6th (which requires a drive angled over water) but also less-engaging brutes like the 478-yard 8th and the 493-yard 9th, two huge, straightaway par 4s. Save for its pair of muscular par 5s and the 244-yard 13th, the inward half is somewhat shorter and reserves its more interesting golf for closers like the soundly bunkered 400-yard 15th, the watery 143-yard 16th and the 411-yard pond-guarded 18th, which includes a particularly nasty back-right pin.

Woodfield Country Club - Boca Raton   ◆◆½

Joe Lee   www.woodfield.org
3650 Club Place, Boca Raton, FL 33496   (561) 994-1000
        7,115 yds   Par 72   Rating: 75.2 / 142   (1987)

A large residential development whose western boundary sits flush against Florida's Turnpike, the Woodfield Country Club was one of the later designs of the prolific Joe Lee – though his touch is less in evidence following a new millennium bunker renovation by Bob Cupp. Save for the 550-yard 1st (a water-guarded right), play opens on a smaller scale, with three sub-400-yard par 4s among the opening five. The action picks up quickly thereafter, however, first at the 561-yard 6th (which dares a long second to a peninsula green), then over a trio of front nine closers that includes the 470-yard dogleg left 7th, the 230-yard 8th and the tightly bunkered 426-yard 9th, which turns sharply right, around a lake. The inward half initially features the 512-yard 11th (a sweeping, watery dogleg left daring an aggressive drive) but peaks over an imposing (if contrived) closing stretch led by the 442-yard dogleg-left 16th (whose final 300 yards are surrounded by water), the 149-yard 17th (played to a bulkheaded island green) and the 447-yard 18th, which includes a narrow putting surface wedged between sand and a man-made creek.

Wycliffe Golf & Country Club (East) - Wellington   ◆◆½

Karl Litten   www.wycliffecc.com
4650 Wycliffe Country Club Blvd, Wellington, FL 33478   (561) 964-9200
        6,917 yds   Par 72   Rating: 74.0 / 147   (1989)

Having jumped quickly into the tournament limelight by hosting the LPGA's old Palm Beach Classic from 1990-1994 (and counting Pat Bradley and Meg Mallon among its early winners), the housing-lined Wycliffe Golf & Country Club is today a 36-hole facility whose Karl Litten-designed courses have been touched up in the new millennium by John Sanford. The tougher East course (upon which Bruce Devlin originally consulted) was the LPGA venue and is a strong test but, like many a Litten design, poses few real strategic questions. Its longer front nine initially crossed Lake Worth Road for a run of five holes highlighted by the 527-yard 2nd (a pond-guarded dogleg right) and the 404-yard pond-affected (but bunkerless) 3rd. The 174-yard over-water 7th is another strong entry before play heads off to a less-imposing back nine anchored by a quirky final four that includes a narrow (if formulaic) double green shared by the 530-yard 15th and the 387-yard 17th, the latter bending rightward around a huge fairway bunker. The 181-yard 16th plays to a tiny sand-fronted putting surface while the 427-yard 18th plays past another massive fairway bunker (this time on the left) en route to a green tucked beyond a front-left lake.

Wycliffe Golf & Country Club (West) - Wellington   ♦♦½

Karl Litten   www.wycliffecc.com
4650 Wycliffe Country Club Blvd, Wellington, FL 33478   (561) 964-9200
            6,641 yds   Par 72   Rating: 73.3 / 150   (1989)

The Wycliffe Golf & Country Club's shorter West course was more heavily renovated by
John Sanford (in 2006) than the club's East course, resulting in more plentiful (and
modern) bunkering, water meaningfully in play on 14 holes and, overall, a rather more
engaging challenge. Given its sub-6,700-yard size, shorter par 4s are a regular presence,
particularly out of the box where the 323-yard 1st plays to a narrow lakeside green and
the 344-yard 2nd dares a tee shot blasted across a swath of right-side sand. The watery
144-yard 3rd is similarly diminutive before the front nine stretches out a bit at the 553-
yard 4th (where a left-side lake affects all three shots) and the 456-yard 6th, a quirky, early
turning dogleg right whose bunkering offers multiple driving options. The much longer
back nine opens with a pair of waste bunker-lined par 4s before playing through a trio of
shortish, water-guarded two-shotters at holes 12-14. The closing stretch is similarly small
and watery, with both the 147-yard 16th and the 485-yard par-5 17th playing to narrow
greens angled along lakes before the 426-yard 18th plays across an over-the-top mix of
sand and water. Though considerably shorter, this may well be the visitor's first choice.

Banyan Cay Resort & Golf - West Palm Beach   N/A

Jack Nicklaus   www.banyancayresort.com
2300 Presidential Way, West Palm Beach, FL 33401   (561) 557-5840

The developing Banyan Cay Resort & Golf project represents a complete overall of the former 36-hole facility known as President Country Club, which traced its earliest golfing roots to the 1970s, but which was overhauled completely by Robert Trent Jones II in 2007. The new development will see the former club's second course (a short 6,158-yard test known as the Patriot) turned into a residential neighborhood, while its main layout, the Eagle, is being completely rebuilt by Jack Nicklaus. The new course (which was well into its construction process at the time of this writing) is projected to measure about 7,200 yards and will retain the great majority of Jones' routing, save for the creation of new 1st and 2nd holes built around a new practice area. A 150-room resort hotel will anchor the facility and is also under construction, as is and a full slate of residential opportunities. The facility's new clubhouse is slated to begin operation in 2019.

Boca Raton Resort & Club (Resort) - Boca Raton   ♦♦½

Gene Bates & Kipp Schulties   www.bocaresort.com
501 East Camino Real, Boca Raton, FL 33432   (561) 447-3419
6,253 yds   Par 71   Rating: 69.5 / 130   (1997)

Since its opening in 1926 (as the Cloister Inn), the Boca Raton Resort & Club has stood among the elite of American resorts, with no less than Tommy Armour and Sam Snead enjoying extended stints as the club's professional. Unfortunately, long gone are a pair of superb William Flynn designs that once graced the property, with the adjacent Royal Palm Yacht & Country Club occupying the site of Flynn's old South course and the present Resort layout lying atop the North. Unlike the South (whose land was sold circa World War II), Flynn's North course was actually renovated out of existence, first by men like Red Lawrence, Robert Tent Jones and Joe Lee, and finally by Gene Bates, who completely overhauled the facility in 1997. Squeezed into a tight, artificially graded site, Bates' version features a pair of strong back-to-back par 4s at the 408-yard 3rd (where a heavily landscaped water hazard flanks the right side) and the 452-yard 4th, but leaves most of the best action for the back nine, where similarly contrived water adds strategic interest at holes 12-14. The 528-yard 16th, which bends around another lake, is also notable before the 380-yard 18th plays to the there's-no-way-there-wouldn't-be-one island green. The history here is dazzling; it just wasn't on this golf course...

Boca Raton Resort & Club (Country Club) - Boca Raton   ♦♦

Joe Lee   www.bocaresort.com
17751 Boca Club Blvd, Boca Raton, FL 33487   (561) 447-3520
         6,714 yds   Par 72   Rating: 73.0 / 141   (1986)

As an off-site alternative, the Boca Raton Resort also offers guests playing privileges at its Country Club course, a 1986 Joe Lee design which had its bunkering re-worked by Gene Bates and Kipp Schulties in 2003. Located five miles northwest of the resort, and just west of Interstate 95, the Country Club is built into a very oddly shaped property as its front nine follows a straight out-and-back routing along a corridor of land so narrow as to yield little possibility for creative or unique holes. The back, on the other hand, embarks on an expansive path that divides the loop into three separate sections within/around a large residential development. After opening with a lake-crossing 318-yard drive-and-pitch, the front is led by a pair of tests played to waterside greens, the 184-yard 5th and the 561-yard 6th. The back then offers solid (if predictable) water holes like the 394-yard 10th (with putting surface jutting into a right-side lake), the 514-yard 14th and the 516-yard 18th, a readily reachable par 5 which culminates in another island green. For the more discerning, the Resort course (*sans* commute) will likely suffice.

The Breakers Golf Club (Ocean) - Palm Beach   ♦♦♦

William Langford   www.thebreakers.com
1 South County Rd, Palm Beach, FL 33480   (561) 655-6611
         6,167 yds   Par 70   Rating: 68.1 / 127   (1926)

Another legendary oceanfront resort along Florida's Gold Coast, The Breakers has existed on its present site for well over a century, beginning life as oil tycoon Henry Flagler's Palm Beach Inn in 1896, and eventually moving (after two catastrophic fires) into today's famed beachfront structure 30 years later. Golf was first played over a primitive Alex Findlay-designed nine in 1897, a loop which would eventually be expanded into Florida's first 18-hole layout before being modified by William Langford in 1926. Renovated substantially by Brian Silva in 2000, the Ocean remains squeezed into a tight, squarish tract immediately adjacent to the hotel, a circumstance which limits size greatly but also provides an old-fashioned, intimate feel. Given the flat, featureless nature of the landscape, water is inevitably the primary hazard, seriously affecting play on 10 holes, mostly in the form of the ponds which protect seven greens. Thus among a fairly even field, favorites include the 440-yard water-fronted 6th, the 221-yard 13th (where a slice may find the hotel's elegant, palm-lined entrance drive), the 212-yard 16th (whose angled green is among the pond-fronted) and the 385-yard 18th (ditto). By no means is this a full-size, challenging test, but Silva's revised layout provides solid resort golf in a uniquely convenient, historic and ambience-filled South Florida setting.

The Breakers Golf Club (Rees Jones) - Palm Beach   ♦♦♦

Willard Byrd   www.thebreakers.com
1550 Flagler Pkwy, West Palm Beach, FL 33411   (561) 653-6320
         7,104 yds   Par 72   Rating: 74.8 / 146   (1968)

Formerly known as Breakers West, today's Rees Jones course lies 10 miles inland from the resort where it was originally built (adjacent to Jack Nicklaus's Mayacoo Lakes) by Willard Byrd in 1970. The higher-profile Jones performed a renovation in 2004, however, and while he retained the entirety of Byrd's residence-lined routing, most everything else was altered; indeed, with its bunkering greatly revised and expanded, and several water hazards being re-shaped, this is one of the area's stronger tests today. Though it initially features the 442-yard 2nd (which plays to one of several greens jutting dangerously into often-reconfigured lakes), the front nine's best stretch doesn't arrive until the 556-yard 6th (whose putting surface is hugged left, right and long by water), the 191-yard lake-crossing 8th, and the 455-yard 9th, a tough dogleg left requiring two substantial water carries. The back nine is slightly longer but also a tad less interesting, though it does offer two early tests played to small greens bulkheaded dangerously above front-right water: the 161-yard 11th and the 514-yard 12th. Amidst a quartet of otherwise-long finishers, also notable is the 326-yard 15th, a heavily bunkered, potentially driveable dogleg left. On the whole, a night-and-day alternative to the resort's cozier Ocean course, but well worth the drive for those more focused on challenge than ambience.   **(GW: #122 Resort)**

PGA National Resort (Fazio) - Palm Beach Gardens   ♦♦½

George & Tom Fazio   www.pgaresort.com
1000 Ave of Champions, Palm Beach Gardens, FL 33418   (561) 627-1800
         7,050 yds   Par 72   Rating: 74.5 / 139   (1980)

Occupying a massive spread adjacent to Florida's Turnpike, far west of the Palm Beach area's better-known coastal addresses, the PGA National Resort has served as the home of the PGA of America since 1981 and offers five housing and water-flanked courses, an impressive four of which play out of a central clubhouse. The first to open was a George and Tom Fazio-designed layout known as the Haig course, a layout which underwent a minor 2012 renovation by Tommy Fazio before being promptly renamed – presumably in the believe that the Fazio name would be more marketable than that of the legendary Walter Hagen. In any event, the youngest Fazio added a bit of length and, to his credit, left the general style of his family's original bunkering largely intact, resulting in a solid (if unspectacular) track that offers a few more engaging moments. After commencing with the 520-yard double dogleg 1st (where water fills both dogleg corners), the front nine is led by the 405-yard dogleg left 6th and the tightly bunkered 440-yard 8th. The stronger back nine leads with the 520-yard lake-flanked 12th before peaking over a trio of longer finishers: the fairly basic 235-yard 16th, the 540-yard lake-fronted 17th and the stiff 465-yard 18th, a tough dogleg right whose entire left side is bordered by a canal.

PGA National Resort (Squire) - Palm Beach Gardens   ♦♦½

George & Tom Fazio   www.pgaresort.com
1000 Ave of Champions, Palm Beach Gardens, FL 33418   (561) 627-1800
6,447 yds   Par 72   Rating: 72.1 / 140   (1981)

Next up chronologically in the PGA National Resort's development was the Team Fazio-designed Squire course, a short test which fans out to the northwest and plays over a non-returning routing that runs through quiet neighborhoods of single-family homes. Measuring less the 6,500 yards, it is perhaps fitting that two of its best holes are diminutive par 5s with tricky lay-up zones, the 497-yard canal-fronted 1st and the 509-yard 18th, whose green is similarly angled behind both water and sand. What lies in between are 16 holes that nicely illustrate George Fazio's style, with most greens being smaller and the bunkering being well positioned, seldom overdone and a bit more penal than strategic. Though few of the par 4s are terribly long, there are several worth noting, including the 419-yard dogleg left 2nd, the 420-yard dogleg left 12th and especially the 307-yard 13th, a potentially driveable entry whose tightly bunkered green is tucked right, behind a pond. The 448-yard dogleg left 14th would surely rate the strongest two-shotter were it not played as the layout's shortest par 5, while the wetlands-flanked 508-yard 5th is another three-shotter of note. This is easily the resort's shortest and lowest-rated layout, but there is still enough here to at least somewhat challenge the better golfer.

PGA National Resort (Palmer) - Palm Beach Gardens   ♦♦½

Arnold Palmer   www.pgaresort.com
1000 Ave of Champions, Palm Beach Gardens, FL 33418   (561) 627-1800
7,079 yds   Par 72   Rating: 74.6 / 141   (1984)

The last of the four central layouts at the PGA National Resort, 1984's Palmer course is the resort's longest and second-toughest track and, like the Squire, it follows a routing which finds its 9th hole far afield. Beginning and ending across the large lake that abuts the clubhouse, its bunkering is somewhat more understated than was the Palmer period norm – though the presence of the odd swath of open sand does differentiate it from its sister layouts. Though in many places uneventful, both nines manage to close strongly, with the outward half featuring the 556-yard 8th (a watery double dogleg whose first turn approaches 90 degrees) and the 423-yard 9th, a dogleg right with water lying short-left of its putting surface. Coming home, the action begins to heat up at short, watery tests like the 156-yard lake-fronted 13th and two slightly awkward par 4s where interceding lakes mandate laid-up drives, the 352-yard 14th and the 373-yard 15th. But once again, the finish is quite strong, and includes the 438-yard 16th (a dogleg right with a large bunker guarding the corner), the 435-yard 17th (where trees and sand narrow the fairway) and the 601-yard 18th, which snakes between water hazards (and a long right-side bunker) to a stonewall-bulkheaded green. Overall, a solid second choice for the better player.

PGA National Resort (Champion) - Palm Beach Gardens ♦♦♦♦

George & Tom Fazio   www.pgaresort.com
1000 Ave of Champions, Palm Beach Gardens, FL 33418   (561) 627-1800
7,045 yds   Par 72   Rating: 75.2 / 148   (1981)

Within its 90 holes of golf, the PGA National Resort's calling card has long been the famed Champion course, site of the 1983 Ryder Cup, Larry Nelson's victory in the 1987 PGA Championship, the Senior PGA Championship from 1982-2000 and, since 2007, the PGA Tour's Honda Classic. But if we are to judge the Champion objectively, we must initially note that it stands in extremely limited company – indeed, only Medinah might clearly exceed it – as a layout which has continued to host major international events despite needing to be significantly redesigned on multiple occasions. Originally the resort's third course to be built by George and Tom Fazio, it survived nearly a decade in its maiden form before Jack Nicklaus was retained to perform a significant renovation in 1990. That project retained virtually all of the Fazio's routing (as with so many Florida courses, surrounding housing limited the options) but numerous less obvious changes were made, both in the bunkering and in a significant recontouring of both fairways and green complexes – and these sorts of not-quite-major changes have continued from time to time ever since. Perhaps the most memorable aspect of Nicklaus's work was the reshaping of holes 15, 16, 17, a run marketed collectively as the "Bear Trap," and which have gained considerable TV fame since the Honda's 2007 arrival. Also noteworthy when observing the pros is the fact that they utilize several tees not listed on the resort scorecard and also convert holes 6 and 10 to par 4s, adding up to a 7,140-yard, par-70 configuration. The Champion's front nine is both shorter and easier than the back and, following the narrow 437-yard 2nd, features a run of three strong entries in its mid-section: the pond-crossing 171-yard 5th, the demanding 488-yard 6th (a water-lined three-shotter which the pros play as a nasty par 4) and the heavily bunkered 226-yard 7th. But the 3,613-yard inward half is another story altogether and it opens in imposing style, first with the 545-yard dogleg right 10th (which the Tour plays as a 508-yard par 4), then at the 450-yard 11th, whose approach is aimed at a bunkerless green angled closely along a front-right lake. The 427-yard 12th (a tightly bunkered dogleg right) immediately follows, and if the 388-yard 13th offers a modest respite, the challenge picks up again at the 465-yard 14th, which bends gently leftward to a green angled along right-side water. The golfer now reaches the much-trumpeted Bear Trap, a watery run composed of the 176-yard 15th (whose green angles dangerously rightward, into a lake), the marginally awkward 434-yard 16th (with interceding water forcing longer hitters to lay up off the tee) and the 172-yard 17th, where a narrow putting surface is again pinched between water and sand in a manner similar to the 15th. It is well worth noting that while both the 15th and 17th greens are indeed scarily positioned, the pros tackle them during the windiest time of the year in South Florida, making the challenge slightly less intimidating for visitors during more benign seasons. And less wind-affected is the 556-yard 18th, a heavily bunkered par 5 which doglegs left, then angles along a large lake en route to a triangular waterside putting surface. A friendly slot on the PGA Tour schedule (combined with many top players residing locally) helped draw some very strong fields during the 2010s, with winners including Major champions like Els, Yang, McIlroy, Harrington and Scott, as well the ever-popular Rickie Fowler. Thus by any measure, the Champion is the obvious choice of the resort's more discerning golfing guests. **(GW: #72 Resort)**

1	2	3	4	5	6	7	8	9	Out
365	437	538	376	171	488	226	427	404	3432
4	4	5	4	3	5	3	4	4	36
10	11	12	13	14	15	16	17	18	In
545	450	427	388	465	176	434	172	556	3613
5	4	4	4	4	3	4	3	5	36

PGA National Resort (Estates) - Palm Beach Gardens   ♦♦

Karl Litten   www.pgaresort.com
7736 Bay Hill Dr, West Palm Beach, FL 33412   (561) 627-2000
6,694 yds   Par 72   Rating: 73.1 / 134   (1984)

Not an original part of the PGA National Resort, what is today known as the Estates course began life in 1984 as the Karl Litten-designed Stonewall Golf Club before being acquired by the PGA four years later. Nominally a private club but open to resort guests, it lies five miles west of the resort's original 72 holes on a narrow, north-to-south-running tract that is divided by numerous rows of single-family homes. The Estates matches two its sister layouts by utilizing a non-returning routing, and it matches most of the then-popular Litten's South Florida work in that its best holes almost invariably rely on water as a primary feature. The front nine offers the more engaging entries, particularly over an early run that includes the 207-yard well-bunkered 3rd, the 420-yard 4th, the 495-yard par-5 5th (which dares a direct over-water route on the second) and the 338-yard lake-fronted 6th. The layout's strongest entry falls at the 551-yard 9th (where water flanks the entire left side and fronts the green) before returning home on a back nine that features the well-bunkered 172-yard 14th, the 407-yard canal-lined 16th, and several prodigiously long cart rides. For the discerning golfer, probably not worth leaving the resort for.

Quail Ridge Country Club (South) - Boynton Beach   ♦♦½

Joe Lee   www.quailridgecc.com
3715 Golf Rd, Boynton Beach, FL 33436   (561) 737-5100
6,715 yds   Par 72   Rating: 72.7 / 131   (1973)

The Quail Ridge Country Club is usually listed as a private facility, but since it now offers vacation rentals (with golfing privileges) to non-members, it is classified as a resort herein. The club features a pair of Joe Lee-designed courses built two years apart on an L-shaped site which straddles Woolbright Road, just southeast of the famed Pine Tree. The older of the two, the South course, is a moderately difficult test built on a rectangular, housing-perforated site along the south side of Woolbright Road. At only 6,715 yards, and with water materially affecting only three holes, this is far closer to high-end functional than it is, for example, to Pine Tree - though as one might expect of the reliably professional Lee, solid entries are certainly plentiful. Going out, these include the 421-yard dogleg right 5th, the 210-yard lake-bordered 6th and the 349-yard 8th, a lake-crossed drive-and-pitch which, despite an impeding condominium or two, might tempt today's longer hitter. Coming home, the 505-yard 15th and 404-yard 16th are enlivened by left-side water, while the 413-yard 14th and the 420-yard dogleg right 18th are strong two-shotters.

Quail Ridge Country Club (North) - Boynton Beach   ◆◆½

Joe Lee   www.quailridgecc.com
3715 Golf Rd, Boynton Beach, FL 33436   (561) 737-5100
          7,003 yds   Par 72   Rating: 74.7 / 139   (1975)

Joe Lee added the Quail Ridge Country Club's North course two years after building the South, this time utilizing another housing-oriented site north of Woolbright Road – but also squeezing in two holes (the 1st and 18th) within the boundaries of the South course in order to provide access to and from the clubhouse. Though Lee's bunkering has been altered over the years, the North remains the stronger track, measuring nearly 250 yards longer and rating two full strokes tougher – yet it possesses an only slightly greater degree of playing interest throughout. The 508-yard 2nd (whose green is tucked leftward, beyond a lake) gets the action going nicely, but the front nine hits peak stride within its closers, the 475-yard par-4 7th, the 410-yard lake-flanked 8th and the 160-yard 9th, with plays across a massive, wildly shaped bunker. The back nine provides another sturdy par 4 at the 424-yard dogleg left 13th, but then matches the outward half by stretching out over a finishing run highlighted by the strong 235-yard 15th, the 542-yard canal-crossing 16th and the 436-yard 18th, which plays to a green angled right-to-left behind sand.

Seagate Country Club - Delray Beach   ◆◆◆

Joe Lee   www.seagategolf.com
3600 Hamlet Dr, Delray Beach, FL 33445   (561) 498-7600
          7,103 yds   Par 72   Rating: 75.0 / 144   (1973)

Recently purchased by the nearby Seagate Hotel & Spa, this, the former Hamlet Golf Club, is one of Palm Beach County's more venerable facilities, having drawn considerable attention in its early days – though this was partially due to an affiliation with LPGA glamour girl Laura Baugh, then at the height of her image-driven fame. Lying one mile west of Interstate 95, the golf course is one of Joe Lee's more engaging creations, its housing-flanked fairways playing to greens which are mostly small, frequently narrow and always very tightly bunkered. Like most Lee designs, clear-cut strategic decisions are limited, but at least on this occasion the bunkering frequently calls for real shotmaking skills on approach. This is especially true at the 214-yard 6th (which plays to a long, very narrow green angled between bunkers) as well as at the 403-yard pond-guarded 7th and the well-bunkered (and newly lengthened) 613-yard 9th. The best golf is mostly reserved for the inward half, however, particularly over a closing stretch which is kicked off by the 506-yard 15th, whose green is flanked by a waterfall which may, perhaps, have been a bit less gimmicky in 1973. The 489-yard par-4 16th is the club's number one stroke hole and sets up the 129-yard 17th (played to a large, pond-flanked putting surface) and the 408-yard 18th, a narrow dogleg right to a green which bends around an invasive front-left bunker. Slightly tame by today's standards, but one of the region's better period designs.

Abacoa Golf Club - Jupiter ♦♦½

Joe Lee   www.abacoagolfclub.com
105 Barbados Dr, Jupiter, FL 33458   (561) 622-0036
            7,200 yds   Par 72   Rating: 75.0 / 142   (1999)

Despite its toney Jupiter address, the Abacoa Golf Club lies well inland, on a compact site wedged between Interstate 95 and the spring training complex shared by the St. Louis Cardinals and Florida Marlins. One of the final courses built by the prolific Joe Lee, the 7,200-yard layout is routed around a central residential neighborhood and, though of the standard Florida style, is quite testing, with water substantially affecting play on 12 holes. With the exception of the 587-yard 6th, the front nine's best entries are a watery quartet which includes the 553-yard 2nd (whose green is tucked left, beyond a pond), the 382-yard 3rd (played from island tees to a narrow peninsula fairway), the 423-yard dogleg right 7th and the 449-yard 9th, whose green is pinched between sand and front-left water. The back then commences with two more water-oriented tests, the 545-yard dogleg left 10th and the 318-yard 11th (whose driveable putting surface is button-hooked around a lake. The 235-yard 13th (angled across the same hazard) is an attention-getter, as are a pair of finishers whose right sides are similarly water-lined, the 546-yard 17th and the 456-yard 18th. Largely unaltered since 1999, this is solid – if not quite unique – stuff.

Atlantic National Golf Club - Lake Worth ♦♦½

Joe Lee   www.atlanticnationalgolfclub.com
6400 Grand Lacuna Blvd, Lake Worth, FL 33467   (561) 969-6600
            6,519 yds   Par 71   Rating: 70.6 / 130   (1985)

Located just west of Florida's Turnpike, the Atlantic National (née Grand Lacuna) Golf Club is a short, not terribly altered Joe Lee design routed around six separate residential neighborhoods. Once owned for more than a decade by Hall-of-Famer Doug Ford, the diminutive layout opens with its longest par 4 (the 430-yard dogleg left 1st) and later includes among its strongest entries the 533-yard 7th (a sweeping dogleg right, around water and a large corner bunker), the 401-yard pond-flanked 9th and the 568-yard 14th, which curls leftward around a lake. But at well under 6,500 yards, this is, inevitably, a course anchored by its smaller holes – a fitting circumstance given that Ford literally wrote the book (in 1963) on how to use a wedge. Shorter pond-affected par 4s are plentiful, with some of the best including the 377-yard creek-crossed 2nd, the potentially driveable 332-yard 3rd, the 391-yard 12th (where right-side water pinches into the fairway) and the 383-yard 13th (ditto). Throw in Lee's tightly bunkered greens and it all adds up to a track which, despite potentially being overlooked by the long-hitting modern player, offers a bit more golf than both the rating and slope might initially suggest.

Atlantis Country Club - Atlantis ◆◆

Robert Simmons   www.atlantiscountryclub.com
190 Atlantis Blvd, Atlantis, FL 33462   (561) 968-1300
               6,610 yds   Par 72   Rating: 71.9 / 133   (1971)

The second regulation facility in this tiny city of only 1.4 square miles (total population: 2,005), the Atlantis Country Club lies immediately north of the private Lost City Golf Club and is slightly newer, having been constructed in 1971 by ex-Dick Wilson sideman Robert Simmons. Though somewhat short in today's game, and taking only sporadic advantage of several native water hazards, the design offers enough obstacles (including trees) to require a fair element of precision. Predictably, much of the best golf tilts toward the small, including par 4s like the 363-yard dogleg left 4th and the tightly bunkered 343-yard 14th, as well as a nice quartet of par 3s led by the 147-yard bunker-ringed 5th, the 170-yard pond-fronted 8th and the 172-yard 17th, whose oddly shaped, tightly bunkered green shows a definite Dick Wilson influence. But several worthwhile longer entries are also present, led by the 419-yard 7th (where water lines the left side), the 525-yard lake-flanked 9th and the 435-yard 15th, whose fairway is pinched by several trees.

Boca Dunes Golf & Country Club - Boca Raton ◆◆

Robert von Hagge & Bruce Devlin   www.bocadunes.com
1400 Country Club Drive, Boca Raton, FL 33428   (561) 451-1600
               6,536 yds   Par 72   Rating: 72.0 / 129   (1970)

A short, mostly wide-open layout which, beyond a recent reconfiguring of its opening hole, hasn't changed too much since 1970, the Boca Dunes Golf & Country Club boasts little of the strategic quirkiness that graces many of von Hagge & Devlin's stronger works, but it offers enough in sand and some very narrow greens to present a decent challenge. Clearly, this was a layout intended for a wide range of golfers, a point driven home by a pair of parallel back nine par 5s (the 532-yard 10th and the 543-yard 18th) that could have utilized the narrow water hazard which separates them far more invasively than they did. Moreover, the average length of the par 4s is only 387 yards, though entries like the 359-yard lake-bordered 4th, the 415-yard 13th and the 372-yard 14th all offer a fairly high level of playing interest. Strongest, perhaps, is a collection of par 3s that includes the 191-yard water-flanked 9th, the 172-yard 11th and especially the 150-yard 17th, whose long but extremely narrow putting surface is squeezed by five bunkers. An adjoining von Hagge & Devlin-designed executive nine has recently been sold off for development.

Boca Greens Country Club - Boca Raton   ♦♦½

Joe Lee   www.bocagreenscountryclub.com
19642 Trophy Dr, Boca Raton, FL 33498   (561) 852-8800
            7,014 yds   Par 72   Rating: 73.2 / 136   (1980)

A residence-oriented facility sitting just over a mile east of the Everglades, the Boca Greens Country Club sports a 1980 Joe Lee-designed layout which, if somewhat Florida-predictable, does provide moments of interesting golf as well as some notably contoured putting surfaces. Though its bunkering has been refurbished, Lee's routing remains undisturbed, leaving water to enhance the challenge significantly on eight holes. The front nine lies north of the clubhouse and is the less exciting half, initially featuring holes like the 419-yard dogleg right 2nd and the tightly trapped 378-yard 5th before closing with the 439-yard 9th, which sweeps rightward around a lake and favors drives laid close to the water. The back initially offers two heavily bunkered short par 4s (the 361-yard 13th and 382-yard 14th) before ratcheting up the scale for a strong trio of finishers: the 220-yard over-water 16th, the 619-yard 17th (a demanding – and very watery - dogleg right) and the 393-yard 18th, whose heavily bunkered green is buffered by so much surrounding land that some may not even recognize it as being situated upon an island.

Boca Raton Municipal Golf Course - Boca Raton   ♦♦

Charles Ankrom   www.myboca.us
8111 Golf Course Rd, Boca Raton, FL 33434   (561) 367-7000
            6,714 yds   Par 72   Rating: 71.8 / 131   (1982)

A shortish but highly functional municipal facility situated just west of Florida's Turnpike, the Boca Raton Municipal Golf Course was built on a lake-dotted, housing-free site by Florida-based architect Charles Ankrom in 1982. In deference to the masses, mostly non-invasive use is made of the numerous water hazards; indeed, not a single forced carry of more than a few yards is required, and only at the 353-yard lake-bothered 6th and the 555-yard 15th (where most competent ball strikers will place their tee shot shy of two encroaching ponds) is the better golfer meaningfully threatened. Favorites initially include the 531-yard dogleg right 1st, the stiff 448-yard 8th and the 389-yard 9th, whose left-side fairway bunkers would be tactically worth flirting with were a cart path not separating them from the fairway. Coming home, bigger tests like the 545-yard 12th and the 415-yard 13th give the action a boost. A nine-hole executive loop (page 131) adjoins.

Links at Boynton Beach - Boynton Beach   ♦♦

Robert von Hagge & Bruce Devlin   www.boynton-beach.org/golf
8020 Jog Rd, Boynton Beach, FL 33472   (561) 742-6501
              6,292 yds   Par 71   Rating: 70.5 / 129   (1984)

Another highly functional municipal facility boasting something for everyone, the Links at Boynton Beach was built by the ever-popular team of von Hagge and Devlin in 1984, and features a compact track whose relatively limited bunkering might fairly allow it to be thought of as von Hagge & Devlin light. There are, however, several somewhat testing water holes present, including a trio of mid-size par 3s: the 186-yard 7th (with water front-left), the 179-yard 15th (angled across a pond) and the 178-yard bunkerless 17th. The 358-yard dogleg right 6th (whose green juts leftward into a lake) is also notable, as are the 307-yard 8th (theoretically driveable but to a sliver of a green tucked dangerously beyond front-right water) and the 374-yard 12th, a sweeping dogleg right daring the direct route over a narrow pond. The 309-yard 14th is another driveable entry, but once again to a very slim green, this time angled behind sand. Also present is strong executive nine (page 131) which offers several holes that would stand out on the main course.

Cypress Creek Country Club - Boynton Beach   ♦♦½

Robert von Hagge   www.cypresscreekcountryclub.com
9400 South Military Trail, Boynton Beach, FL 33436   (561) 732-4202
              6,531 yds   Par 72   Rating: 71.7 / 131   (1964)

Originally built in what was then undeveloped country three and a half miles inland from the Atlantic, the Cypress Creek Country Club is today marked by residential development both on its perimeters and within several small neighborhoods that dot its interior. It is also notable as the first solo design of Robert von Hagge, predating his partnership with Bruce Devlin by four years – though his maiden effort was favorably enough received to entertain the LPGA in both 1967 and 1968, with the latter event being won by Mickey Wright. Aside from von Hagge's bunkering having lost much of its rougher-edged flavor, little else has changed here, leaving a course which mixes some interesting, challenging holes with a smattering of more basic ones. The front nine features a run of three strong outlying entries: the 530-yard lake-guarded 3rd, the 404-yard 4th (where ideal drives flirt with right-side out-of-bounds) and the watery 357-yard 5th, which once shared a double green with the 3rd when such things were more novel. A pair of holes fronted by a canal (the 370-yard 13th and the 195-yard 14th) then lead a 3,158-yard back nine which later closes strongly with the 439-yard 18th, a gentle tree-lined dogleg right.

Delray Beach Golf Club - Delray Beach   ♦♦½

Donald Ross / Red Lawrence   www.delraybeachgolfclub.com
2200 Highland Ave, Delray Beach, FL 33445   (561) 243-7380
                6,907 yds   Par 72   Rating: 72.2 / 119   (1926)

Located two miles inland from the Atlantic Ocean and just west of Interstate 95, the Delray Beach Golf Club dates to a 1926 Donald Ross nine (today's inward half) which straddles the prominent El Rio canal. The present front nine was only added in 1950, apparently by Red Lawrence, and possibly to Ross's original routing. (A third loop, built by Dick Wilson and Robert Bruce Harris in 1962, today lies buried beneath a vast corporate development on the club's northeastern side.) Lawrence's slightly longer front nine plays through a range of modern-era bunkering and is led by holes like 401-yard 2nd (a dogleg left around a pond), the 451-yard 4th and the 528-yard 9th, a sharp and tightly bunkered dogleg left. Drawing the lion's share of interest, the Ross nine has seen major alteration to its early holes (the 561-yard canal-crossing 12th, for example, began life as a par 4) as well as to virtually all of its bunkering. Thus while holes like the 225-yard 13th, the 433-yard dogleg left 16th and the 417-yard straightaway 18th are strong enough entries, their ties to Ross are at this point attenuated at best. The golfing landscape has clearly changed, but there is enough history here – with names like Armour, Sarazen, Hogan and Snead having been regular prewar visitors – to make for an interesting stop.

Forest Oaks Golf Club - Lake Worth   ♦½

Unknown   www.forestoaksgc.com
144 Lucerne Lakes Blvd N, Lake Worth, FL 33467   (561) 967-6810
                5,823 yds   Par 71   Rating: 67.9 / 118   (1971)

A short and rather rudimentary track dating to 1971, the Forest Oaks Golf Club is a real estate-oriented layout which manages a par of 71 only by counting five sub-475-yard holes as par 5s (including the 410-yard 7th and the 443-yard 18th) as well as the 240-yard 3rd as a par 4. Predictably then, the golf is of a lower-octane variety, with better entries including the 412-yard 1st (a genuinely tough straightaway two-shotter), the 466-yard par-5 2nd (pinched between a creek left and out-of-bounds right), the 330-yard 4th (where a pond eats up much of the landing zone) and the over-classified 7th, which would otherwise be a strong, pond-fronted two-shotter. On the back nine, mature trees affect both the 470-yard 10th and the narrow 483-yard 12th, while the similarly tree-squeezed 380-yard 15th bends rightward, between water and condominiums.

Golf Club of Jupiter - Jupiter   ♦♦½

Lamar Smith   www.golfclubofjupiter.com
1800 South Central Blvd, Jupiter, FL 33458   (561) 747-6262
        6,235 yds   Par 70   Rating: 67.9 / 125   (1981)

Another unpretentious facility lacking a significant architectural pedigree, the Golf Club of Jupiter lies off the eastern flank of Interstate 95, where it sports one of the region's more uneven designs, blending numerous short, basic holes with a handful of gigantic and/or interesting ones. Going out, the latter category is led by a pair of back-to-back par 5s on opposite sides of a lake, the genuinely strong 545-yard 4th and the 495-yard 5th, where a water carry is necessary to successfully get home in two. The back nine saves its brighter moments for the late going, first at the 600-yard pond-flanked 14th, then with a closing trio composed of the 404-yard dogleg left 16th (where water lurks right of the green), the 383-yard 17th (a condominium- and bunker-tightened dogleg right) and the 408-yard 18th, where more condos line the left side and water sits right of the green.

Lake Worth Municipal Golf Course - Lake Worth   ♦♦½

William Langford / Dick Wilson   fwv
One 7th Ave North, Lake Worth, FL 33460   (561) 582-9713
        6,184 yds   Par 70   Rating: 69.2 / 121   (1925)

One of the best located municipal golf courses in the nation, the Lake Worth Muni fills over a mile of narrow Intracoastal Waterway frontage, a spot which provides both cooling breezes and a view across to the southern end of Palm Beach. Golf began here in 1925 with a much-chronicled William Langford-designed nine and has evolved – largely at the postwar hand of Dick Wilson – into the short, compact 18 in play today. While five holes parallel the Waterway, only the 533-yard 1st sits close enough to truly utilize it as a prominent hazard – though the 405-yard 10th and the 477-yard 7th are strong enough tests regardless. For many, most enjoyable will be a quintet of par 3s led by the 204-yard 4th, the 170-yard 9th (whose narrow, tightly bunkered green sits near a pond on the south side of the clubhouse), the 149-yard 14th (backdropped by the Waterway) and the tightly bunkered 150-yard 8th. Like several other Golden Age layouts in the region, Lake Worth's Collectability Rating lies as much in its venerability as the quality of its golf – with the facility's history being boosted by a four-year LPGA run (1957-1960) that counted Hall-of-Famers Betsy Rawls (twice) and Marlene Hagge among its champions.

Links at Madison Green - West Palm Beach   ◆◆◆

John Sanford   www.madisongreengolf.com
2001 Crestwood Blvd N, West Palm Beach, FL 33411   (561) 784-5225
7,000 yds   Par 72   Rating: 73.9 / 152   (2001)

A tough layout built in an area which sounds coastal but actually lies 12 miles inland from the Atlantic, the Links at Madison Green is a modern, hazards-everywhere sort of design routed among several large neighborhoods of single-family homes. Water significantly affects some 14 holes and bunkers of every shape and size are similarly prominent, providing plenty of chances for the average player to run up some big numbers. The longer front nine is led by a pair of mid-size par 3s (the 197-yard 4th and 194-yard 6th) played across large, angled bunkers, as well as the 508-yard lake-guarded 8th, where a centerline bunker also complicates the lay-up zone. Its most tactically inclined test, however, is the less attention-grabbing 381-yard 3rd, where drives across right-side water take a left-side pond out of play on approach. The back opens with the 449-yard 10th (which curves around more water) before featuring two potentially driveable par 4s, the 332-yard pond-narrowed 12th and the tricky 341-yard 15th. Play then concludes with a third par 3 angled over sand (the 211-yard 16th) followed by the 402-yard 17th (where the ideal drive skirts left-side water) and the 427-yard 18th, whose drive and approach are threatened first left, then right, by lakes. This is a cut above most public fare challenge-wise and, despite its myriad hazards, poses a fair number of strategic questions as well.

North Palm Beach Country Club - North Palm Beach   ◆◆◆

Jack Nicklaus   www.npbcc.org
951 U.S. Hwy 1, North Palm Beach, FL 33408   (561) 691-3420
7,028 yds   Par 71   Rating: 73.8 / 140   (2006)

Another modern South Florida municipal course with historic on-site roots, the North Palm Beach Country Club sits on land once occupied by the Palm Beach Winter Club, an exclusive 1926 MacDonald & Raynor layout which was slowly renovated out of existence after World War II. The present layout owes to a *pro bono* Jack Nicklaus re-design which resulted in one of the tougher munis around, a stiff test marked by a set of heavily contoured greens and bunkers which are both plentiful and punishing. Blessed with more rolling terrain than is the area norm, this is also a strategically inclined track, with fairway bunkering (including several prominent centerline hazards) often delineating tactically advantageous lines of play. Most memorable for many are a pair of holes bordering the Intracoastal Waterway (the 203-yard 5th and 430-yard 6th), but they are but a part of a front nine which also features the 606-yard pond-guarded 3rd, the 447-yard tree-narrowed 4th, the 373-yard 8th (which bends right, around more water) and the smartly bunkered 430-yard 9th. The back is longer and more heavily bunkered, with oversized sand affecting holes like the 358-yard 11th, the 444-yard 14th (a sharp dogleg left) and the 494-yard pond-guarded 16th, an imposing par 4. Water, for its part, appears meaningfully at the 511-yard 13th (right of the green) and on the 210-yard all-carry 17th. Though criticized by some for its difficulty, this is a vastly more engaging track than the largely mundane layout it replaced, and one of the stronger munis in the country.

Okeeheelee Golf Course - West Palm Beach ♦♦

Roy Case   www.pbcokeeheeleegolf.com
7715 Forest Hill Blvd, West Palm Beach, FL 33413   (561) 964-4653
          Heron/Eagle: 6,882 yds   Par 72   Rating: 74.2 / 136   (1995)
          Osprey: 3,301 yds   Par 36   Rating: 36.5 / 139   (1995)

The centerpiece of a large county park along the eastern side of Florida's Turnpike, the Okeeheelee Golf Course is a municipally operated facility offering 27 mid-size holes built by Roy Case in 1995. Its highest-rated combination pairs the Heron and Osprey nines, with the former leading with a pair of strong back-to-back par 4s at the 419-yard water-flanked 3rd and the 445-yard 4th before later closing with three holes whose utilization of a central lake is more scenic than strategic: the 395-yard dogleg left 7th, the 355-yard 8th (where a small pond also sits awkwardly in the center of the fairway) and the 203-yard 9th. The Eagle nine, meanwhile, is wedged into the property's northwestern corner, where, following the 512-yard pond-guarded 1st, it plays through a series of tightly dovetailed par 4s led by the 413-yard dogleg right 4th. The 508-yard dogleg left 8th then sets the table for the 464-yard dogleg right 9th, a demanding par 4 which sweeps sharply right, around the central lake and past a huge, short-right bunker. The Osprey loop is arguably the least interesting of the three and is led by a trio of solid par 5s: the 518-yard lake-flanked 1st, the 527-yard 5th (a sharp dogleg right that turns past a lake and the maintenance yard) and the 539-yard 9th, which twists between two lakes (and very close to the maintenance area) en route to a shallow bunkerless green.

Osprey Point Golf Course - Boca Raton   ♦♦

Roy Case   www.pbcospreypointgolf.com
12551 Glades Rd, Boca Raton, FL 33498   (561) 482-2868
          Falcon/Raven: 6,786 yds   Par 72   Rating: 72.6 / 136   (2010)
          Hawk: 3,312 yds   Par 36   Rating: 35.4 / 126   (2010)

Another Roy Case-designed 27-hole municipal facility, the Osprey Point Golf Course is a part of South County Regional Park, a multi-purpose facility built upon the site of a former strip mine adjacent to the Everglades. Given the limited portion of the park set aside for golf, there was little choice but for this to be a compact layout, a point demonstrated by the fact that its top-rated pairing – the Falcon and Raven nines – measure under 6,800 yards. The former runs out to the site's northern tip where it offers a pair of strong holes whose waste bunkers in spots double as cart paths (something of a trademark here), the 538-yard pond-bothered 3rd and the 325-yard wetlands-fronted 4th. The loop also closes in style with the 510-yard 9th, a double dogleg daring a long second across a corner of the park's central lake. The Raven is the longest nine and shows its (relative) muscle over a trio of holes in its mid-section (the 437-yard waste bunker-crossed 4th, the 600-yard 5th and the 222-yard 7th) before closing with the 333-yard pond-squeezed 9th. The Hawk fills the southernmost part of the park and is pretty solid stuff as "third" nines go, initially challenging with the 577-yard canal-lined 2nd before closing with a strong, varied trio: the 300-yard 7th (played to a wide, very shallow green), the 190-yard 8th (angled across the lake) and the 555-yard split-fairway 9th, which features a waste bunker-divided fairway and a lake-guarded green. Solid municipal fare made more enticing by a complete lack of development around all but its southern edges.

Palm Beach National Golf Club - Lake Worth   ♦♦½

Porter Gibson   www.palmbeachnational.com
7500 St. Andrews Rd, Lake Worth, FL 33467   (561) 965-3381
              6,734 yds   Par 72   Rating: 73.1 / 133   (1962)

Lying along Florida's Turnpike, immediately south of Okeeheelee Park, the Palm Beach National Golf Club was among the more ambitious designs of North Carolina-based architect J. Porter Gibson, its island-green 3rd hole in particular being somewhat ahead of its time back in 1962. Filling a rectangular site with multiple residential neighborhoods extending into it from the perimeter, the layout had numerous bunkers added by Joe Lee during a 1978 renovation and is today a mid-size track offering a more established feel than many in the region. Though hardly of the all-or-nothing TPC Sawgrass variety, the front nine's showpiece remains the flashy 165-yard 3rd, with the rest of the loop being anchored by a trio of mid-size par 4s: the 407-yard 4th, the 426-yard dogleg right 5th and the 414-yard sand-narrowed 6th. The inward half (which includes only one par 3 and one par 5) is a touch less engaging, with its best entries being a pair of late sub-400-yard par 4s: the 390-yard 15th (where aggressive drives carry right-side water) and the 358-yard 18th, whose green features railroad tie bulkheading added by Lee. Though often viewed (and marketed) as a Joe Lee design, this remains mostly Porter Gibson's work.

Park Ridge Golf Course - Lake Worth   ♦♦

Roy Case   www.pbcparkridgegolf.com
9191 Lantana Rd, Lake Worth, FL 33467   (561) 966-7044
              6,707 yds   Par 72   Rating: 72.2 / 123   (2007)

A new millennium project built on the site of a retired landfill, the municipally owned and operated Park Ridge Golf Course utilizes the "natural" features of the land, resulting in far more rolling golfing terrain than one generally finds in these parts. The property's treeless nature also played nicely into the idea of a *faux* links design, a logical concept which, with the exception of the brief use of an existing lake and some flowery bunkering definitely *not* borrowed from the St Andrews, is how Roy Case's 2007 work turned out. Though play opens with a 597-yard par 5, the majority of the layout's muscle comes later, particularly through a middle stretch that includes the 439-yard 8th (a dogleg left to a green wedged into the property's southeast corner), a pair of imposingly large par 3s at the 237-yard 9th and the 238-yard 11th, and the 524-yard 12th, where the lake hugs nearly the entire left side. On the whole, a layout which may not rate among the region's very best, but which certainly provides something different – and quite ecologically useful – on a site where such productive results were hardly guaranteed.

Polo Trace Golf Club - Delray Beach   ♦♦½

Karl Litten & Joey Sindelar   www.polotracegolf.com
13479 Hagen Ranch Rd, Delray Beach, FL 33446   (561) 495-5300
              7,068 yds   Par 72   Rating: 74.6 / 139   (1990)

Still another facility built in the shadow of Florida's Turnpike, the Polo Trace Golf Club also represents yet another venture into the fruitless world of attempting to replicate links golf – but while no one is likely to confuse this with St Andrews or Muirfield, there is some interesting action here. The front nine remains within the property's core, well away from the housing which flanks only the southern and western sides. Initially offering a pair of watery, stonewall-buttressed par 3s at the 136-yard 2nd and the 190-yard 5th, its interest level peaks towards the close, where the 429-yard dogleg right 8th bends around a huge bunker and the 566-yard 9th is an imposing, water-crossing par 5. The routing actually includes three par 5s in succession as both the 10th and 11th are lake-dotted three-shotters lying outside the adjacent housing, the latter running parallel to the Turnpike. Thereafter, the inward half is headed by a trio of water-oriented tests: the 162-yard 12th, the 437-yard pond-guarded 14th and the 440-yard finisher, whose green is guarded right by both a lake and a long, narrow bunker. One of Karl Litten's more appealing designs – perhaps due to input from Champions Tour player Joey Sindelar?

Polo West Golf Club - Delray Beach   ♦½

Ted McAnlis   www.polowestgolf.com
2470 Greenview Cove Dr, Wellington, FL 33414   (561) 328-3800
              3,271 yds   Par 36   Rating: 36.2 / 138   (1980)

Originally operating under the name Greenview Cove, today's Polo West Golf Club began life as an 18-hole facility laid out upon a large, U-shaped site in a then-rapidly developing area by Ted McAnlis in 1980. The club ran into financial problems in the mid-2000s, however, actually closing for several years before being revived as a nine-hole track in 2012. Gone are the nine holes that filled the eastern side of the U, leaving a short loop that remains largely as it was designed, minus several large (but not terribly relevant) bunkers. Following an out-and-back routing up the west side of the U, it is led by the 385-yard water-lined 2nd, the 470-yard par-5 3rd (whose green is tucked beyond front-left water) and the 353-yard 7th, a gentle dogleg left dotted with occasionally invasive trees.

Sandhill Crane Golf Club - Palm Beach Gardens   ◆◆

Roy Case   www.pbgfl.com
11401 Northlake Blvd, Palm Beach Gardens, FL 33412   (561) 630-1160
            6,504 yds   Par 72   Rating: 72.0 / 136   (1992)

A municipally owned and operated facility in the city's less developed western reaches, this, the former Palm Beach Gardens Golf Course, is a short but fairly challenging layout shoehorned into a narrow, wetlands-laced property sitting diagonally across Northlake Boulevard from the PGA National Resort's Estates course. Originally laid out by Roy Case in 1992, it was renovated by former Greg Norman associate Matthew Dusenberry in 2013 – though given the compact, wetlands-squeezed nature of the routing, that job was primarily about rebunkering on a smaller scale. The front nine is routed south of the clubhouse and offers mostly basic, functional design save for a trio of holes built around a pair of central lakes: the 504-yard dogleg right 1st, the 391-yard dogleg left 6th and the 480-yard dogleg left 9th, which dares the better player to attempt a bold carry off the tee. The back ventures into the wetlands, with the marshes significantly affecting favorites like the 428-yard 11th (squeezed between wetlands and out-of-bounds), the 471-yard double dogleg 13th and especially the 546-yard 18th, an imposing marsh-crossing finisher.

Southwinds Golf Course - Boca Raton   ◆½

Unknown   www.southwindsgolfcourse.com
19557 Lyons Rd, Boca Raton, FL 33434   (561) 483-1305
            6,018 yds   Par 70   Rating: 68.8 / 127   (1977)

A short, manageable layout located across Lake Windermere from the western flank of Florida's Turnpike, the Southwinds Golf Course enjoys an absence of housing within the layout itself and is routed among a network of interrelated water hazards – virtually none of which affect play in too direct a fashion. Lacking a design pedigree and weighing in at just a shade over 6,000 yards, it is a layout upon which longer holes come at a premium, though the 426-yard 1st, the 539-yard 5th (where water lingers right) and the 509-yard pond-crossing 10th are sizeable enough. But thereafter, favorites are all of the shorter variety, with better entries including a decent trio to close out the front nine: the 189-yard 7th, the 367-yard 8th (where the ideal drive challenges left-side water) and the 175-yard well-bunkered 9th. Most noteworthy on the inward half is the 377-yard 15th, the entirety of which is an island within the largest of the lakes.

Sugar Cane Golf Club - Belle Glade   ♦♦

Unknown / Gary Player & Karl Litten
2619 West Canal St, Belle Glade, FL 33430   (561) 996-6605
                6,558 yds   Par 72   Rating: 71.3 / 126   (1946)

By far the most inland course in Palm Beach County, the Sugar Cane Golf Club lies near the southeast shore of Lake Okeechobee, in an area responsible for nearly half of America's annual sugar cane output. The course began life as the nine-hole Belle Glade Municipal immediately after World War II, then had a second nine added – half a mile down West Lake Road – by Gary Player and Karl Litten in 1987. Nearly surrounded by cane fields, it is thus a course in two parts, with the older front nine offering smaller greens, a more basic design and only two somewhat significant holes: the 521-yard creek-crossed 2nd and the pond- and creek-guarded 469-yard 5th, a tough par 4. Player and Litten's back nine, on the other hand, measures 3,461 yards and is built to a more modern (if lightly bunkered) standard, with a pair of pond-guarded openers (the 569-yard 10th and the 411-yard 11th) initially raising the bar, and the 376-yard 15th (which dares a long, angled carry across water) leading the charge thereafter.

Village Golf Club - Royal Palm Beach   ♦♦

Mark Mahannah   www.thevillagegolfclub.com
122 Country Club Dr, Royal Palm Beach, FL 33411   (561) 793-1400
                6,860 yds   Par 72   Rating: 72.7 / 134   (1975)

Located in the county's only inland municipality to use "Beach" in its name, the Village Golf Club actually lies 12 miles inland from the Atlantic Ocean where it was built by popular regional designer Mark Mahannah on a narrow, residence-lined site in 1975. Though missing a number of original bunkers (especially on the back nine), it remains a decent test, but one which provides ample playing room by utilizing water frequently, but mostly along its flanks. The front nine runs out to the north and is led by a pair of mid-size par 4s (the 428-yard 1st and the 421-yard lake-bothered 4th) as well as the 510-yard 9th, where left-side water keeps the lay up honest. The back quickly provides some muscle of its own at the 529-yard 11th and the 449-yard 12th before including two of the club's more water-oriented tests (the 194-yard 14th and the 182-yard 17th) followed by a big finish at the 567-yard 18th, a dogleg left with water down much of its left side.

West Palm Beach Golf Course - West Palm Beach   ◆◆◆

Dick Wilson   www.wpalmbeachgc.com
7001 Parker Ave, West Palm Beach, FL 33405   (561) 582-2019
7,002 yds   Par 71   Rating: 73.0 / 128   (1947)

Built in 1947 near the banks of the Palm Beach Canal (today's adjacent Interstate 95 was not yet even a dream), the West Palm Beach Golf Course is historically important both as the building block of South Florida's eventual postwar golf boom and as the course most directly responsible for launching Dick Wilson's prolific design career. Initially operating in relative obscurity, the layout came to national attention by hosting the PGA Tour's old West Palm Beach Open from 1955-1962 (the first three unofficially), with Arnold Palmer, Gay Brewer and Gardner Dickinson included among the winners. Wilson's design added no water hazards to the rolling (for Florida) site, and its initial routing remains completely intact today. The landscape (and bunkering) have been altered quite a bit, however, as a 2009 Mark McCumber renovation removed numerous trees and created wide swaths of "native" sand between holes, resulting in an imposing and attractive (if somewhat contrived) aesthetic. McCumber's revamped bunkering may be little match for Wilson's, but the course retains plenty of backbone in its collection of longer par 4s, led by the 465-yard uphill 4th, the 435-yard 6th, the 440-yard 9th and the 478-yard dogleg right 10th. Also notable are two long par 5s (the 588-yard straightaway 2nd and the 565-yard uphill 18th) as well as the driveable (but tightly bunkered) 326-yard 5th, which backs up against the interstate. History accounted for, this is palpably strong municipal stuff.

Westchester Golf & Country Club - Boynton Beach   ◆◆

Karl Litten   www.westchestercc.com
12250 Westchester Club Dr, Boynton Beach, FL 33437   (561) 369-1000
Red/Blue: 6,772 yds   Par 72   Rating: 72.3 / 143   (1988)
Gold: 3,310 yds   Par 36   Rating: 35.8 / 138   (1988)

A residential facility whose 27 holes were built by Karl Litten, the Westchester Golf & Country Club's three nines fan out in different directions but are all squeezed in around the edges (and occasionally through the heart) of vast collections of single-family houses. With numerous sharp doglegs thus a fact of life throughout, the top-rated combination of nines pairs the Red and Blue, with the Red starting with the club's most imposing hole, a 573-yard par 5 which bends nearly 90 degrees around a pond. The loop's remaining (shorter) favorites include the 333-yard 5th (whose green is tucked behind right-side water) and two more pond-guarded tests, the 380-yard 7th and the 389-yard 9th. The Blue runs out to the east where, beyond the 201-yard 7th (all carry across a pond), it is led by a trio of mid-size, water-bothered par 4s: the 404-yard 2nd (a 90-degree dogleg left) the 383-yard bunkerless 5th and especially the 420-yard 9th, which bends rightward, along a large lake to a heavily bunkered green. The Gold nine is situated a short cart ride north of the clubhouse and, after the lake-flanked 420-yard 1st, features the 360-yard dogleg right 4th (where a row of bunkers guards the aggressive driving line), the 493-yard 5th (another 90-degree dogleg around a lake), the 506-yard water-lined 16th and the 385-out-of-bounds-flanked 18th, whose fairway narrows greatly the longer one's drive.

Club at Winston Trails - Lake Worth   ◆◆

Joe Lee   www.winstontrailsgolfclub.com
6101 Winston Trails Blvd, Lake Worth, FL   33463   (561) 439-3700
        7,084 yds   Par 72   Rating: 74.1 / 134   (1993)

One of Joe Lee's later designs, the Club at Winston Trails has a somewhat more modern look about it, mostly due to its cape-and-bay-style bunkering which, while hardly wild by contemporary standards, is flashier than the well-established Lee norm. A real estate-oriented layout to its core, the course is routed in two clockwise circles around vast residential neighborhoods and, though challenging enough, offers fairly little in the way of major tactical questions. The front nine in particular is mostly functional, its lone true highlight coming at the 569-yard 9th, a vast dogleg right around a lake. With water more regularly a factor on the back, the interest level picks up noticeably, first at the 469-yard dogleg right 11th (where a large lake again fills the corner), then towards the close at the 529-yard yard 15th (a sharp, soundly bunkered dogleg right around another lake) and the 380-yard 16th, yet another hole which curls rightward around water. Like most Joe Lee layouts, this is dependably solid – even if the bunkering is a stylistic mystery.

Boca Delray Golf & Country Club - Delray Beach   ♦½

Karl Litten   www.bocadelray.net
5483 Boca Delray Blvd, Delray Beach, FL 33484   (561) 495-1597
              3,197 yds   Par 60   Rating: 56.5 / 96   (1983)

A private 18-hole executive facility, Boca Delray is a 1983 Karl Litten design whose expansive routing meanders through a residential community. Six par 4s are present, led by two which require dangerous over-water approaches, the 277-yard 2nd and the 333-yard 16th. Among the one-shotters, favorites include the 133-yard 11th and the 119-yard 14th (which play to shallow, bulkheaded greens) and the tiny 94-yard 15th, which hops more water en route to one last narrow, railroad-tied putting surface.

Boca Raton Municipal Golf Course - Boca Raton   ♦½

Charles Ankrom   www.ci.boca-raton.fl.us/rec/golf
8111 Golf Course Rd, Boca Raton, FL 33434   (561) 483-5226
              1,877 yds   Par 30   Rating: - / -   (1982)

Like the regulation half of Boca Raton's municipal golf facility, this, an adjacent executive nine offers solid muni fare over the course of its 1,877 yards. As with the full-size layout, several lakes are utilized more scenically than invasively, but there is plenty of relevant bunkering present, as are three par 4s in excess of 300 yards. Among the loop's best are the 330-yard 1st, the 310-yard 4th (where the angle of a slender green encourages tee shots skirting a right-side lake), the 160-yard 5th and the 122-yard tightly bunkered 6th.

Links at Boynton Beach (Family) - Boynton Beach   ♦♦

Robert von Hagge & Bruce Devlin   www.boynton-beach.org
8020 Jog Rd, Boynton Beach, FL 33437   (561) 742-6502
              1,940 yds   Par 30   Rating: 30.2 / 103   (1984)

Though obviously of a dramatically smaller scale, nine-hole Family course at the Links at Boynton Beach bears the odd (but pleasant) distinction of possibly being more interesting than the regulation layout it abuts. Notably, the loop includes three good-size par 4s (measuring 348, 380 and 351 yards), but it is within a group of water-affected par 3s that the most engaging golf is found. Tops among these are the 139-yard 3rd, the 122-yard 4th (played to a forgiving near-island green), the 172-yard lakeside 6th and the 158-yard 7th.

Cypress Lakes - West Palm Beach   ♦

Ron Garl
3445 Cypress Trail, West Palm Beach, FL 33417   (561) 640-1044
             1,763 yds   Par 57   Rating: - / -   (1988)

A private executive layout which includes only three par 4s among its 18 holes, Cypress Lakes is credited to Ron Garl but shows little of the modern flair and styling typical of his work. Indeed, occupying a narrow, mostly dry strip of land along the western flank of a residential development, it is mostly short and basic, offering only a rudimentary level of play as it runs along/around several neighborhoods of small, single-family homes.

Jupiter Dunes Golf Course - Jupiter   ♦½

Bob Erickson   www.jupiterdunesgolf.com
401 North A1A, Jupiter, FL 33477   (561) 746-6654
             2,036 yds   Par 54   Rating: 65.0 / 100   (1973)

One of the region's more admirably situated par 3 layouts, the Jupiter Dunes Golf Course lies only yards from the Atlantic, where its two nines straddle Jupiter Beach Road and run among lakes, estuaries and, alas, condominiums. Renovated (though not hugely) by ex-Jack Nicklaus associate Thomas Pearson in 2003, its design is actually of a fairly basic standard, though its bunker shaping and overall aesthetic rise somewhat above the short-course norm. While a pair of tiny front nine entries (the 70-yard 3rd and 90-yard 4th) require water carries, equally favored are a pair of straight-ahead holes which border an inlet of the Loxahatchee River, the 133-yard 13th and the 135-yard 14th.

Kings Point Golf (Executive) - Delray Beach   ♦♦

Robert Trent Jones   www.kingspointdelray.com
7000 West Atlantic Ave, Delray Beach, FL 33446   (561) 499-7840
             3,794 yds   Par 60   Rating: 59.2 / 103   (1972)

Planted within a veritable sea of condominiums, Kings Point Golf is rather a unique facility, boasting a pair of short courses – one executive, one par 3 – built by the venerable Robert Trent Jones. As one might expect, the standard of design is thus somewhat higher here than on many such layouts, particularly on the Executive course, which winds amidst a network of lakes and includes among its six par 4s the 388-yard lake-flanked 5th, the 341-yard pond-fronted 8th and the 331-yard sand- and pond-guarded 17th. Even more engaging is a group of par 3s whose frontal and angled bunkering creates some genuine playing interest, including the 179-yard 12th and the 122-yard 16th.

Kings Point Golf (Par 3) - Delray Beach   ♦½

Robert Trent Jones   www.kingspointdelray.com
7000 West Atlantic Ave, Delray Beach, FL 33446   (561) 499-7840
            2,094 yds   Par 54   Rating: 52.1 / -   (1973)

Kings Point Golf's Par 3 course lies a quarter-mile to the northwest of the club's executive
layout where it occupies an L-shaped tract and is less ambitious in its approach. Indeed,
with water in play (and then only moderately) on three occasions, and only two holes in
excess of 140 yards, this is a layout which relies entirely on greenside bunkering for
playing interest. Thankfully, there is a good variety of it here.

Lakeview Golf Club - Delray Beach   ♦

John Walker   www.lakeviewgcdelray.com
1200 Dover Rd, Delray Beach, FL 33445   (561) 498-3229
            3,006 yds   Par 60   Rating: 57.4 / 90   (1972)

Occupying a long, narrow tract which runs through a neighborhood of single-family
homes, the Lakeview Golf Club is presumably named for the large water hazard which
flanks its 4th and 5th holes, then cuts awkwardly in front of the green at the 232-yard 6th –
because there are no other lakes in sight. The design is fairly basic and quite short, the
longest of its six par 4s measuring all of 284-yards. That, however, is the more appealing
8th, which doglegs sharply left around a pond, daring an aggressive drive.

Leisureville Community Golf Course - Boynton Beach   ♦

Unknown
1007 Ocean Dr, Boynton Beach, FL 33426   (561) 732-0593
            1,839 yds   Par 54   Rating: - / -   (1970)

Situated half a mile west of Interstate 95, in the northwestern corner of this Boynton
Beach retirement community, the Leisureville Community Golf Course is a private, 18-
hole par-3 facility routed around a central lake. A slightly more engaging design than its
sister Leisureville nine in Pompano Beach, it is routed to allow the lake to flank more than
half the holes, though never too closely. But this watery ambience notwithstanding, with
few exceptions, the overall standard of play remains pretty rudimentary.

The Little Club - Delray Beach   ◆◆

Joe Lee
100 Little Club Rd, Delray Beach, FL 33483   (561) 278-5830
                    2,102 yds   Par 54   Rating: - / -   (1969)

A private 18-hole par 3 facility of some repute, the Joe Lee-designed Little Club sits upon
some very expensive Delray Beach real estate, with its western boundary being the
Intracoastal Waterway and the Atlantic Ocean washing ashore just a mid-iron away to
the east. The course features holes ranging from 74 to 177 yards, with water often
visible but rarely affecting the competent ball-striker. Two holes which border the
Intracoastal (the 150-yard 11th and the 120-yard 17th) are perhaps the most memorable,
but tightly bunkered tests like the 107-yard 5th and the 116-yard 6th, plus the two lake-
guarded entries (the 131-yard 14th and 119-yard 18th) offer the most engaging golf.

Lone Pine Golf Course - West Palm Beach   ◆

Richard LaConte & Ted McAnlis   www.lonepinegolfclub.com
6251 North Military Trail, West Palm Beach, FL 33407   (561) 285-3854
                    4,120 yds   Par 62   Rating: 58.7 / 85   (1981)

The rare completely bunkerless layout in Southeast Florida, the Lone Pine Golf Course is
an executive track routed among single-family homes less than a mile west of Interstate
95. As this is no Royal Ashdown Forest, the lack of sand makes for some decidedly
rudimentary golf, resulting in a round briefly enlivened by four holes which make passing
use of two lakes: the 295-yard 3rd, the 150-yard 4th, the 370-yard 13th (comfortably the
club's longest) and the 165-yard 14th. Overall, as basic as its bunker count suggests.

Palm Beach Par 3 Golf Course - Palm Beach   ◆◆

Dick Wilson   www.golfontheocean.com
2345 South Ocean Blvd, Palm Beach, FL 33480   (561) 547-0598
                    2,572 yds   Par 54   Rating: - / -   (1961)

Joining Seminole and Gulf Stream as the region's only courses to have holes built directly
into seaside dunes, the Palm Beach Par 3 Golf Course fills an incalculably valuable 27-acre
site stretching across Palm Beach from the Atlantic to the Intracoastal Waterway, with
Ocean Boulevard slashing through its center. Holding a mixed-gender professional event
(won by Louise Suggs) upon its 1961 opening, the once-private layout is today owned by
the city and was modernized heavily by Raymond Floyd in 2009. Floyd added various
bells and whistles but the golf is still fairly basic, with highlights including a trio of holes
perched along the Waterway (numbers 5, 6 and 7) and, of course, the three that lie
beachside: the 171-yard 13th, the 129-yard 14th and the 179-yard 18th.

Poinciana Country Club - Lake Worth   ♦♦

Joe Lee   www.poincianacc.com
3536 Via Poinciana, Lake Worth, FL 33467   (561) 439-4721
          4,561 yds   Par 64   Rating: 60.9 / 103   (1974)

Though measuring only 4,135 yards, the Joe Lee-designed Poinciana Country Club might almost be called the world's shortest regulation-size golf course, for how many executive layouts include a 400-yard par 4 and a trio of par 5s, one measuring 550 yards? Several of these (especially the 400-yard canal crossed 9th and the 470-yard 10th) would fit nicely on most regulation-size layouts and there are relatively few weak entries throughout, with Lee's aggressive greenside bunkering lifting this well above standard short-course fare. Beyond the 9th and 10th, the 162-yard 11th (played to a narrow, angled green) and the 375-yard pond-flanked 15th are particularly worthy of note. Elite of its type.

Red Reef Executive Golf Course - Boca Raton

Charles Ankrom   www.mybocaparks.org
1221 North Ocean Blvd, Boca Raton, FL 33434   (561) 391-5014
          1,357 yds   Par 32   Rating: - / -   (1961)

Given its marvelous seaside location (the 86-yard 7th and 165-yard 8th holes sit just above the beach), the Charles Ankrom-designed Red Reef Golf Course is surprisingly unknown outside of its immediate neighborhood. Of course, much of this anonymity lies in the basic nature of its design, and the fact that its par of 32 really ought to be 27, as its "par 4s" range from 165 to 227 yards. Basic fare, then, but in an anything-but-basic setting.

St. Andrews Club - Delray Beach   ♦♦

Pete & Alice Dye   www.standrewsclub.org
4475 North Ocean Blvd, Delray Beach, FL 33483   (561) 272-5050
          1,784 yds   Par 54   Rating: - / -   (1973)

A private, 18-hole par-3 facility built by Pete and Alice Dye, the St. Andrews Club sits along the Intracoastal Waterway where, though devoid of most of Dye's traditional flashy trimmings, it features a pleasant tropical ambience and plenty of solid, well-bunkered holes. The front nine runs along the property's perimeter and is led by two entries which sit flush to the Waterway, the 82-yard 3rd and the 172-yard 5th. The shorter inward half then negotiates several interior lakes, peaking with two waterside closers, the 90-yard 17th and the 94-yard 18th. Though the average hole length is only 99 yards, a pleasant (if quick) round – and one blessed with an uncommon design pedigree for a par-3 layout.

Sherwood Park Golf Course - Delray Beach   ◆

William Amick

170 Sherwood Forest Dr, Delray Beach, FL 33445   (561) 499-3559

3,438 yds   Par 62   Rating: - / -   (1968)

Though designed by well-known Florida architect William Amick, the Sherwood Park Golf Course is a mostly rudimentary executive facility, its 3,438-yard 18 boasting less than 10 bunkers and no water hazards — though two lakes and the narrow canal which today is partially piped underground affected play when the layout opened in 1959. The course's maturity has allowed for significant tree growth, however, which adds challenge, particularly on dogleg holes like the 289-yard 3rd and the 312-yard 16th.

MARTIN COUNTY

Dye Preserve Golf Club - Jupiter   ♦♦♦½

Pete Dye   www.thedyepreserve.com
1808 Colony Way, Jupiter, FL 33478   (561) 575-7891
          7,301 yds   Par 72   Rating: 76.0 / 151   (1988)

Originally known as Cypress Links, the secluded Dye Preserve Golf Club sits four miles
west of Interstate 95 and has been in existence since 1988 - though its reputation jumped
significantly following a Pete Dye renovation in 2002. While Dye retained all of his own
original routing, numerous smaller changes were made, resulting in a more playable, less
manufactured layout, yet also one whose challenge remains quite high – as a 76.0 rating
and several very long par 4s suggest. The 566-yard double-dogleg opener draws its share
of praise but the highly compact front nine is also highlighted by three more early holes:
the 170-yard 3rd (angled along a left-side pond, but with bailout room available), the 469-
yard 4th (where more water sits left of the fairway and right of the green) and especially
the tempting 299-yard 5th, a driveable lakeside par 4 whose approach is tightly squeezed
between bunkers. Both the 508-yard 9th and the 429-yard 11th (where water and sand
encroach front-left of the putting surface) are high octane two-shotters, and set up an
inward half led by a pair of deluxe par 3s, the heavily bunkered 230-yard 12th (described
by Dye as a "semi-Redan," and played to a demanding plateau green) and the 240-yard
17th, which angles over water to a railroad tie-buttressed target angling into the hazard.
Cap it all off with the 461-yard 18th and one is left with a track which may not rate among
the absolute Dye elite, but whose mix of strong holes, minimal trickery, lots of room to
hit the driver and limited housing (all situated well back from lines of play) make Dye
Preserve one of South Florida's more desirable options.   (GD: #23 State)

Floridian - Palm City   ♦♦♦½

Tom Fazio   www.floridian.cc
3700 SE Floridian Dr, Palm City, FL 34990   (772) 781-1000
          7,114 yds   Par 71   Rating: 74.7 / 145   (2012)

Situated at the tip of a peninsula extending into the St. Lucie River (where much of its
acreage actually lies in St. Lucie County), the Floridian was the mid-1990s brainchild of
South Florida sports magnate H. Wayne Huizenga, who hired Gary Player to build a golf
course to anchor his under-the-radar ultra-private hideout. But in 2010 Huizenga sold
the club to Houston Astros owner Jim Crane, who began turning it into a more traditional
sort of operation, and quickly hired Tom Fazio to undertake a significant golf course
makeover. In truth, some of today's design credit still belongs with Player, for large
chunks of his routing remain intact - but with several entirely new holes and significant
stylistic changes, in play, the layout can more reasonably be called Fazio's now. The
biggest aesthetic change is the conversion of bunkering from Player's wild, often over-
the-top hazards to smaller, more traditional-looking ones, such as the centerline bunker
fronting the green at the demanding 454-yard 3rd. But sand notwithstanding, it is water
which defines several of the front nine's best, including the 182-yard lakeside 4th, the
301-yard driveable 6th and the 153-yard pond-crossing 8th. The back begins in similar
fashion, with the 448-yard 11th bending along a left-side pond and the 194-yard 12th
doubling back over the same hazard. At the close, the 385-yard 17th requires a long
wetlands carry en route to a riverside green, while the 493-yard 18th is a huge par 4
routed directly along the shoreline. A more stylish track than Player's original, this seems
likely to rise in stature in the years ahead. (GD: #18 State   GW: #142 Modern)

The Fox Club - Palm City ♦♦½

Roy Case
10664 Whooping Crane Way, Palm City, FL 34990
7,115 yds   Par 72   Rating: 74.5 / 148   (1989)

www.foxclubfl.com
(772) 597-4222

Occupying an inland site which borders the northbound side of Interstate 95, and whose northern boundary is the St. Lucie County line, The Fox Club was initially built as the anchor of a relatively low-density housing development by Roy Case in 1989. But in 2004, a new ownership hired future British Open champion Darren Clarke and 1989 Walker Cup participant Eoghan O'Connell to perform a renovation – a job which retained all of Case's original routing and green complexes but added length and downsized bunkering, leaving a more polished, classic-feeling track in their wake. Play opens with four holes running southward along the Interstate (the strongest being the 439-yard lakeside 3rd) before the action picks up as the backdrop quiets, with remaining outgoing favorites including the 203-yard pond crossing 7th and the 536-yard 8th, a water-menaced dogleg left. The longer back nine is most memorable for its 162-yard near-island green 15th and the 586-yard 18th (which bends 90 degrees leftward around a lake) but the loop also includes several strong par 4s, led by the 438-yard wetlands-flanked 10th, the 444-yard 11th, the 427-yard bunker- and water-pinched 14th, and the 440-yard dogleg right 16th. Given several long, wetlands-necessitated treks between greens and tee, it is strictly cartball here.

Hobe Sound Golf Club - Hobe Sound ♦♦½

Joe Lee
11671 SE Plandome Drive, Hobe Sound, FL 33455
6,664 yds   Par 72   Rating: 72.3 / 144   (1988)

www.hobesoundgolfclub.com
(772) 546-4600

Lying nearly two miles inland, where most of its flanks are buffered by jungle and other undeveloped terrain, the Hobe Sound Golf Club draws far less attention than neighbors like the McArthur and Medalist Clubs, perhaps due to the relative shortness of Joe Lee's 1988 design. But Lee's largely unaltered creation is, like most entries in his long portfolio, eminently solid, offering plenty of interesting golf – albeit on a somewhat limited scale. The front nine works its way around a small neighborhood of single-family homes in the property's northern half, where a fairly staid list of favorites includes the 345-yard 2nd (a tempting dogleg left around a lake), the 392-yard 4th (one of the least imposing number one stroke holes around) and the 528-yard pond-flanked 8th. The back picks up the pace a bit, starting with the 362-yard 11th (where stronger drives flirt with a right-side lake) and the 516-yard 12th, a sharp dogleg right around wetlands, with part of the hazard invasively filling the corner. The 402-yard 13th doglegs right, around a prominent corner bunker, while the close in led by the 217-yard 17th and the 388-yard finisher, where a right-side pond threatens full drives and lies before a shallow, angled putting surface.

Jupiter Hills Club (Hills) - Tequesta   ◆◆◆◆

George Fazio   www.jupiterhillsclub.org
11800 SE Hill Club Terrace, Tequesta, FL 33469   (561) 746-5151
7,344 yds   Par 70   Rating: 77.1 / 150   (1970)

It can be argued that no postwar golf facility in the history of South Florida drew as much attention in its early years as George Fazio's original Hills course at the Jupiter Hills Club, attention which manifested itself not just in articles and photos but also in its being ranked among *Golf Digest's* top 30 in America during the mid-1970s. But while the Hills course certainly maintains a significant national profile today, *that* level adoration would eventually prove fleeting, arguably because it was rooted in two qualities whose novelty would lessen in later years. First, Jupiter Hills was the exceedingly rare Florida layout to utilize major undulations within its design, with sections of the course climbing Conch Bar Hill, a sand dune-covered ridge rising as high as 70 feet (a true geographic quirk given that the site lies only 200 yards from the Intracoastal Waterway). Indeed, the property offers so much variance that noted architect/critic Tom Doak has called it "a bit too hilly" – not a charge that's frequently thrown about in the Sunshine State. Jupiter Hills' second major 1970 uniqueness – one which has become commonplace today - was that it was the first modern Florida course to substantially incorporate the state's natural sandy terrain in its design, as Fazio chose not to grass over the hole surrounds, leaving native, scrub-filled sand to separate the fairways. Yet even with much of its novelty value lost, the Hills course still stands today as one of the state's stronger courses, being a long, highly demanding test which can be stretched to an unlisted 7,344 yards, but which more regularly plays at 7,147. Play begins and ends on high ground, with the downhill 493-yard 1st (generally a par 5 for member play) and the 469-yard 2nd setting a fast early pace. The 187-yard 3rd, however, breaks somewhat from the rustic mode, being an all-carry test played across a man-made lake. Once play has ascended back to the clubhouse area at the 6th green, one then embarks on a three-hole loop that is not original, as numbers 7-9 were built in 1976 when three other holes were commandeered in order to allow the new Village course to begin and end at the clubhouse. The downhill dogleg left 7th is a sort of mirror image of Dr. MacKenzie's famous 6th at Royal Melbourne, while the 442-yard 8th is just plain difficult. But both of these are overshadowed by the 211-yard 9th, which requires a long carry over a rough Pine Valley-like expanse to a small, elevated green with no real bailout area; there are few stronger or more memorable one-shotters in all of South Florida. One fair criticism of the Hills course is the relative repetitiveness of its par 3s for beyond the 9th, both the 197-yard 11th and the 214-yard 14th follow the lead of the 3rd, playing in opposite directions off the same ridge top to greens guarded by more man-made water. Similarly contrived is the 408-yard 15th, which sweeps tightly leftward around a large irrigation lake, and offers several options (none entirely easy) off the tee. But more fitting down the stretch are the 357-yard 16th (another hole reconfigured in 1976, and now featuring a left-side line of five ascending bunkers) as well as the stiff 420-yard 18th, a patently demanding finisher requiring a long, uphill approach – and which can be stretched as far as 486 yards. Aside from hosting Billy Mayfair's victory at the 1987 U.S. Amateur (the event's Sunshine State debut), Jupiter Hills has long existed outside of the major event spotlight. Yet it remains one of the strongest and most groundbreaking designs of an inartistic era - and, for the visitor, one of Florida's most distinctive and desirable stops.   **(GD: #130 USA, #6 State GW: #95 Modern)**

1	2	3	4	5	6	7	8	9	Out
493	469	187	578	457	377	424	442	211	3638
4	4	3	5	4	4	4	4	3	35
10	11	12	13	14	15	16	17	18	In
424	197	441	545	219	408	357	498	420	3509
4	3	4	5	3	4	4	4	4	35

Jupiter Hills Club (Village) - Tequesta   ◆◆◆

George Fazio   www.jupiterhillsclub.org
11800 SE Hill Club Terrace, Tequesta, FL 33469   (561) 746-5151
6,812 yds   Par 72   Rating: 72.7 / 140   (1976)

Nephew Tom joined George Fazio in building the Jupiter Hills Club's Village course, which debuted with nine holes (three borrowed from the original Hills' routing) in 1976, before nine more were added two years later. Though commencing from the same elevated clubhouse, and offering its own heavy doses of native sand, the Village is a very different golf course, this owing to the presence of wall-to-wall housing within its mid-section. Following a non-returning routing over the property's southern half, this is pretty strong stuff as "second" courses go, though it is largely devoid of the sort of top-shelf holes that dot the Hills. The shorter, less-engaging front nine, for example, is led by solid mid-range par 4s like the 417-yard 5th and the 400-yard 7th (where out-of-bound flanks both sides), as well as the highly tempting 282-yard 6th, a potentially driveable two-shotter which makes a late right turn to a tiny, closely bunkered target. The longer inward half initially favors the heavily bunkered 508-yard 12th and the 385-yard 14th (whose green bends rightward, along a pond) before closing strongly with the 560-yard dogleg left 16th, the lake-fronted 191-yard 17th and - following a noticeably long cart ride - the 420-yard 18th, which climbs to a narrow green angled among bunkers. Though *Golf Digest* has been known to rank the Village at the tail end of its Florida top 30, the visiting golfer may prefer to play the Hills course a second time before teeing it up here.

Jupiter Island Club - Hobe Sound   ◆◆½

William Diddel   www.thejic.com
1 Estrada Rd, Hobe Sound, FL 33455   (772) 546-1000
6,109 yds   Par 72   Rating: 70.2 / 132   (1958)

One of Florida's most affluent, out-of-the-limelight facilities, the Jupiter Island Club sits along the Intracoastal Waterway amidst an exclusive oceanside residential enclave, where it was designed by William Diddel during the late 1950s. Because it is shoehorned rather tightly among some of Florida's most expensive homes, Diddel's routing remains completely intact, but much of what is in play today hazard-wise owes to renovative work performed by P.B. Dye. The result is not especially Dye-like in appearance, however, particularly at the 342-yard 7th and the 364-yard 8th, which march, single-file, between Gomez and South Beach Roads (and their flanking estates) in old-fashioned style. While quite short by modern standards, the combination of water and the ever-present sea breeze can make Jupiter Island somewhat challenging. For the most part, however, the most memorable golf is confined to the back nine, where the 455-yard par-5 11th and 155-yard 12th skirt the Waterway, and holes 13-16 occupy an island within it . Tops among this watery quartet are the 178-yard 14th (whose green complex juts far out into the Intracoastal, requiring a shot angled across an inlet) and the 326-yard 16th.

Loblolly Golf Club - Hobe Sound ◆◆◆½

P.B. Dye
7407 SE Hill Terrace, Hobe Sound, FL 33455
6,930 yds   Par 72   Rating: 74.9 / 145   (1988)

www.loblollyinfo.com
(772) 546-8700

Built along Dixie Highway on a narrow, triangular tract separated by Peck Lake from the Atlantic, the Loblolly Golf Club utilizes some tight corridors of play due to flanking residential development, and features enough shaping to create contours atypical of South Florida golf. The course was built by Pete Dye's younger son P.B. and while only mid-size by modern standards, it is both demanding (witness its 74.9 rating) and engaging enough to include virtually no mundane holes. The outward half measures a stout 3,607 yards and is driven by a number of muscular entries, including a pair of fine early par 4s (the 461-yard 3rd - an early turning dogleg right - and the 436-yard dogleg left 5th) as well as both of its par 5s, the 573-yard 6th (which sweeps almost 90 degrees right to a water-backed putting surface) and the exciting 540-yard 8th, a reachable three-shotter twisting between two lakes. The much shorter back nine fills the narrow end of the triangle and, while a tad less engaging than the front, initially features the 263-yard 13th, a tiny, driveable par 4 whose green is tucked beyond a long right-side bunker. The finishers are predictably demanding and include the daunting 195-yard 16th (routed along a *deep* right-side bunker), the 591-yard lakeside 17th and the 405-yard 18th, a gentle dogleg right where driving close to flanking water opens the best line of approach. Loblolly is widely viewed as P.B. Dye's best work, and though he may have borrowed a thing or two from his father, replicating classics was never held against Seth Raynor or C.B. Macdonald, so why should one be critical here?   **(GD:** #198 USA, #17 State   **GW:** #123 Modern)

Mariner Sands Country Club (Green) - Stuart ◆◆

Frank Duane
6500 SE Mariner Sands Dr, Stuart, FL 34997
6,803 yds   Par 72   Rating: 73.2 / 132   (1973)

www.marinersands.com
(772) 221-7300

Occupying a large property which stretches from Federal Highway across to Route A1A, the 36-hole Mariner Sands Country Club began in 1973 with its Green course, a layout whose architectural lineage has an element of murkiness; indeed, Cornish & Whitten credit Arnold Palmer and his then-partner Frank Duane as co-designers, while the club, passing on the easier marketing angle, lists it as a Duane solo job. In any case, the Green is a mid-size, housing-lined test which primarily offers functional golf, with the occasional brighter moment thrown in. Few of these better entries appear on the shorter front nine, but worthy of note is the 379-yard 2nd, a sharp, early turning dogleg right around water whose obvious shortcut route has a somewhat gimmicky line of trees deliberately impeding its line. Things kick up somewhat on the back nine, however, first at the 528-yard 10th (water right) and the 412-yard 11th (water left), then more significantly at the 311-yard dogleg right 12th, which dares an over-water carry to successfully reach the very driveable green. But overall, this is basic, non-threatening Florida golf.

Mariner Sands Country Club (Gold) - Stuart   ◆◆½

Tom Fazio   www.marinersands.com
6500 SE Mariner Sands Dr, Stuart, FL 34997   (772) 221-7300
        6,811 yds   Par 72   Rating: 73.2 / 140   (1981)

The Mariner Sands Country Club's second course, the Gold, was one of a young Tom Fazio's earlier solo projects, opening for business on the property's southern half in 1981. Though carrying an identical rating to its sister Green layout, this is a track which most visiting golfers will find rather more engaging, as Fazio's use of both water and sand is far more strategic in nature than the more basic work of Frank Duane next door. Play opens on the stronger side as three of the first four holes are solid par 4s of at least 415 yards, led by the 423-yard 4th, the number one stroke hole. The remainder of the outward half picks up steam at the 145-yard waterside 6th before going large again at the 471-yard par-4 7th and the 500-yard 9th, a sweeping dogleg right which bends around a lake and several prominent trees. The back gets going at the 529-yard 11th (one of several holes featuring slightly gimmicky patches of rough within otherwise desirable areas of the fairway) before offering a particularly strong test at the 436-yard 13th, which bends right around two prominent corner bunkers. Play also closes on a high note with both the 389-yard 17th and the 509-yard 18th being closely guarded by greenside water.

McArthur Golf Club - Hobe Sound   ◆◆◆½

Tom Fazio & Nick Price   www.mcarthurgolf.com
6550 SE Osprey St, Hobe Sound, FL 33455   (772) 545-3838
        7,251 yds   Par 72   Rating: 75.4 / 145   (2002)

Occupying a 990-acre woods- and wetlands-filled tract lying on the western edge of developed Hobe Sound, the McArthur Golf Club is an admirably secluded golf-only facility featuring a strong layout designed by the pairing of Tom Fazio and Hall-of-Famer Nick Price. Not surprisingly, while it was Price who was the original designer hired by the developer, this sort of landscape (which includes nearly 300 preserved acres) proved a good fit for Fazio's ultra-polished/natural look, with native stretches of sand and marsh making for some striking images – though seldom are these potentially fine hazards actually brought directly into play. Man-made lakes routinely are, however, notably at the 397-yard 7th (where aggressive drives must flirt with a left-side hazard) and the 533-yard 9th (ditto, on both drive and second) - though the front nine's strongest entry is very likely the 594-yard dogleg right 5th, which requires a long tee shot angled across native wetlands. The back nine is the longer and more engaging half, and begins with the 592-yard 10th (which sweeps rightward, past all manner of native and man-made hazards), a pair of solid par 4s (the 460-yard 11th and 439-yard 12th) and the 188-yard 13th, which plays to an S-like, waterside green. The closers are equally testing, led by the watery 542-yard 15th (which dares a gusty second) and the 474-yard 18th, where water flanks the entire left side while scrub-filled sand lines the right. Throw in some vividly contoured greens, plus the layout's housing-free nature, and it's no wonder this has emerged as one of South Florida's top stops. (**GD:** #176 USA, #14 State GW: #160 Modern**)**

Medalist Golf Club - Hobe Sound ♦♦♦½

Pete Dye & Greg Norman   www.medalistgolfclub.org
9908 SE Cottage Ln, Hobe Sound, FL 33455   (772) 545-9600
                7,571 yds   Par 72   Rating: 77.9 / 155   (1995)

The McArthur Golf Club's immediate southern neighbor, the Medalist Golf Club was initially viewed as a modern classic, its innovative Pete Dye & Greg Norman design wandering across the scruffy, marsh-dotted landscape, often culminating in elevated greens whose sculpted surrounds drew comparisons to Pinehurst. But club co-founder Norman altered many of Dye's unique features over the ensuing years, and when Bobby Weed was brought aboard to turn things around, Norman departed the scene altogether - though notably, Dye joined him in requesting that his name also be removed from the design masthead. Among other changes, Weed added tees that stretched the layout to nearly 7,600 yards, though many a discerning golfer has found the revised layout less appealing than the original, regardless. The best of the current track today includes the 496-yard wetlands-hopping 2nd, the 203-yard pond-guarded 8th and the 494-yard 9th, a dogleg left requiring a long marsh carry off the tee. The back nine first offers a pair of driveable par 4s, the 335-yard 11th and the 318-yard 14th, the latter bending leftward, along water, to a tiny putting surface. The close, on the other hand, is a bit brawnier, led by the 497-yard 15th (where water and sand line the entire left side), the 444-yard dogleg right 17th (which dares a long carry over more wetlands) and the once-again-imposing 484-yard 18th, which is back to playing as a stiff two-shotter after an ill-fated experiment as a short par 5. The Medalist has climbed back among the state's elite in most rater's eyes, and thus surely rates among Southeast Florida's very best. **(GD: #11 State)**

Monarch Country Club - Palm City ♦♦½

Arnold Palmer   www.clubcorp.org
1801 SW Monarch Club Dr, Palm City, FL 34990   (772) 286-8447
                6,890 yds   Par 72   Rating: 73.8 / 145   (1987)

A real estate-oriented facility located half a mile off the South Fork of the St. Lucie River, the Monarch Country Club features a mid-size 1987 Arnold Palmer-designed 18 whose holes proceed, single file, through the standard regional tableau of single-family homes. Little changed (save for the build out of the housing) since its opening, it is a layout that was clearly created with the recreational golfer in mind, though there is enough bite present to at least keep the better player on his toes most of the time. The slightly longer front nine is fairly straight-ahead in nature, its most noteworthy moments coming at the 203-yard 2nd (played to a tightly bunkered T-shaped green) and the 436-yard dogleg right 7th. The back then carries on in similar style before reaching the featured 527-yard 14th, a reachable par 5 whose island green lies far enough out in a lake that laid-up seconds will leave a fairly substantial third. The 390-yard 15th is a split-fairway test (the left side offering the best approach angle) before play wraps up over a pair of closers with water down their left sides, the 388-yard 17th and the 563-yard 18th.

Sailfish Point Golf Club - Stuart   ◆◆◆

Jack Nicklaus   www.sailfishpoint.com
2203 Sailfish Point Blvd, Stuart, FL 34996   (772) 225-1500
              7,088 yds   Par 72   Rating: 75.0 / 143   (1981)

Remarkably situated on its own barrier island just a short distance north of Hobe Sound, the Sailfish Point Golf Club represents one of the more unique golf-oriented developments in the often repetitive South Florida market. Given the limited size of the property and the fact that virtually the entire waterfront perimeter was reserved for housing, Jack Nicklaus & Co. were left to fashion a solid and challenging layout routed throughout the interior, a track which was completely rebunkered in the mid-2000s but which still has water in play on 16 holes. Not coincidentally, two of the most memorable are the only ones that actually reach the shoreline, the slightly awkward 614-yard 14th (which requires one to lay up shy of a wide waterway en route to a green backed up against St. Lucie Inlet) and the 443-yard 18th, a gentle dogleg right which bends along a vast bunker to a green framed by the Atlantic. Beyond these, there are plenty of demanding holes but few real standouts, with the front nine featuring the 405-yard 3rd (a soundly bunkered lakeside test) and the quirky 315-yard 7th (where a lake and fairway bunkering make for a tricky lay up), while the back offers the 187-yard 12th, which plays diagonally across a waterway. The location does somewhat outshine the tactical merits of the layout (within the region, only Miami's Indian Creek enjoys a comparable island setting) but as with most Nicklaus layouts, the golf itself is still strong enough not to let down the side.

Turtle Creek Club - Tequesta   ◆◆◆

Joe Lee   www.turtlecreekclub.com
2 Club Circle, Tequesta, FL 33469   (561) 746-8371
              6,831 yds   Par 72   Rating: 74.8 / 146   (1970)

A somewhat overlooked Joe Lee design dating to 1970, the Turtle Creek Club sits in a residential neighborhood close to the Loxahatchee River, some two miles inland from the Atlantic where, despite its limited size, it offers quite a bit of interesting, often watery golf. Heavily bunkered and occasionally separated from adjacent fairways by swaths of open sand, the layout includes a set of dry holes that are of a dependable Lee standard, their strongest entry being the 452-yard dogleg right 7th. The water holes, on the other hand, are not terribly long but they frequently are dangerous, with front nine favorites including the 550-yard 4th (whose putting surface is tucked behind a front-left pond) and the 412-yard 9th, where a central lake menaces the tee shot before angling in front-left of the green. Following the 532-yard dogleg right 10th, the back nine features the layout's most memorable entry at the 405-yard 11th, a near-90-degree dogleg left around/across a large lake. The close offers several similarly testing moments via a final trio of water holes: the tricky 372-yard pond-fronted 14th, the 399-yard 15th (which doglegs left to a green guarded front-right by a pond) and the 410-yard 18th, a lake-flanked dogleg right where the hazard again angles in before the green. Justifiably overshadowed by nearby Jupiter Hills, and not quite long enough to really push better players, still worth a look.

Willoughby Golf Club - Stuart   ♦♦½

Arthur Hills   www.willoughbygolfclub.com
3001 SE Doubleton Dr, Stuart, FL 34997   (772) 220-6000
                    6,591 yds   Par 72   Rating: 73.0 / 138   (1989)

Built upon a wetlands- and lake-dotted site four miles inland from the Atlantic, the
Willoughby Golf Club offers a 1989 Arthur Hills-designed layout which, despite its obvious
shortness today, utilizes Hills' occasionally quirky stylings to provide an often-interesting
test. Decidedly less of that playing interest is found on the front nine, however, for after
the 520-yard 2nd (a wetlands narrowed dogleg right), the loop's best come late, first at
the 364-yard lake-fronted 8th (one of the shorter number one stroke holes around), then
at the 509-yard 9th, a sweeping dogleg left whose green extends leftward into a lake. The
back nine, however, is well-stocked with more appealing entries, beginning with an early
trio of water-oriented tests: the 426-yard 11th (which curls rightward along a lake), the
181-yard 12th (angled across the corner of a large pond) and the 503-yard 13th, a gentle
dogleg right to a green tucked beyond more front-right water. The scale of play drops off
soon thereafter, with the final quartet composed of the 318-yard 15th, the 149-yard 16th,
the 484-yard 17th (whose crescent-like green curves rightward, behind some larger trees)
and the 385-yard 18th, where the tee shot angles across the edge of right-side wetlands.

Yacht & Country Club - Stuart   ♦♦

Charles Martin   www.yccstuart.org
3883 SE Fairway East, Stuart, FL 34997   (772) 287-3736
                    6,463 yds   Par 71   Rating: 71.7 / 128   (1971)

Its property bisected by a canal-like inlet off the St. Lucie River, Stuart's Yacht & Country
Club is something of an architectural mystery, with the club claiming Dick Wilson as its
original designer while Cornish & Whitten (among others) cite a none-too-prolific period
Florida practitioner named Charlie Martin. Regardless, as the banks of the inlet were
reserved exclusively for housing, the prospects were perhaps a bit limited here, with the
end result being a short, housing-lined track whose collection of solid sub-400-yard par 4s
makes it well suited to senior play. On the front side, several such short two-shotters are
affected by ponds (e.g., the 364-yard 2nd, the 387-yard 5th and the 356-yard 9th), though
equally memorable are the 380-yard 6th (where several very mature trees narrow the
fairway) and, on the longer side, the 581-yard 4th, where a pond again fronts the green.
The back nine lies mostly on the west side of the inlet but is the less-engaging half, its
favorites including the strong 420-yard 12th and the 329-yard tree-narrowed 18th.

Piper's Landing Yacht & Country Club - Palm City   ♦♦

Joe Lee   www.piperslanding.com
6160 SW Thistle Terrace, Palm City, FL 34990   (772) 283-7000
            6,922 yds   Par 72   Rating: 74.2 / 149   (1982)

Though otherwise considered a private facility, the Piper's Landing Yacht & Country Club advertises on-site rentals (with golfing privileges) to non-members and thus, while by no means a traditional resort, it is so listed here. Located off a wide bend in the St. Lucie River, some six miles inland from the Atlantic, the club features a relatively challenging, housing-lined layout originally built by Joe Lee in 1984, but which was later renovated by Gene Bates in 2007. Aside from creating a handful of new holes on the back nine, Bates basically retained Lee's routing, but he also toughened things significantly by replacing numerous Lee bunkers sitting along fairway's edge with new hazards far more invasive to their driving zones. The result is a track whose par 4s are frequently on the shorter side yet are fairly demanding, with favorites including the 404-yard tree-menaced 10th, the 351-yard 11th (which bends leftward around a lake), the 421-yard 16th (mostly a longer version of the 11th) and the especially tightly bunkered 394-yard 18th. Among regional layouts recently renovated, this may thus be more friendly to senior golfers than most.

Champions Club at Summerfield - Stuart   ♦♦½

Tom Fazio   www.thechampionsclubgolf.com
3400 SE Summerfield Way, Stuart, FL   34997   (772) 283-1500
            6,890 yds   Par 72   Rating: 72.8 / 135   (1994)

One of several South Florida projects completed by Tom Fazio before he perfected his more sophisticated polished/rough aesthetic, the Champions Club at Summerfield is routed over a wetlands-laced property, with single-family homes occupying what *terra firma* was definable along a number of fairways. Given its timing, the layout is far less flashy than many a Fazio project to follow, but the frequent wetlands presence (they meaningfully affect the majority of holes) is enough to lift this among the region's better daily fee layouts. And the wetlands make their mark quickly, first fronting the green at the 197-yard forced-carry 2nd, then forcing longer hitters to throttle down as they pinch both sides of the fairway at the 432-yard 3rd, the number one stroke hole. The 528-yard dogleg right 8th dares a wetlands shortcut off the tee, setting up the slightly awkward 393-yard dogleg left 9th, where interceding marshes again force a lay up off the tee. Tactically, the inward half may be less interesting but beginning at the 216-yard 12th, it enjoys a run of housing-free golf among the wetlands, the highlight of which is the 552-yard 13th, a late-turning dogleg left which dares a tree and wetlands carry on the second.

Eagle Marsh Golf Club - Jensen Beach   ♦♦♦

Tommy Fazio   www.eaglemarsh.com
3869 NW Royal Oak Dr, Jensen Beach, FL   34957   (772) 692-3322
            6,918 yds   Par 72   Rating: 73.4 / 139   (1997)

Another 1990s layout built on a wetlands-heavy site, the Eagle Marsh Golf Club borders the St. Lucie County Line and includes a somewhat reduced housing element, once again due to a relatively limited amount of dry land available along many fairways. The course was designed by Tom Fazio's nephew Tommy, who surely had his routing freedom at least somewhat limited by the environmentally sensitive landscape, but the third-generation Fazio designer managed to produce one of the more highly thought of public courses in the area. Though it opens with a 545-yard wetlands-bordered par 5 and a 400-yard lake-squeezed par 4, the front nine is more than 200 yards shorter than the back and includes four par 4s under 400 yards, none of which are genuine standouts. But the story changes immediately upon making the turn, as the inward half opens with the 420-yard 10th (where drives flirting with left-side sand yield the best line to a wetlands-flanked green) and the 535-yard dogleg right 11th, which requires a long, marsh-carrying drive from the tips and features a dual-fairway lay-up zone. Also imposing are the loop's pair of muscular par 3s, the 236-yard 13th (angling over water from the back tees) and the 227-yard 17th, whose small green moves leftward behind two large bunkers. Also highly notable is the 454-yard 18th, which turns sharply right before crossing wetlands – but which also includes a somewhat gimmicky alternative green measuring 351-yards.

Evergreen Club - Palm City

◆◆½

Charles Martin   www.theevergreenclub.com
4225 SW Bimini Circle S, Palm City, FL 34990   (772) 242-4124
6,910 yds   Par 72   Rating: 73.0 / 134   (1982)

Bordering the County Line Canal on its northern flank, the Evergreen Club is another Martin County facility situated directly along the St. Lucie County border, in this case occupying a very narrow east-west-oriented site encircled by housing. Local designer Charlie Martin is the architect of record and while his work may never have drawn major national attention, this is a layout which continues to hold its own relative to most South Florida creations of its period. The front nine follows a nearly symmetrical path around a central neighborhood of low-density single-family homes and offers a bit of early muscle at the 538-yard 1st (played to a tightly bunkered green), the 482-yard par-4 2nd (where water parallels the left side) and the 441-yard 6th, a straightaway test played to a narrow, angled pear-shaped putting surface. The action downsizes through the turn (holes 7-10 are the only ones not routed directly east-west) before picking up again at the 603-yard 11th (where right-side water touches the lay-up zone) and the 379-yard tree-narrowed 12th. The 339-yard pond-narrowed 14th reaches the property's eastern tip before the march home culminates in the 544-yard pond-fronted 17th and the 447-yard finisher.

The Florida Club - Stuart

◆◆◆

Dick Gray   www.floridaclubgolf.com
9005 SW Old Royal Dr, Stuart, FL 34997   (772) 287-3680
6,909 yds   Par 72   Rating: 74.2 / 141   (1996)

Another facility which might draw a bit more attention were it located in Palm Beach or Miami, the Florida Club sits just west of Interstate 95 where it was laid out by former Pete Dye sideman Dick Gray, an apparently capable designer whose career was instead rooted more in greenkeeping. In no sense is Gray's work here original in scope; indeed, at first glance, one might well assume it to be a product of the Dye clan in nearly every respect. But in the same way that the Dyes can seldom be accused of building a dull golf course, there is lots of interesting (if derivative) golf to be found within this housing-lined layout. Scale-wise, play begins somewhat slowly, with the only early hole to flex much muscle being the 209-yard 3rd, the first of four par 3s to play to greens somewhat similarly angled beyond long, narrow waste bunkers. The outward half ends strongly, however, with the 529-yard 8th curling leftward along a lake and the 436-yard 9th bending rightward past three long waste bunkers. The longer and stronger back nine begins with the 392-yard centerline-bunkered 10th as well as the 457-yard 12th, where the maximum carry across angled wetlands yields the ideal second shot. A varied finish is then led by the 323-yard 16th (driveable but along/across a right-side waste bunker), the 224-yard lakeside 17th (the last of the waste-bunkered par 3s) and the 472-yard 18th, a slightly awkward dogleg left which requires a wetlands crossing on the second.

Hammock Creek Golf Club - Palm City   ♦♦½

Jack Nicklaus & Jack Nicklaus II   www.hammockcreekgolfclub.com
2400 SW Golden Brea Ln, Palm City, FL 34990   (772) 220-2599
                7,131 yds   Par 72   Rating: 74.6 / 143   (1996)

Occupying a housing-permeated site that lies along the eastern side of Florida's Turnpike, the Hammock Creek Golf Club is a Nicklaus father-and-son production which, though of solid proportion and challenge, appears to have been created with a higher-volume daily fee audience in mind. Indeed, very little of the fairway bunkering can be called invasive and only on the tee shot at the 400-yard 4th is anything resembling a significant water carry required. Of course, the downside of such an arrangement is that Hammock Creek thus lacks some of the tactical excitement that defines most Nicklaus designs, with clear decision-making really only required at the 380-yard 5th (where drives angled across a small right-side pond open the ideal angle of approach), the 389-yard 13th (whose centerline fairway bunker mandates thought off the tee) and the 393-yard 16th, upon which a tee shot carrying a right-side bunker takes a left-side pond out of play a yields a wide-open pitch. A fair amount of length is consumed by a trio of longer par 5s (the 577-yard 9th, the 564-yard 15th and the 555-yard 17th), leaving the longest two-shotters to be the 443-yard dogleg right 3rd, the 454-yard 11th and the 447-yard 18th, none of which pose major strategic questions with their muscle. Still, this is eminently solid public golf.

Heritage Ridge Golf Club - Hobe Sound   ♦♦

Dick LeConte / Charles Ankrom   www.heritageridgegolf.com
6510 SE Heritage Blvd, Hobe Sound, FL 33455   (772) 546-2800
                6,014 yds   Par 70   Rating: 69.6 / 129   (1980)

Wedged in between the private Mariner Sands and Loblolly Pines, and between Federal Highway and Route A1A, the Heritage Ridge Golf Club was built in two parts, with one Dick LeConte building the front nine in 1980, and Charles Ankrom squeezing the much shorter inward half into limited acreage two years later. Despite some modest touching up in recent years by Dom Fazio, there remains nearly 500 yards of difference between the two loops. The par-36 outward half includes a pair of par 3s in excess of 210 yards (as well as the 180-yard lake-fronted 2nd) as well as a trio of full-size par 5s led by the 515-yard dogleg right 5th and the 535-yard 8th, where the same lake represents a forced-carry hazard on both the second and third. Though palpably undersized at 2,762 yards, the par-34 back nine does include several stronger holes, led by the effectively bunkered 201-yard 12th, the 510-yard 13th (whose green angles tightly beyond a front-right pond) and one more long and testing par 3, the well-bunkered 213-yard 16th.

Indianwood Golf & Country Club - Indiantown   ♦½

Ted McAnlis   www.indianwoodgolfclub.com
14007 Golf Club Dr, Indiantown, FL 34956   (772) 597-3794
6,008 yds   Par 70   Rating: 69.1 / 129   (1984)

By far the most inland of Martin County's courses, the Indianwood Golf & Country Club is located far closer to Lake Okeechobee (15 miles) than to the Atlantic Ocean (35), where it sits along the northern edge of this small town (population 6,083) that began life as a Seminole trading post in the mid-19th century. The obviously short Ted McAnlis-designed golf course is actually a layout in two parts, with the front nine covering the site's larger eastern side where, amidst a number of fairly basic holes, it includes the 506-yard 4th (an engaging dogleg right around a central lake), the 518-yard wetlands-flanked 8th and the 394-yard pond-guarded 9th. The 2,805-yard inward half is then squeezed into much tighter acreage on the west side of Golf Club Drive, where tree-lined holes are routed in a mostly back-and-forth manner. Notable, however, are its finishers, the 140-yard over-water 17th and the 414-yard 18th, a narrow dogleg left and the club's longest par 4.

Lost Lake Golf Club - Hobe Sound   ♦♦½

Jim & Tommy Fazio   www.lostlakegolfclub.com
8300 SE Fazio Dr, Hobe Sound, FL 34455   (772) 220-6666
6,850 yds   Par 72   Rating: 73.9 / 138   (1993)

Anchoring a good-size real estate development which extends somewhat incongruously into the boundaries of Atlantic Ridge Preserve State Park, the Lost Lake Golf Club is a housing-lined track constructed in the early 1990s by most of the third generation of Team Fazio. With water or wetlands meaningfully affecting a majority of holes, there is plenty of challenging golf here, though as the sometimes disjointed routing suggests, there are also places where either environmental restrictions or the priority given to housing may have put a limit on things. This is particularly apparent early on (where holes 2-4 are squeezed around a small, semi-circular neighborhood) before the front nine picks up at the 542-yard 5th (which sweeps leftward, between wetlands and a lake), the 205-yard 6th (played to a shallow, sand-fronted target) and the 485-yard par-5 7th, an obviously reachable three-shotter complicated by its narrow green being flanked left, right and long by water. The back then opens on a longer note, first with the 548-yard 10th (a water-flanked double dogleg), then via the 415-yard lakeside 11th and the 502-yard 12th, where a creek curls in front-left of a bunkerless green. Among the closers, the 203-yard waterside 14th and the 65-yard swale-guarded 16th are engaging entries, while the 441-yard 18th bends leftward between left-side wetlands and a right-side lake.

Martin County Golf Course (Red/White) - Stuart   ♦½

William Langford   www.martincountygolfcourse.com
2000 SE St. Lucie Blvd, Stuart, FL 34996   (772) 320-4653
              6,436 yds   Par 72   Rating: 70.6 / 123   (1925)

By more than six decades the older half of this 36-hole municipal facility, the Martin
County Golf Course's Red/White course has a somewhat blurry design history, with the
club claiming that William Langford laid out the original Golden Age layout, while Cornish
& Whitten cite Langford as redesigning an early nine and adding nine more in 1951. But
either way, the Langford credit is more about marketing at this point as later renovations
have left little more than a few of his corridors of play intact. What remains, then, is a
shortish, soundly bunkered course which, though far more functional than exciting, does
offer a few more somewhat more memorable moments. Among these are the 406-yard
dogleg left 2nd, the 507-yard 4th (where a creek cuts before the putting surface), the 200-
yard 6th (played across a pair of diagonal bunkers) and the 424-yard 9th, the layout's
longest par 4. On the back, the 290-yard lakeside 11th is temptingly short par 4.

Martin County Golf Course (Gold/Blue) - Stuart   ♦½

Ron Garl   www.martincountygolfcourse.com
2000 SE St. Lucie Blvd, Stuart, FL 34996   (772) 320-4653
              6,137 yds   Par 72   Rating: 70.0 / 122   (1988)

The (much) newer half of this municipal complex, the Martin County Golf Course's Blue/
Gold course bears several oddities for a modern-era addition, not the least of which is
the fact that Ron Garl's 1988 design is nearly 300 yards shorter than it's much older
sibling. But even more notable is that rather than reconfigure the existing 18 to allow for
both courses to begin and end at the clubhouse, Garls creation features a pair nines that
not only lie a good 800 yards from the clubhouse, they also are positioned about 600
yards from each other, occupying the more wooded eastern and southern flanks of the
adjacent Witham Field Airport. With nearly every hole being on the shorter side, this is
clearly user-friendly municipal golf, though the front nine does include the 329-yard 5th
(whose tee shot is aimed diagonally across a lake), the 521-yard 7th (where right-side
water threatens the second) and the layout's toughest overall test, the 400-yard 9th, a
dogleg right with a prominent lake lurking dangerously/awkwardly beyond the corner.

Martin Downs Golf Club (Banyan Creek) - Palm City   N/A

Charles Ankrom   www.martindownsgolfclub.com
3801 SW Greenwood Way, Palm City, FL 34990   (772) 286-6818

The older half of this 36-hole facility situated along the east side of Florida's Turnpike, the former Crane Creek course is still closed as it undergoes a significant renovation (and rebranding) at the time of this writing. The project has been undertaken by Jupiter-based architect Harry Bowers and, given the long-established housing that frames the majority of holes (usually at reasonable distance), nearly all of Charles Ankrom's original corridors of play will be retained. Whereas the course was previously a typical, fully turfed Florida layout, the revised edition will have numerous areas of "native" sand exposed, making it more visually appealing, but also less expensive to maintain. A fairly challenging track pre-renovation, it certainly doesn't figure to get any easier now.

Martin Downs Golf Club (Osprey Creek) - Palm City   ♦♦½

Charles Ankrom   www.martindownsgolfclub.com
3801 SW Greenwood Way, Palm City, FL 34990   (772) 286-6818
                6,868 yds   Par 72   Rating: 72.6 / 134   (1981)

Popular area designer Charles Ankrom built the Martin Downs Golf Club's Osprey Creek course nine years after the now-former Crane Creek layout, routing it through multiple residential neighborhoods on the southern half of the property. Unlike many a regional facility, water is seldom a major factor here, meaningfully affecting the competent ball striker on no more than five occasions. Sand, however, is another story, as roughly 80 bunkers perforate the landscape, defining nearly every hole and occasionally offering a strategic aspect as well. On the front side, water is the primary factor at the 381-yard 2nd (which doglegs left around a lake) but thereafter the loop's best include the 407-yard dogleg right 5th (which dares an aggressive line across a prominent corner bunker), the 528-yard heavily bunkered 8th and the stiff 216-yard 9th. The inward half offers its early water hole at the 178-yard all-carry 11th before running through a quartet of strong, mid-size entries that includes the fairly basic 442-yard 12th, the 537-yard 13th (where two huge frontal bunkers limit run-up possibilities), the 424-yard 15th and the 400-yard 18th, a straightaway test whose green angles along a front-right pond.

Palm Cove Golf & Yacht Club - Palm City   ♦♦

Gary Player   www.palmcovegolf.com
2363 SW Carriage Hill Terrace, Palm City, FL 34990   (772) 287-5605
                6,340 yds   Par 71   Rating: 69.6 / 139   (1990)

A short housing-oriented layout located where the County Line Canal meets the St. Lucie River (and just across the water from the very private Floridian), the Palm Cove Golf & Yacht Club was originally laid out by Gary Player in 1990, but was later renovated by the ever-popular Chi Chi Rodriguez early in the new millennium. Though the routing of the back nine remained 100% intact, Rodriguez's work completely reconfigured the outward half, though it remains a short, highly compact, housing-lined loop whose most notable holes include two particularly narrow entries (the 421-yard dogleg right 3rd and the 498-yard 6th) as well as the 192-yard wetlands-crossing 8th. The par-37 back then ventures out to the west where, after opening with a trio of shorter par 4s, it crosses Mapp Road for a run of three stronger holes: the 353-yard 13th (where a significant wetlands carry is required off the tee), the 553-yard dogleg left 14th and the 182-yard over-water 15th. With right-side water affecting one's second, the 540-yard dogleg left 18th is a solid closer – provided that one's drive avoids the houses which dangerously fill the corner.

Eaglewood Country Club - Hobe Sound   ♦½

Ward Northrup   www.eaglewoodhoa.net
85000 SE Eaglewood Way, Hobe Sound, FL 33455   (772) 546-3656
             3,142 yds   Par 57   Rating: 54.0 / 80   (1990)

An above average executive layout in most every respect, the Eaglewood Country Club is a private, residence-driven facility located just a short par 4 west of Federal Highway. Laid out by Ward Northrup, it is routed in and around housing and includes three par 4s, though the layout's strength really lies in its collection of fairly diverse par 3s. Water affects the competent ball striker on six holes, the most testing of which include the 126-yard pond-crossing 5th (played a bulkheaded green), the 125-yard 10th and especially the 190-yard 13th, where a lake runs the entirety of the left side.

The Little Club - Tequesta   ♦

Unknown
9601 SE Little Club Way N, Tequesta, FL 33469   (561) 746-1869

Not to be confused in style, substance or location with the same-named Joe Lee-designed facility in Delray Beach, this Little Club is a private facility which publishes no rating or slope information. The nine-hole golf course is of the back yard variety, being routed among a line of single-family houses to the south and rows of multi-story condominiums to the north. Water appears on four occasions but never terribly pressingly, allowing this to be pleasant back yard golf, and a reasonably good facility of this type.

Miles Grant Country Club - Stuart   ♦½

Mark Mahannah   www.milesgrantcc.com
5101 SE Miles Grant Rd, Stuart, FL 34997   (772) 286-2220
             4,712 yds   Par 64   Rating: 63.0 / 108   (1972)

The centerpiece of a residential community admirably located off a large inlet of the St. Lucie River known as Great Pocket, the Miles Grant Country Club boasts a full-size executive course – that is, a track measuring over 4,700 yards which includes two par 5s, two par 4s in excess of 400 yards, and a total of six two-shotters averaging 385. The standard of Mark Mahannah's design is a relatively high one, and while water only affects the 370-yard 17th and 483-yard 18th, bunkering is plentiful, with 50 hazards coming into play. The 10 par 3s aren't overwhelming in length but with legitimately solid par 4s like the 420-yard 6th and the 410-yard 10th around, they don't really need to be.

Monterey Yacht & Country Club - Stuart   ◆

Unknown   www.montereyyachtandcountryclub.com
1991 SW Palm City Rd, Stuart, FL 34994   (772) 283-7600
            1,219 yds   Par 30   Rating: - / -   (1970)

Another private executive facility, the Monterey Yacht & Country Club sits along the
South Fork of the St. Lucie River, where its nine-hole executive course is routed among
rows of multi-story condominiums. Despite the presence of six ponds, there are only two
forced water carries present (at the 125-yard 5th and the 78-yard 8th) and bunkering is
nearly nonexistent. Further, this is really a par-3 course as the listed par of 30 is achieved
by counting holes measuring 200, 168 and 160 yards as par 4s. But the often tree-lined
ambience is pleasant, making this a nice back yard amenity for residents.

North River Golf Club - Stuart   ◆

Art Young   www.northrivergc.com
1827 NW Pine Lake Dr, Stuart, FL 34994   (772) 692-0346
            4,439 yds   Par 66   Rating: - / -   (1970)

Situated just inland from the St. Lucie River, and nearly adjacent to the St. Lucie County
line, the North River (née Pine Lakes) Golf Club offers an executive 18 that is impressive
on the scorecard but which, despite the presence of a dozen par 4s, most offers just basic
fundamental golf. The primary reason for this is that the layout is completely bunkerless,
though water does make two relevant appearances, first flanking the entire left side of
the 328-yard 3rd (a legitimately testing two-shotter if one is susceptible to hooking), then
catching only missed tee shots to the right of the 277-yard dogleg right 10th.

Ocean Club - Stuart   ◆◆

Charles Ankrom   www.marriott.com
555 NE Ocean Blvd, Stuart, FL 34996   (772) 225-6819
            4,022 yds   Par 61   Rating: - / -   (1990)

Enjoying a spectacular location on Hutchinson Island, a large barrier landmass in the
Atlantic, the Charles Ankrom-designed Ocean Club is the recreational centerpiece of a
Marriott Resort and one of the strongest executive course one is likely to encounter.
Routed among condominiums, resort housing and several larger, man-made lakes, the
heavily bunkered layout includes five par 4s and one par 5 (the 484-yard pond-fronted
18th) and initially features the 148-yard 2nd (which backs up against the Indian River), the
205-yard 6th and the 166-yard island green 8th. Similarly watery is the 133-yard 13th,
while both the 335-yard 15th and the par-5 18th are solid, regulation size entries.

Riverbend Golf Club - Tequesta

Tom Fazio   www.riverbendfl.com
9300 SE Riverfront Terrace, Tequesta, FL 33469   (561) 746-5108
4,402 yds   Par 64   Rating: 62.6 / 115   (1971)

Residing across Country Club Drive from the neighboring Turtle Creek Country Club, just north of the Palm Beach County line, the Riverbend Golf Club is old enough to be from an era when Tom Fazio would still take on an executive project. Of course, that also means that the layout is too old to carry the careful polish of Fazio's later work, leaving it as a fairly basic 18 routed around and among condominiums. Basically bunkered and routed with a non-returning 9th hole, its best entries are almost all watery in nature, led by the 335-yard pond-guarded 8th, the 314-yard 11th (where a right-side lake affects the drive) and the 460-yard par-5 17th (ditto). This is eminently solid stuff in the world of executive golf; just don't arrive in search of the modern, polished Tom Fazio experience.

INDEX

Abacoa GC	117	Deer Creek GC	51
Aberdeen G&CC	66	Deering Bay Yacht & CC	20
Addison Reserve	66	Del Aire CC	78
Adios GC	38	Delray Beach GC	121
C at Admiral's Cove (East)	67	Delray Dunes G&CC	78
C at Admiral's Cove (Village)	67	Diplomat G Resort & Spa	43
Atlantic National GC	117	Dye Preserve GC	138
Atlantis CC	118	Eaglewood CC	155
Ballenisles CC (East)	68	Eagle Marsh GC	148
Ballenisles CC (North)	68	Eastpointe CC (East)	79
Ballenisles CC (South)	69	Eastpointe CC (West)	79
Banyan GC	69	Eco GC	60
Banyan Cay Resort & Golf	110	Emerald Dunes GC	80
Bear Lakes CC (Lakes)	70	C at Emerald Hills	52
Bear Lakes CC (Links)	70	The Everglades C	80
The Bear's C	71	Evergreen C	149
Biltmore GC	23	Falls G&CC	81
Boca Delray G&CC	131	L at Fisher Island	23
Boca Dunes G&CC	118	Flamingo Lakes CC	52
Boca Greens CC	119	CC of Florida	81
Boca Grove G&TC	71	Florida C	149
Boca Lago CC	72	Florida Keys CC	16
C at Boca Pointe	72	Floridian	138
Boca Raton Muni GC	119	Forest Oaks GC	121
Boca Raton Muni GC (Exec)	131	Ft Lauderdale CC (North)	39
Boca Raton Res (Country Club)	111	Ft Lauderdale CC (South)	39
Boca Raton Res (Resort)	110	Fountains CC (South)	82
Boca Rio GC	73	Fountains CC (West)	82
Boca West CC (Palmer I)	73	Fox C	139
Boca West CC (Fazio II)	74	Frenchman's Creek (North)	83
Boca West CC (Palmer III)	74	Frenchman's Creek (South)	83
Boca West CC (Dye IV)	75	Frenchman's Reserve	84
Boca Woods CC (Lakes)	76	Gleneagles CC (Legends)	84
Boca Woods CC (Woods)	75	Gleneagles CC (Victory)	85
Bocaire CC	76	Granada GC	30
Bonaventure CC	43	Grand Palms G Resort	44
L at Boynton Beach	120	Grande Oaks GC	40
L at Boynton Beach (Family)	131	Greynolds Park GC	30
The Breakers GC (Ocean)	111	Gulf Stream GC	85
The Breakers GC (Rees Jones)	112	Hammock Creek GC	150
Briar Bay GC	36	Heritage Ridge GC	150
Broken Sound C (Club)	77	Heron Bay GC	44
Broken Sound C (Old)	77	High Ridge CC	86
Card Sound GC	14	Hillsboro C Par 3	60
The Carolina C	49	Hobe Sound FC	139
Champions C at Summerfield	148	Hollybrook GC	40
Cheeca Lodge & Spa GC	17	Hollybrook GC (Par 3)	60
Colony West CC	49	Hollywood Beach G Resort	45
Colony West CC (Glades)	59	Hunters Run (East)	87
Cooper Colony CC	59	Hunters Run (North)	87
Coral Ridge CC	38	Hunters Run (South)	86
Coral Ridge CC (Rees)	59	C at Ibis (Heritage)	88
CC of Coral Springs	50	C at Ibis (Legend)	88
Costa Del Sol GC	29	C at Ibis (Tradition)	89
Crandon G Key Biscayne	29	Indianwood G&CC	151
Crystal Lake CC	50	Indian Creek CC	21
Cypress Creek CC	120	Indian Spring CC (East)	89
Cypress Lakes	132	Indian Spring CC (West)	90
Davie GC	51	International Links GC	31

Inverrary Resort (East)	45	Ocean C	156
Inverrary Resort (West)	46	Ocean Reef C (Dolphin)	15
Jacaranda GC (East)	46	Ocean Reef C (Hammock)	15
Jacaranda GC (West)	47	Okeeheelee GC	124
Jonathan's Landing GC (Fazio)	91	Old Marsh GC	96
Jonathan's Landing GC (Hills)	91	Old Palm GC	97
Jonathan's Landing GC (Village)	90	Orangebrook G&CC (East)	53
Jupiter CC	92	Orangebrook G&CC (West)	53
Jupiter Hills C (Hills)	140	Oriole GC	54
Jupiter Hills C (Village)	141	Osprey Point GC	124
Jupiter Island C	141	Palm-Aire CC (Cypress)	48
Jupiter Dunes GC	132	Palm-Aire CC (Oaks)	48
GC of Jupiter	122	Palm-Aire CC (Palms)	47
Key Colony Beach GC	17	Palm Beach CC	97
Key West GC	16	Palm Beach National G&CC	125
Killian Greens GC	31	Palm Beach Par 3 GC	134
Kings Point G (Exec)	132	Palm Beach Polo C (Cypress)	98
Kings Point G (Par 3)	133	Palm Beach Polo C (Dunes)	98
La Gorce CC	20	Palm Cove G & Yacht C	154
Lago Mar CC	41	Palmetto GC	35
Lake Worth Muni GC	122	Park Ridge GC	125
Lakeview GC	133	Parkland GC	41
Lauderhill GC	61	Pembroke Lakes GC	54
Leisureville Com Assoc	61	PGA National Res (Champion)	114
Leisureville Com GC	133	PGA National Res (Estates)	115
The Little C	134	PGA National Res (Fazio)	112
The Little C – Tequesta	155	PGA National Res (Palmer)	113
Loblolly GC	142	PGA National Res (Squire)	113
Lone Pine GC	134	Pine Island Ridge CC	62
Lost City GC	92	Pine Tree GC	99
Lost Lake GC	151	Piper's Landing Yacht & CC	147
Lost Tree C	93	Plantation Preserve GC	55
Loxahatchee C	93	Poinciana CC	135
L at Madison Green	123	Polo C Boca Raton (Club)	100
Margate Executive GC	61	Polo C Boca Raton (Equestrian)	100
Mariner Sands CC (Gold)	143	Polo Trace G&CC	126
Mariner Sands CC (Green)	142	Polo West GC	126
Martin Co. GC (Gold/Blue)	152	Pompano Beach GC (Palms)	55
Martin Co. GC (Red/White)	152	Pompano Beach GC (Pines)	56
Martin Downs GC (Banyan)	153	Perserve at Ironhorse	101
Martin Downs GC (Oprey)	153	Quail Ridge CC (North)	116
Mayacoo Lakes CC	94	Quail Ridge CC (South)	115
McArthur GC	143	Red Reef Executive GC	135
Medalist C	144	Redland G&CC	35
CC of Miami (East)	32	Riverbend GC	157
CC of Miami (West)	32	Riviera CC	22
Miami Beach GC	33	Royal Palm Yacht & CC	101
Miami Shores CC	33	St Andrews C	135
Miami Springs G&CC	34	St Andrews CC (Fazio II)	102
Miccosukee G&CC	24	St Andrews CC (Palmer)	102
Miles Grant CC	155	Sailfish Point GC	145
CC at Mirasol (Sunrise)	95	Sandhill Crane GC	127
CC at Mirasol (Sunset)	94	Seagate CC	116
Mizner CC	95	Seminole GC	103
Monarch CC	144	Seven Bridges at Springtree	62
Monterey Yacht & CC	156	Sherwood Park GC	136
Normandy Shores GC	34	Shula's Hotel & GC	24
North Palm Beach CC	123	Southwinds GC	127
North River GC	156	Stonebridge G&CC	104

Sugar Cane GC	128	Wanderers C	107
Sunrise Lakes Phase 3 GC	62	Wellington National GC	107
Sunrise Lakes Phase 4 GC	63	West Palm Beach GC	129
Tequesta CC	104	Westchester G&CC	129
TPC Eagle Trace	56	Weston Hills CC (Players)	42
Trump Int'l GC	105	Weston Hills CC (Tour)	42
Trump Int'l GC (Trump 9)	105	Willoughby GC	146
Trump Doral (Blue Monster)	26	Woodfield CC	108
Trump Doral (Golden Palm)	25	Woodlands CC (East)	57
Trump Doral (Red Tiger)	25	Woodlands CC (West)	57
Trump Doral (Silver Fox)	27	Woodmont CC	58
Trump National Jupiter	106	C at Winston Trails	130
Turnberry Isle Resort (Miller)	28	Wycliffe G&CC (East)	108
Turnberry Isle Resort (Soffer)	27	Wycliffe G&CC (West)	109
Turtle Creek C	145	Wynmoor GC	63
Via Mizner GC	106	Yacht & CC	146
Village GC	128		

Made in the USA
Middletown, DE
23 October 2018